Aeschylus

THE EARLIER PLAYS AND RELATED STUDIES

This volume complements D.J. Conacher's two earlier studies of Aeschylus, *Aeschylus' 'Prometheus Bound'* (1980) and *Aeschylus' 'Oresteia'* (1987), and completes his literary commentary on the extant plays of Aeschylus.

In this volume Conacher provides a detailed running commentary on the three earlier plays (*The Persians, The Seven against Thebes,* and *The Suppliants*), as well as an analysis of their themes, structure, and dramatic techniques and devices. In two more general studies he reviews Aeschylus' dramatic uses of the Chorus and of imagery.

Conacher's close readings of the text and sensitive analysis of the main problems in the plays will be of benefit to students, especially those encountering these plays for the first time, either in Greek or in translation. He provides a thorough overview of the various interpretative and philological problems and opinions encountered in Aeschylean scholarship, which will be of interest to senior scholars as well as students.

D.J. CONACHER is Professor Emeritus in the Department of Classics at the University of Toronto.

UNIVERSITY OF TORONTO PRESS

Toronto   Buffalo   London

D.J. CONACHER

Aeschylus

THE EARLIER PLAYS
AND RELATED STUDIES

© University of Toronto Press Incorporated 1996
Toronto Buffalo London
Printed in Canada

ISBN 0-8020-0796-1 cloth
ISBN 0-8020-7155-4 paper

∞

Printed on acid-free paper

Canadian Cataloguing in Publication Data

Conacher, D.J., 1918–
Aeschylus: the earlier plays and related studies

Includes bibliographical references.
ISBN 0-8020-0796-1 (bound)   ISBN 0-8020-7155-4 (pbk.)

1. Aeschylus – Criticism and interpretation.
2. Aeschylus – Technique. I. Title.

PA3829.C65 1996   882'.01   C96-930920-1

University of Toronto Press acknowledges the financial assistance to its
publishing program of the Canada Council and the Ontario Arts Council.

To my wife

γυνή ... ἀρίστη τῶν ὑφ' ἡλίῳ μακρῷ

Euripides, *Alcestis* 151

Contents

Preface

Students of Aeschylus (and not a few teachers of classics) often concentrate their study of the dramatist on his most celebrated work (and only extant trilogy), the *Oresteia*, and on the *Prometheus Vinctus*, which is arguably the most influential, but whose authenticity (at least *in toto*) is now undergoing considerable uncertainty. There are, however, several features of Aeschylus' earlier plays, to be discussed in this study, which no one interested in the first of the great tragic poets can afford to neglect.

In view of the small number of plays (seven) in the Aeschylean canon of extant plays, it may seem arbitrary to distinguish the *Persae* (472 BC), the *Septem* (467 BC), and the *Supplices* (463 BC, at the latest) as 'earlier plays' from the three plays of the *Oresteia* (458 BC) and the *Prometheus Vinctus* (456 BC?). Most critics would agree (though not always for the same reasons) that there are clear contrasts between the *Persae* and the *Septem*, on the one hand, and the *Oresteia*, on the other. The *Supplices* (the only extant play of the Danaid trilogy), which one critic, at least, firmly aligns with the 'later' plays,[1] I would regard as 'transitional,' or at least as manifesting, in its themes and structure, dramaturgy, and imagery, certain affinities with both groups.

---

1 See Herington *Aeschylus* chap 5; see also his article 'The Last Phase.' While agreeing with many of this fine critic's contrasts between the earlier and later plays of Aeschylus, I find it difficult to agree entirely with the main principle of his division: the alleged fundamental change in the poet's view of the nature and workings of the cosmos. It is Herington's belief in this fundamental change (which, he argues, coincided with 'the violent struggle to replace the old constitution [at Athens] by the radical democracy') which leads him to place the *Supplices* with plays of 'the last phase.'

Discussion of the themes of these earlier tragedies will obviously have to await the detailed analyses in the following chapters. In general terms, these themes (including that of the *Supplices*) may be said to be simple, but strong and clearly defined. Sometimes, the dearth of dramatic action (as we tend to understand the term) will require a kind of dramatic structure very different, but very effective in this circumstance, from what we may think of as ideal tragic structure as sanctified by Aristotle.

Other thematic features of these earlier tragedies we shall find to be more typical of the poet's work in general (at least to the limited degree to which we can know it); indeed, it is in the observation of such elements that we find interesting anticipations of themes and techniques which Aeschylus is to develop more richly in the *Oresteia*. Among these elements are some of the great social and ethical themes, which were not necessarily original with Aeschylus but to which he gave new power and meaning by his dramatic treatments of them. Such themes include the almost superstitious fear of great wealth, and of ostentation, a Solonian conviction to which Aeschylus usually added his own insistence on the act of outrage, of going beyond one's *moira*, or allotted destiny or role in life, before the inevitable catastrophe ensues. This theme is prominent in both forms in the tragedy of Xerxes, 'the Great King,' in the *Persae*. The theme of dangerous wealth appears also with (as we shall see) questionable relevance in the *Septem*, as the Chorus hymns the background, in the legend of Oedipus, of Eteocles' tragedy. Such passages are precursors of the more explicit expression of the *choros-hybris-atê* theme (great wealth leading to an act of violent outrage ... and disaster) in the celebrated 'ethical coda' which the Chorus sings at *Agamemnon* 750 ff Even in the *Agamemnon*, however, there are passages (for instance, at vv 773 ff and 1008 ff) which hint at the dangers of great wealth alone.

Other celebrated Aeschylean themes such as the fulfilment (in the *Persae*) of familial dooms long prophesied, or of family curses for ancestral sins (as in the mythical background of the *Septem*), make their first appearance in these earlier plays. It may indeed have been the proper deployment of such themes – the ancestral curse working through three generations of the house of Labdacus – which led Aeschylus to invent the connected trilogy for his tragedies. Unfortunately, only the *Septem* remains of his 'Labdacid trilogy,' but enough can be gleaned from it, and from our knowledge of the myth, to provide an interesting anticipation of the more complex development of such a theme in the *Oresteia* trilogy.

So, too, it is with the more tantalizing problems of the Danaid trilogy, of which only the *Supplices* remains extant. Again (as in the case of the *Septem*) some knowledge of the larger myth (in its various forms) and other fragmentary evidence allow us to attempt at least a hypothetical reconstruction of the trilogy. Once again it seems likely that another element of the *Oresteia* trilogy (violence, counter-violence, and resolution, to express the matter in over-simple terms) may be anticipated in an earlier and perhaps more 'archaic' form in the Danaid trilogy.

In our discussion of the formal and structural features of these early plays, we shall be concerned primarily with considering, in the case of each play, how effective these features are in achieving the dramatic expression of the theme. Nevertheless, there will inevitably be certain features (particularly in the use and deployment of the Chorus) which strike us as peculiar to, or at least indicative of, the earlier stages of tragedy, and others which seem to anticipate techniques and effects more fully developed later, in the *Oresteia*. Funereal lamentations, for example, such as we find at the end of the *Septem*, may well reflect, as some critics have thought, the original function of the tragic and even the pre-tragic Chorus. There are, of course, other uses of the Chorus which occur only in these earlier extant plays. Among such are its use (again in the *Septem*) to indicate mob terror, in a passage which comes as close as tragedy can to violent on-stage action, and its use (this time in the *Supplices*) to achieve the turning point in the action by the choral 'persuasion,' bullying even, of the protagonist. These uses are, however, as much a feature of the dramatic situation as of the limitations of early tragic structure, and indeed the latter example provides a sort of ironic anticipation of a more peaceful passage of persuasion, this time of the Chorus by an actor, at the end of Aeschylus' *Eumenides*.

In our earliest extant tragedy, Aeschylus' *Persae*, we shall be noting occasional abrupt shifts, at certain moments in the action, from exchanges between Chorus (or the Chorus-Leader) and an actor to dialogue between two actors – a procedure which, as one critic has suggested, may indicate the fairly recent introduction of a second actor to tragedy.[2] Elsewhere, however, in these earlier plays of Aeschylus, we shall be noting skilful uses of exchanges between the Chorus (or the Chorus-Leader) and an actor to advance the dramatic action, or even (in the *Septem*, though at a quite elementary level) to illuminate the character

2 See Michelini *Tradition and Dramatic Form in the Persians of Aeschylus*; cf also Belloni *Eschilo I, Persiani, Introduzioni* pp liv–lviii.

of the protagonist. This technique of Chorus-inspired dramatic action is, of course, particularly prominent (and used to particularly exciting effect) in the *Supplices*, where, owing to the poet's choice of dramatic presentation, there is only one actor and the Chorus, in a sense, assumes the role of protagonist. However, we shall notice the same technique in operation in the *Septem*, where, indeed, the dramatic climax of the play, the protagonist's fateful decision, becomes the subject of a dialogue between the protagonist and the Chorus, which becomes '*epirrhematic*' (that is, the Chorus singing and the actor speaking) when, at more excited moments, the whole Chorus takes over from the Chorus-Leader. Again, it is in such examples as these that we find the dramatist's technique, in these earlier plays, anticipating its later deployment in such passages as the exchanges between Clytemnestra and the Chorus toward the end of the *Agamemnon*, between Electra, Orestes, and the Chorus in the 'great kommos' of the *Choephori*, and between the Chorus and Athena at the end of the *Eumenides*.

There are, however, other instances, more easily recognizable, where prominent features of one of the earlier plays will be seen to anticipate the use of similar devices in the *Oresteia*. Two excellent examples of this are to be found in the *Persae* and the *Agamemnon*. One is the use of the Chorus early in both plays to set up a sort of tragic rhythm with songs whose initial confidence and power gradually fade to premonitions of disaster. The other is the dramatic appearance of a prophetic figure (the *Persae*'s ghostly King Darius anticipating the Apollo-inspired Cassandra of the *Agamemnon*) to expound the tragic fulfilment of an ancestral doom.

In the two concluding chapters of these studies, some attempt will be made to compare and contrast the poet's dramatic uses of imagery (in chapter 4) and of the Chorus (in chapter 5), both in the plays discussed in the preceding chapters and (to a lesser degree in the case of 'imagery') in Aeschylus' extant work as a whole. In both these discussions there will inevitably be some repetition of (and cross-references to) points made in the preceding chapters; however, in both cases an overall view may be found to be of some interest. In the case of 'imagery,' although I argue strongly for the specific dramatic function which the poet's images play in their immediate context, it has seemed worthwhile to set down within one chapter certain distinctive uses of imagery noted in different plays, and to ask whether any significant development in this matter can be noted even in the limited number of extant plays of the Aeschylean corpus. (Imagery in the *Oresteia* has, of course, received generous treatment by various excellent scholars, and this part of my chapter will be limited mainly to a discussion of some of these studies.

In the case of the *Prometheus Vinctus*, doubts about its authenticity, in whole or in part, inhibit the comparative or 'developmental' aspect of the discussion.) With regard to the Chorus, a review of its structural and thematic functions, not only in the three plays studied in the preceding chapters but also in the *Oresteia* and (for somewhat different reasons) in the *Prometheus Vinctus*, should help us to see the role of the Chorus in the 'earlier plays' in the context of the poet's dramatic use of the Chorus in general. Though that role is always fashioned to suit the theme and structure of the play which it serves, certain striking similarities in choral technique will be noted in comparable passages in different plays where a similar choral effect is called for. Moreover, apart from the intrinsic interests of the specific comparisons and contrasts involved, it seems appropriate to conclude this study with a general appreciation of what is perhaps the most striking feature of Aeschylus' tragedies.

The studies in this book are designed primarily for students, both graduate and undergraduate. However, I would hope that all who seek to appreciate Aeschylus by close readings of his texts might find something of value in them. The tragedies of Aeschylus can be discussed in many ways but I have restricted myself, in my discussions of his earlier plays, to one major purpose: to provide detailed analyses of these plays, indicating the structures and the various poetic devices by which the dramatist expresses their individual themes and, within those structures, the essential elements (choral, dramatic, and spectacular) which contribute to the tragic action and tragic meaning of their respective plays. The reader of this book should not, however, expect to find in it startlingly new meanings, new interpretations of plays which have been admired and enjoyed (surely not always for the wrong reasons) for many centuries. The extant tragedies of Aeschylus, like those of many great tragedians, concern important but often fairly simple themes. What makes them great is how the poet *expresses* these themes so that the audience (or, at one remove, the reader) receives them with the immediacy which only the tragic experience can provide. It is with this 'how' that the following chapters are concerned.

Many readers will be aware (and others should be advised) that much critical work on Greek tragedy, as on literature generally, has taken rather different directions from the 'formal' approach indicated above. Among these new directions in criticism, we may mention the work of the structuralists, the deconstructionists, and (particularly important for Aeschylean studies) the recent emphasis on the visual, the theatrical, aspect of Greek tragedy. (It should be made clear, however, that by no means all recent critics of Greek tragedy fall into one or another of these categories.) Much in these approaches, however valuable in themselves, is not relevant, for one reason or another, to what I am attempting in the present studies. An important aspect of structuralism, for example, is its interest in discovering in what ways the works being studied reflect the social structures, and their development, of their time. With regard to Aeschylean drama, this legitimate and often exciting approach is, perhaps, most useful in connection with the *Oresteia*, though I shall have occasion to refer to one of its followers in connection with the *Septem* and the *Supplices* as well.

If the approach of the structuralists differs in its subject matter from that of the present approach, the deconstructionists seem to me (though here I tread on somewhat uncertain ground) to differ both in the object of study and (perhaps more important) in the means employed to achieve that object. Deconstructionists show much less confidence than do traditional critics (and certainly less than the common reader) in ascertaining 'meaning' (or, if that is not the proper word, 'the thing signified') in a literary work, or, indeed, in any passage in it. In the deconstructionists' view of a play, many factors, some affecting the choice of words by a character, others affecting the audience or the reader receiving those words, inhibit the more naive interpretations such as are employed in the following pages. Nevertheless, I have found much of value in this connection in Simon Goldhill's *Reading Greek Tragedy* (which might be called an introduction to this approach for classicists) and, particularly with regard to communication in the *Oresteia*, in his *Language, Sexuality and Narrative: The Oresteia*.

The third of the recent critical approaches which I have mentioned is highlighted (as it was to a considerable degree initiated, at least in English-language studies) by Oliver Taplin's *The Stagecraft of Aeschylus*, published in 1977. This valuable work provides a constant and sometimes chiding reminder (not only, I imagine, to this writer) of the importance, in writing about Greek tragedy, of keeping the theatrical element constantly in mind. Of the many impressive features of Taplin's work, the one which stands out particularly is the success with which he relates his discussions of the visual aspects of a tragedy to his understanding of the play as a whole. This properly 'integrated' approach enables him to show, to a degree not previously recognized, how the structure of a play is dependent on, or at least is indicated by, stage movements. Taplin's detailed work in his *Stagecraft of Aeschylus* has, in many cases, left little more to say on the visual and theatrical aspects of the extant plays of Aeschylus. For the most part, therefore, except in places where I have ventured disagreement, I have (with frequent references to Taplin's work) left these aspects of Aeschylean tragedy to him.

One further point, relating to the manner in which material is presented in these studies, needs perhaps a word of explanation. In the case of a poet as complex in expression as Aeschylus, and as far removed in time, culture, and language, I have found it necessary occasionally to supplement my analyses of the plays with discussions of textual problems, of interpretation of vexed passages, of mythological background, and the like. Some of these discussions, to be sure, will be of more interest to the specialist than to the general reader; partly for this reason, and partly so that they may not interfere with the sequence of the dramatic analyses, I have fairly rigorously relegated these discussions to the notes and appendices to my chapters. Nevertheless, I regard this 'undergrowth' to my text (if I may so term it), and the research involved in it, as an important part of the total presentation, for without such discussions (which literary studies sometimes lack) it is often difficult to achieve an informed appreciation of the plays. In the case of contentious problems arising in this material, my aim has been to make the reader aware of the major issues and of scholarly opinion on them, and to indicate what I think to be the best solution, whether my own or my reasoned choice among conflicting views.

An earlier version (now revised and 'up-dated') of chapter 1 ('The *Persae*') was published as an article, 'Aeschylus' *Persae*: A Literary Commentary,' in *Serta Turyniana* (a festschrift in honour of Alexander Turyn), edited by John Heller (University of Illinois Press, 1974), pp 143–68. Chapter 3 (The *Supplices*) incorporates material from a lecture given at the Institute for Advanced Study at Princeton in 1987. A small part of chapter 5 ('The Chorus') incorporates material from a short paper delivered at an international colloquium at the University of Toulouse in 1991 and subsequently published as 'Rapports entre le choeur et la structure dramatique dans les tragédies d'Eschyle,' in the *Actes* of this colloquium, in *Pallas, Revue des Etudes Antiques* (1992), pp 153–60.

I should like to thank Trinity College, University of Toronto, and its administrators, for generously providing me with an office during retirement years, when much of the work on this book was completed. I should also like to thank the University of Toronto Press, and particularly my editor, Ms Joan Bulger, for their faithful support during various vicissitudes in the process of seeing this work through to publication.

PART ONE

CHAPTER ONE

Persae (The Persians)[1]

The *Persae* of Aeschylus, a fine play which has been much misunderstood and undervalued, is of great interest to us for many reasons. Not the least of these is the fact that it is the only extant Greek tragedy based not on ancient myth but on nearly contemporary history, and so is the first historical play in extant Western literature. More important still, perhaps, is the point that it shows us, even at this early period in the history of Greek drama (the *Persae*, at 472 BC, is now generally admitted to be the earliest Greek play that we possess),[2] just how historical material should be approached, if it be approached at all, by the writer of imaginative literature. The tragic poet, if he follows Aeschylus' example, will select only historical events of sufficient grandeur to have seized the popular imagination in such a way that they have already acquired something of a mythic quality – that is, events which seem to imply causes or meanings (however defined) belonging to a higher order of reality than the particular events themselves. Second (and this is, perhaps, merely the subjective side of the same observation),

---

1 This chapter is a revised and extended version, with further bibliographical material, of an article which originally appeared as 'Aeschylus' *Persae*: A Literary Commentary' in *Serta Turyniana* ed John L. Heller, pp 143–68.

2 The previously alleged earlier date of Aeschylus' *Supplices* has now, of course, been generally discredited; see *P Oxy* 2256 (1952) fr 3, and the lucid account of its significance in dating the *Supplices* by Garvie, *Aeschylus' Supplices: Play and Trilogy* chap. 1.

For an interesting discussion of certain of the *Persae*'s stylistic features regarded as stemming from its literary-historical position in a newly evolving genre, see Michelini *Tradition and Dramatic Form in the Persians of Aeschylus*; cf also the more general discussion in Belloni *Eschilo I, Persiani, Introduzione* pp liv–lviii.

our tragic poet will choose only such historical events as provide, in his own poetic or imaginative reaction to them, a striking example, almost as good as myth itself, of some great truth or insight about life which he finds fundamental to his own view of tragic experience. This implies, of course, that the element of choice on the poet's part does not end with the choice of a historical subject that suits his theme. However, before exercising the necessary freedom of the artist, the poet of contemporary history has also to recognize a certain responsibility: he must present events in such a way that they are acceptable to those familiar with the actual happenings. Herein lies the limiting or restrictive element in composing historical drama, but it is, in a sense, the debt which the poet owes to the great events he has borrowed in order to exploit them for his own (quite legitimate) purposes; for, as I have indicated, much of the play's authority, of its grip on the popular imagination, depends initially on the impact which these events have made upon it. Moreover, if the reader or member of the audience is so irritated by a distortion of events with which he is familiar that he cannot attend to the new event (what the poet makes of his historical material), then the poet has lost credibility in more senses than one.[3] Still more important, perhaps, for the student of the *Persae* is the consideration of the freedom with which a poet may be expected to approach his historical material. Once the minimum of historical responsibility (of the kind suggested above) has been met, the poet of a historical tragedy must continue to exercise his privilege of choice by selecting and emphasizing, or even by distorting and repressing, various aspects of the events, which belong to history, in the interest of the theme, which belongs to the poet alone. More, he must invent qualities in his

3 'The willing suspension of disbelief' cannot be expected to extend indefinitely in the treatment of events which have radically affected the lives of the audience. As Richmond Lattimore has observed of the *Persae* in this connection, '... we have no right to assume that the Athenians would award first prize to a tragic poet for dealing wildly with known facts in a contemporary theme' (Lattimore 'Aeschylus on the defeat of Xerxes' p 87).

Among recent historical plays, Hochhuth's *Soldiers* is a good example of a borderline case. This play, while making no claim to historical accuracy, undoubtedly owed much of its initial grip on the audience's imagination to its realistic and recognizable presentation of Winston Churchill and of certain historical situations and events more or less (sometimes less) familiar to the audience. Some viewers were so incensed with what they regarded as distortion of the character and decisions of the *historical* Churchill that they could not attend to the fascinating poetic truth which the playwright was attempting to express through his dramatic treatment of historical characters and situations.

'historical' characters and supporting details in his 'historical' events to suit his theme and the dramatic personalities which he has created to express it.

This sort of adaptation, transformation rather, of particular events and their circumstances is what the critics have in mind when they speak of Aeschylus' 'mythologizing' of history for his purposes. In this way he so converts particular events as to make them express, more powerfully than they would in their original form, the general pattern or idea about human experience, or about the ways of Zeus with man, which he wishes to express.[4]

Whether history unadapted can ever provide the stuff of tragedy is debatable;[5] certainly it could never produce a tragedy as powerful as the *Persae*. Nevertheless, the simple historical facts of Xerxes' Greek experience, viewed in the light of Greek ethical thought, clearly suggest the theme of divine nemesis. On the one hand, we have the Solonian

4 This familiar distinction between 'poetry' and 'history' (cf Aristotle *Poetics* 1451b5–7) should perhaps need no comment except that the numerous comparisons made between the poetic and the historical treatments of Xerxes' enterprise have tended to muddy the distinction. Compare for example Snell's suggestion in *Aischylos und das Handeln im Drama* p 66 that in Aeschylus' time there was no clearcut distinction between myth and history with Deichgräber's refutation of this view in 'Die *Persae* des Aischylos' pp 200–1. Contrast also Gomme's comparison of Herodotus and Aeschylus in *Greek Attitudes to Poetry and History* p 98 with Murray's comparison in *Aeschylus, the Creator of Tragedy* p 125.

Defenders of the historicity of the *Persae* have not, indeed, been lacking. See again Deichgräber (in a more recent publication) *Die Persertetralogie des Aischylos* pp 36–40, who believes that Aeschylus was influenced by the writings of Hecataeus. Cf also Belloni *I Persiani* pp xlv–vi, and various places in his notes, who also shows confidence in the historical aspects of the play, especially with regard to the battle of Salamis. (On this matter, indeed, he is joined by numerous historical critics; see below, n 30.) An interestingly new approach to an old topic has been provided recently in Edith Hall's *Inventing the Barbarian* pp 62–76. Hall (pp 64 ff), like this writer, rejects the view that the Greeks failed to distinguish between myth and recent history. (She also provides good arguments against taking too seriously Deichgräber's view of the influence of Hecataeus on Aeschylus.) Nevertheless, in illustrating her thesis 'that Greek writing about barbarians is usually an exercise in self-definition' (p 1), Hall provides much judicial discussion (with up-to-date bibliographical documentation) of various issues concerning what might be called 'the historical ambience' of the *Persae*. Other views of the 'historicity' of the *Persae*, particularly with regard to the treatment of Darius, will be considered later, as we come to the relevant parts of the play.

5 Cf Murray's comment (126): 'If one Greek general had been named the play would have become modern and exposed to all the small temporary emotions of the immediate present, the gratified vanity, the annoyance, the inevitable criticism.'

doctrine[6] concerning the dangerously changeable quality of great good fortune and particularly of fortunes unjustly acquired beyond one's right or *moira*; on the other hand, we have the extraordinary fact of the Persian defeat by the Greeks, which must have seemed (to victors and vanquished alike) impossible without the hand of God – and the combination, in the tragic sufferer, of Persian despotism and overreaching ambition made Xerxes a perfect subject for the Solonian lesson. Possibly it is the very simplicity of the *koros-hybris-atê* theme (great wealth, feeding on pride and greed, tempted by the gods to the fateful and ruinous overstepping of the *moira* which the gods have themselves set down) which leads some critics to replace it with other themes (the celebration of Athenian triumph, for example, or the vindication of the policies and cunning of Themistocles) which are, at best, peripheral to the tragic meaning of the play. There is, in any case, a tendency in recent Aeschylean criticism generally to reject such simple ethical formulations of Aeschylean themes as that suggested above.[7] Sometimes it is argued that Aeschylus had little idea of any element of human responsibility in his depiction of the ruin of tragic heroes.

6 See Solon fr 1 (Diehl); cf fr 3.
7 The ethical *'hybris-atê'* formulations of Aeschylean themes have been questioned, from one aspect or another, by several scholars in the past few decades; cf, for example, Page's edition of Aeschylus *Agamemnon* pp xx–xxix; Lloyd-Jones 'Zeus in Aeschylus' pp 55–67 and 'The Guilt of Agamemnon' pp 187–9; Dawe 'Inconsistency of Plot and Character in Aeschylus' pp 47 ff, 61; and 'Some Reflections on *Atê* and *Hamartia*' pp 108–11. Cf also n 39, below. Some more recent commentators on the *Persae* appear to take a similar view, as far as Xerxes' downfall is concerned. Garvie 'Aeschylus' Simple Plots' pp 68 ff regards the basic contrast of the play to be that between Xerxes' former splendour and present ruin, and emphatically rejects the view of *'hybris* punished' as the theme of the play; Gagarin *Aeschylean Drama* pp 36–7, takes a similar view and plays down (pp 47–52) suggestions of impiety and *hybris* on Xerxes' part. (Broadhead, by contrast *The Persae of Aeschylus* pp xxi–ii, gives proper emphasis to Darius' criticisms of Xerxes' impiety and *hybris*.) Rosenmeyer *The Art of Aeschylus* pp 261 f, despite his statement that Xerxes' suffering is, from the beginning of the play, 'defined as punishment,' remains curiously vague about the provenance of that punishment. The more traditional, 'ethical' interpretations of Aeschylean tragedy which one associates with Murray, Kitto, Lesky, and, to some degree, Reinhardt, have not, however, been completely abandoned with regard to the *Persae*; see, for example, Winnington-Ingram *Studies in Aeschylus* chap. 1, 'Zeus in *Persae*,' and other references later in this chapter. See also Hall *Inventing the Barbarian* pp 70–3 for discussion of opposing views as to whether 'the *hybris-atê* theme' in the *Persae* is to be regarded as of 'universal application' or whether (as Hall's own emphasis tends to suggest) it is to be regarded as an essential part of the depiction of 'the barbarians.'

It is possible that behind these recent rejections lies a certain boredom with the constant restatement of what is, after all, a very simple theme (the divine nemesis which overtakes the hybristic man) and a certain irritation with scholars who feel that that is really all that need be said about much Aeschylean tragedy. This irritation is understandable, but the point which needs making is not that the traditional critics have got the theme wrong, but that it is not merely the theme but also the way in which a dramatist makes his audience experience his theme which determines the greatness of a play. Thus, though the theme of the *Persae* can be quickly understood or at least mentally pigeon-holed by any schoolboy who can read a handbook, it cannot be experienced as Aeschylus meant us to experience it, in this instance, until every fibre of its simple but powerful structure has been grasped as bearing, each time from some new direction, on the same central pathos which we are asked to share with Xerxes. It is this intensive centripetal character of the play which is completely missed by those critics who, feeling that the play needs some apology for the simplicity of its theme and its lack of complication, developing action, and the like, praise its vivid passages of descriptive narrative, its moving and theatrical incidents (such as the evocation of Darius) as if these were bonuses by which the play is made acceptable even though they do little to advance the action.[8]

Both the setting of the play and the most obvious adaptations which Aeschylus makes in historical events and personages serve as a preliminary indication of the centre of dramatic interest. The scene is set in Susa in the Persian court for the obvious purpose that we may experience the action and share the sufferings of Xerxes as much as possible through Persian eyes and ears and minds and hearts. Tragic experience must always be vicarious, but clearly, to reach a tragic sufferer as distant as Xerxes, we shall need such intermediaries as these. Further advantages

8 See, for example, Smythe *Aeschylean Tragedy* p 82 and chap. 3 passim. Cf Dawe 'Inconsistency' (above, n 7), who seems to regard the Darius scene, in part at least, as 'a skilful way of making a limited amount of material stretch a long way without tedium.' Such views of the *Persae*'s structure are not, of course, shared by all critics of the play. Several critics have stressed as a major effect of that structure (and as a function, at least, of all its parts) the focus on the ruined Xerxes which is achieved in the final scene. (See, for example, Smethurst *The Artistry of Aeschylus and Zeami* pp 81, 94–6, 101; Else [to whom Smethurst refers, p 97, n 36, in this connection] *The Origins and Early Form of Greek Tragedy* p 87; cf also Thalmann 'Xerxes' Rags' passim, whose observation of various dramatic 'preparations' for the final scene suggests, at least, a similar view of the play's structure.)

of this setting, quite necessary to the play's effect, appear as the structure of the play unfolds.

The three or four most obvious liberties with history which the dramatist has taken all clearly point in the same direction. The depiction of Xerxes as the only Persian king personally to lead an army from Asia into mainland Europe; the contrasting of Xerxes with his father Darius, presented as the wise restrained ruler who understood the *moira* which the gods allow the Persians – these two features, however unhistorical,[9] mark the Xerxes of this play as the egregiously hybristic one who alone has put himself and his people in such awful jeopardy. The incontinent flight of Xerxes immediately after the defeat at Salamis; the playing-down (though not the omission) of the battle at Plataea – these distortions render the central dramatic catastrophe at Salamis more simple, swift, and absolute; and, finally, the freezing, then melting, of the River Strymon to drown the remnants of Xerxes' army limping home – this invention (or partial invention)[10] of the poet serves to isolate the god-inflicted aspect of the ruin in a way which was impossible at Salamis, where Greek and particularly Athenian *aretê* joins with the *daimôn* in bringing catastrophe upon the King.

The theme of the *Persae*, then, is simply the demonstration of divine nemesis answering the overreaching ambition of human greed and puffed-up confidence in power and wealth, the old sequence of *koros-hybris-atê* familiar to the Athenian audience since Solon's day. Even Aeschylus' recurrent paradoxes – divine temptation to abet human transgression, doom preordained to balance human choice – succeed (more clearly than elsewhere in Aeschylus) in complementing the ethical theme. Both the basic idea and the action (the defeat of Xerxes) by which it is to be demonstrated, are known to the audience and in

9 The treatment of King Darius both through his own ghostly utterances and through the words of the Chorus about his rule provide the most interesting and, in some details, the most difficult of Aeschylus' departures from 'history' in the play. Various specific details will be considered as we come to them in our analysis.

10 There seems little doubt that the disaster at the River Strymon as related at *Persae* 495 ff is an Aeschylean invention. It does not appear in Herodotus' account of the return of Xerxes and his army (Herod VIII.115–20) and is particularly well suited to Aeschylus' tragic treatment of his theme. See also Broadhead's note to *Persae* 495–7 (which agrees with this conclusion) and references to supporting views there given. Still, that *something* happened to Xerxes' force, or part of it, at or near the River Strymon, seems probable when we consider, in addition to the episode narrated in the *Persae*, the account of a storm assailing Xerxes' ship at the mouth of the Strymon, in a tale told to Herodotus (VIII.18), though Herodotus has his own reasons for not believing fully in this account (VIII.19–20).

any case the movements of ships and troops can never be confused with the movements of a drama. Thus in a play such as the *Persae*, there will be little occasion for forward-moving or linear action and none at all for a complex development of plot. (Among Greek tragedies, the *Persians* stands at the exact opposite pole to, say, the *Philoctetes* of Sophocles.) What we must look for, rather, are the ways by which Aeschylus, starting from the Persian position of, it would seem, absolute power and confidence, imposes his theme dramatically with ever-increasing intensity and fullness of meaning on the consciousness of his audience. While there is little linear plot development ('historically,' the defeat of Xerxes must already have happened before the initial pondering of the Chorus in the parodos), the theme is developed, as if in a symphonic tone-poem, from premonitory hints of disaster in the parodos (soon to be lost in a rush of triumphant brass), through the central portions of the play where every instrument is tuned to the disaster, to the final lament of the King himself as he sings his grief and guilt antiphonally with the Chorus's questioning. In this progression, the theme is viewed from four different aspects, each view adding something which could not be achieved before. In the first, the anticipatory, movement of the play, the *hybris-atê* theme can only be hinted at by the waiting Persian court, and the most sinister hints are introduced almost unconsciously, with only the audience aware of their dread significance. The second movement presents the fulfilment of these dramatic expectations, news of the actual disaster itself in the Messenger's eye-witness report of Salamis and further Persian woes. Next, the Ghost of Darius looks back upon his son's exploit and now for the first time the premonitions of the Queen and the Chorus and the hints of the Messenger about the hand of God are fully realized in these ghostly revelations. Anticipation, fulfilment, retrospection, and finally, with the long-awaited appearance of Xerxes himself, the awful evidence, in the person of the ruined King, of the operation of justice from the gods.

We are called the trusted ones, the guardians of the Persians whose warriors have gone forth against the land of Greece; guardians of Persia's rich and gold-encrusted royal seat, chosen, for our years, by Xerxes himself, King and son of a King, Darius, to keep watch over this land.[11]

11 Belloni *I Persiani, Introduzione* makes much of the Chorus's role as guardians in relation to Xerxes and his dynastic rule, even comparing them in this respect (li–ii) to

But about the King's return and the return of his army rich in gold even now my evilly prophetic heart is troubled (for the whole strength of the Asian people has fared forth with him) and mutters [βαΰζει] against my youthful King. For no messenger and no horseman has reached the city of the Persians. (*Persae*, 1–15)

An opening heavy with foreboding. Even before the prophetic spirit of the Chorus voices its fears for the absent host, Persian riches and gold (Aeschylean danger-signs)[12] have been mentioned thrice. 'Xerxes, King and son of a King, Darius,' is soon to become a sinister contrast and already in βαΰζει, a complaining word, the Chorus of Elders anticipates its final role as the Great King's inquisitors.[13]

A glorious roster of the Persian army, its leaders and allies ('men like Amistres or Artaphernes, Megabates or Astaspes, fearful to look upon, terrible in battle') sweeps away the Chorus's worries for fifty marching, anapaestic lines. Splendid processional to match the final grim recessional.[14] Even so, sinister words keep creeping in: πολύχρυσος again (45), ἁβροδίαιτοι (41) of the Lydians (some compound of ἁβρός –

Artabanus whom, Herodotus tells us (VII.52), Xerxes left as a guardian of his house and power in his absence.

12 Cf Finley *Pindar and Aeschylus* pp 210 ff

13 βαΰζει, v 13, is admittedly difficult. I follow J.T. Sheppard in taking θυμός (the Chorus's troubled spirit), in v 11, as subject. Most editors, however, punctuate so as to take ἰσχὺς 'Ασιατογενής as subject of βαΰζει in a new sentence, though Page marks a missing line (which would, presumably, have contained the subject of βαΰζει) after v 13. There are further uncertainties concerning the text and the precise meaning of βαΰζει in the context. Roussel *Eschyle, Les Perses* somewhat improbably reads νυὸς for νέον (or possibly ἐὸν, depending on how we divide the words in v 13), and translates '*la jeune épouse appelle de ces cris son mari.*' But apart from this surprising intrusion of a 'young wife' at this point, one would expect βαΰζει to have a hostile overtone, as its use in a similar context at *Ag* 449 (cf Sidgwick's note, *ad loc.*) indicates. This objection also applies to Murray's more interesting translation 'baying' (like enthusiastic dogs around their master), agreeing with ἰσχὺς 'Ασιατογενής as subject. The only alleged parallel quoted (Heracl B97 D-K) has dogs barking in a *hostile* way, and that is precisely the sense which must be avoided if the glorious departing army (and not the worrying Chorus, waiting for news) is to be the subject. See also Broadhead's note *ad loc* and his supplementary notes, pp 249–50, for a summary of various interpretations of this difficult passage.

14 Michelini *Tradition and Dramatic Form* p 8 (and cf p 77) comments on the profusion of catalogues in the *Persae*, a feature which she regards as indicative of early tragedy's close association with epic. (With regard to this particular catalogue, at vv 16–58, Roussel rather captiously complains of the omission of certain 'historical' allies of Xerxes.) Hall, who has a good section (*Inventing the Barbarian* pp 6–9) on Aeschylus' alleged attempts to suggest various sound effects of Persian speech, mentions his 'cacophanous catalogues' (p 78) as an outstanding example of this. But contrast

a soft word for fighting men – is to be used no less than five times of the Persian host),[15] φοβερός (48) and δεινός (40, 58), both used 'bravely' here, have uncomfortably ambiguous overtones (Xerxes' summons will turn out 'dread' indeed). Words for the army too are unfortunate, to say the least: ὄχλος (42) is meant to emphasize the number of the Lydians but anticipates the disordered rabble (see 422, 470) which the whole host is to become; τοιόνδ' ἄνθος Περσῖδος αἴας / οἴχεται ἀνδρῶν (59–60) is a pretty phrase for the departed youth of Persia but bloom suggests fading, blossoms suggest picking, and οἴχεται can be used of one who makes the last departure. (τὸ Περσῶν δ' ἄνθος οἴχεται πεσόν: these words of the Messenger at 252 soon fulfil the ironic meanings latent here.)[16]

The Chorus, as if depressed by its own overtones, shifts to full mourning in the closing lines of these 'triumphant' anapaests:

Such is the power of the Persian land which has left us, warriors whom all the land of Asia, their nurse, now bemoans with violent longing; parents and wives alike tremble with fear at the ever-lengthening stretch of days. (59–64)

In the lyric part of the parodos, the variations in mood follow a similar decline from martial confidence through uncertainty to outright fear, for now the fear becomes specific as some hint of danger from the gods makes its first appearance. The first two strophic pairs give stirring pictures of Xerxes (θούριος ἄρχων, 73)[17] crossing the Hellespont

---

Lattimore's more favourable view (see below, n 28) of the sound effect of the battle catalogues in the *Persae*.

15 Cf Stanford *Aeschylus in His Style* p 113.

16 On οἴχομαι in the *Persae*, see also Avery 'Dramatic Devices in Aeschylus' *Persae*' pp 173 ff, and Winnington-Ingram *Studies in Aeschylus* pp 198–9, appendix A, 'A Word in *Persae*.' Winnington-Ingram establishes conclusively, in my opinion, the initially ambiguous and increasingly sinister uses of οἴχομαι at vv 1, 12–13, 59 ff, 252, 546 ff, and 916. (Winnington-Ingram's note on οἴχομαι first appeared in *BICS* 20 (1973) 37 f. Both this note and his 'Zeus in *Persae*' [= chap. 1 of his *Studies in Aeschylus*] appeared after the earlier version of this chapter had gone to press. Retrospectively I can only add that I would clearly have profited from an earlier perusal of this excellent study with which I am in substantial agreement.)

17 Both this expression, θούριος ἄρχων, and διχόθεν (76) in this same sentence, used of Xerxes and his double thrust, will remind readers of the *Agamemnon* of the θούριος ὄρνις of the *Agamemnon*'s eagle portent and of the twin-throned power of the Atreidae (*Ag* 12 and 108, respectively). Other anticipations of the *Agamemnon* in the *Persae* are to be found in the recurrent use of significant and sinister images. For 'yoke' and

on his bridge of boats and of the whole host sweeping into Greece: irresistible army under a king who

> glaring about him with a dragon's murderous glare, 'mid myriad ships and myriad arms, on Syrian chariot onward speeds, bringing war of bowmen against famed warriors of spear. (81–6)

But again, dangerous ambiguities gleam through the shining façade. Xerxes is περσέπτολις (65), but *whose* city will he destroy? He is ἰσόθεος (80), innocent in epic but not in tragic imitation of epic, and sprung, through Danaë, from Zeus' golden seed (79–80: more dangerous gold). More sinister (if unconsciously so) is the Chorus's first reference to Xerxes' bridging of the Hellespont: 'casting a yoke on the sea's neck' (72) picks up the expression used a moment before of the planned enslaving of Greece (ζυγὸν ἀμφιβαλεῖν δούλιον Ἑλλάδι, 50; ζυγός is another of the thematic 'danger-words' in this play),[18] and the careful reminder 'Helle, child of Athamas' (for the Hellespont) underlines the personal aspect of the sea's enslavement. Finally, at the end of this triumphant passage, Xerxes' 'invincible' host is called a flood (ῥεῦμα) which no man can withstand, 'an irresistible wave of the sea' (87–90). All these unconscious anticipations are later to be grimly and fully realized.[19]

Suddenly, with one of those exciting leaps in which Aeschylean lyrics excel (often to the despair of textual critics),[20] the suppressed fears of the Chorus rise to the surface:

'net' images so used, compare *Persae* 50, 72, 107–14, with *Ag* 44, 218, 358–61, 866–8, 1116, 1382.

18 Cf Stanford's list (*Aeschylus in His Style* p 96 ff), with line references, of dominant images and image-sequences in various Aeschylean plays, and his comment, 'In varying degrees, each dominant image has some literal reference to an important aspect of the action in five of the plays.' (His examples are drawn from *Suppl, Pers, Sept, PV, Ag*.) This indicates, Stanford argues, 'a close interplay between the world of symbol and the world of fact.'

19 Cf Wardman's comment ('Tactics and Tradition in the Persian Wars' p 53) that it is proper and just that Xerxes' defeat should actually occur on the insulted element. Alexanderson ('Darius in *The Persians*' p 4) is, I think, wrong in arguing that the first suggestion of danger in Xerxes' bridge comes with Darius' pronouncements. This may be the first clear and overt statement of that danger but the sinister aspect of Xerxes' yoking of the Hellespont is certainly hinted at (with increasing awareness on the part of the Chorus) in the passages just cited and in the complementary one at 93–114 (in the original line sequence of the MSS).

20 Müller, Murray, and others transpose vv 93–100 to follow vv 101–14. Among more recent editions, they are followed by Broadhead, Roussel and West (but not by Page). Both sequences make sense, though the sequence of the MSS provides

Guileful deception of god, what man can avoid it? What man, be he ever so nimble, can leap such a leap to escape it? For Atê, false-smiling, gulls man into nets of destruction, whence no one unscathed can escape. (93–100)

Whence this sudden panic? The Chorus has remembered that land, not sea, is the god-given Persian element (πολέμους πυργοδαΐκτους ... ἱππιοχάρμας τε κλόνους: marvellous, untranslatable Aeschylus for 'rampart-smashing wars' and 'the uproar of cavalry battle'); the strophe ends with a final terrified glance at swirling waves beneath the slender fastenings of Xerxes' fatal bridge (108–14). This, then, is the net of destruction, as the sequel and later the ghostly Darius are to show us; already the god-fearing language of the Chorus hints at more flagrant ways in which the Persian *moira* (101) has been transgressed.[21]

The Chorus now gives itself over to unrelieved foreboding ('now shudders my black-robed heart ...,' 115 ff), to pictures of the city greeting the dreadful news (no hint of which has yet reached them) with tears and lamentation. The confident and powerful water-images (μεγάλῳ ῥεύματι φωτῶν, 88; ἄμαχον κῦμα θαλάσσας, 90, for the Persian army) now give way to terrestrial images ('like a swarm of bees,' 128), but this *land* army (as the image impresses on us) has now irrevocably crossed the sea (130–2). And so the lyric ends in deeper gloom than did the anapaests, as the Chorus now sings of Persian wives softly grieving

---

a more striking example of Aeschylean technique. There is certainly no compelling reason for accepting Müller's transposition. See also Sidgwick's defence of the original line sequence in his notes on vv 91 and 101 ff, with which I agree, except for his exaggerated suggestion about 'the whole play being the glorification of Salamis.' (On Winnington-Ingram's view of the whole passage, see the following note.)

21 Winnington-Ingram *Studies* pp 3–4 (cf pp 1–2) defends Müller's transposition of vv 93–100 to follow 101–14: he finds this sequence easier to relate to his argument that in this, the first part of the play, human disasters are treated according to 'quite unmoralized' notions such as divine jealousy of (Persian) prosperity and the resulting 'crafty deception of god,' while in the second part (ie, in the Darius Scene) such disasters are treated as due to 'the stern punishment of *hubris*.' In a somewhat complex interpretation of the whole passage (as rearranged in Müller's text), he finds the Chorus expressing the former view, while the audience *may*, by contrast, interpret their words in accordance with the moralistic view of disaster. (Winnington-Ingram makes the interesting suggestion, ibid 1, that this ambiguity between prosperity and *hubris* as the source of human disaster is present in the *Persae* but had disappeared in favour of the latter explanation by the time of the *Oresteia* [458 BC]. However, a touch of the old ambiguity would still seem to remain if we consider *Ag* 772 ff and esp 1001–16, as well as *Ag* 750 ff.)

(ἀβροπενθεῖς) in their lonely beds (133 ff), a poignant contrast to the martial vigour of its opening.

It is the Queen's role to repeat in dramatic terms the apprehensions which the Chorus has expressed in lyrics. A neat transitional passage (140–9, much belaboured by the critics) precedes her entry: the Chorus begins to debate, in solemn conclave, whether Persian arrows or Greek spears will prevail, only to be interrupted by the Queen who, with her premonitions, dreams, and omens, provides the only sort of answer which the Chorus's questions can, at this stage, receive.[22]

The Queen travels in a few lines the same distance which it has taken the Chorus a full lyric to traverse. Leaving 'her gold-decked chambers,' she trembles, 'lest Wealth [retaining πλοῦτος, as in the MSS] rushing headlong, may trip and overthrow, mid clouds of dust, the prosperity which Darius reaped with some god's help' (163–4). Wealth is at the heart of the Queen's fear: her thought is Solonian in its ambiguity – a good reason for retaining πλοῦτος at v 163, for in Solon wealth can lead to the overthrow of the very prosperity which it brings; it is left to the play to add the Aeschylean emphasis that not without some deed of *hybris* will wealth bring ruin.[23]

22 Critics worried about what they regard as the quite abortive nature (at least from the dramatic point of view) of the Chorus's proposed session of deep thought, at 140 ff, on Xerxes' prospects have sought to explain it in terms far removed from the dramatic context. Stoessl 'Die *Phoinissen* des Phrynichos und die *Perser* des Aischylos' p 150, followed by Lesky (*Die tragische Dichtung* p 62), thinks that the proposed pondering of the Chorus of Elders is introduced merely in slavish imitation of the *Phoenissae* of Phrynichus: the Alexandrian Hypothesis to the *Persae* quotes one Glaucus as saying that Aeschylus imitated Phrynichus in this play and we learn from the same hypothesis that a eunuch tells of the defeat of Xerxes as he prepares the seats for a Council of Elders' meeting, presumably to discuss this crisis. Wilamowitz's explanation, 'Die *Perser* des Aischylos' pp 382–3, that the passage is simply a flaw, a sign of a developing poet, is still less convincing. Taplin (*Stagecraft* p 65) finds it reasonable (from 'the exhoration to sit' at 140–1) that the Chorus are to be thought of as inside a council chamber, though he does not insist that this is meant to recall the scene-setting of Phrynichus' *Persians* and, indeed, deprecates the need for seeking too insistently for motivations for the entrances and exits of Choruses and characters in Aeschylean tragedy.

23 Cf Solon fr 1 (Diehl), esp vv 7–32, 71 ff, and Aesch *Ag* 750 ff. In the present passage, Queen Atossa goes on to express two supplementary fears suggestive of the whole Persian dilemma: the fear that wealth without manpower is not to be honoured (this will be Xerxes' situation after his defeat) and the fear that without wealth a man's true strength cannot shine forth (165–7). However, vv 163–4 in particular are puzzling. Most editors retain πλοῦτος (recognizing that by wrong use of excess wealth one may put an end to prosperity), but it is difficult to see how wealth 'kicks

The Persian catastrophe (as we know) has already happened. The dramatic action cannot affect it; prophetic dreams and visions must replace action in the opening episodes of plays like this. The ominous import of Atossa's visions (the Greek woman, yoked to the Persian one, who overthrows her would-be master; the eagle fleeing for safety before the little falcon) is clear enough but the language and details of the Queen's narration heighten their significance. Xerxes' yoking of the mares (ζεύγνυσιν αὐτὼ καὶ λέπαδν' ἐπ' αὐχένων / τίθησι, 191–2) echoes the King's yoking of the Hellespont (ζυγὸν ἀμφιβαλὼν αὐχένι πόντου, 72) as well as his intention of yoking Greece in slavery (ζυγὸν ἀμφιβαλεῖν δούλιον Ἑλλάδι, 50) – and both ζυγόν and λέπαδνον are words which Aeschylus uses elsewhere with sinister overtones.[24] In the telling of the same dream-omen, two telling cameos appear with the instant completeness of dream-imagery: one is the image of the Persian mare preening herself (ἐπυργοῦτο, 192, is the untranslatable word) in the luxury of her enslavement; the other is the image of Xerxes' despair, 'rending his robes' (199) when the Greek mare overthrows him, while father Darius looks down in pity. This emphasis on the relation of raiment to Persian pride and Persian ruin is to recur (832–6, 846 ff, 1030, 1060) at the climactic moments of the play.

Before the arrival of Xerxes' Messenger, another brief transition (230–45) prepares us for the switch from the Persian court to the battle in Greece. Three points in the Chorus's answers about the distant enemy heighten the tragic expectation: Greece's distance ('by the setting of the sun's decline,' 232) plays up the overreaching quality of Asiatic Xerxes; Greece's wealth, θησαυρὸς χθονός, 'the land's own treasure house' (238), contrasts with the Persian ruler's individual magnificence,[25] Greek

---

up clouds of dust.' Perhaps the best explanation (short of Broadhead's suggestion of textual corruption) is David Sansone's in 'Aeschylus, *Persae* 163' pp 115–16. He cites several passages supporting his view that we have here a wrestling metaphor, which would explain both the presence of dust and of tripping (allowed in Greek wrestling).

24 Cf, for example, *Ag* 218 and *Ag* 1071. Cf also Smethurst's good comment (*Artistry* p 113) on this whole passage: 'A structural function of the dream report in the *Persians* is to delay, but also to prepare for, a report of the actual event [ie, the defeat at Salamis] by the messenger and a performance "event", Xerxes' appearance and lament.'

25 Cf Finley *Pindar and Aeschylus* p 210, who comments on the contrast between Persian gold and Greek silver as paralleling the contrast between Persian *hybris* and Greek piety (for the Athenians used *their* wealth for the defence of their country). On this latter point, cf Podlecki *The Political Background of Aeschylean Tragedy* p 15; he reminds

freedom opposes Persian despotism – and yet its army 'subject to no man' has once before prevailed (241–4, 236).[26]

> O Persian land ... at one stroke our great fortune is destroyed, the bloom of Persian manhood turned to dust. (250–2)

This 'final' announcement of the Messenger's, at the very moment of his entry, epitomizes the nature and effect of the *Persae*'s special structure: the four discrete but related aspects of Xerxes' fall so placed that we may grasp them, *in toto et in partibus*, in a single dramatic experience. During the Messenger Scene we are as close to the actual catastrophe as the dramatic scope (let alone the dramatic convention) of the play can tolerate. Once again (as in the preparatory movement) lyric precedes dramatic treatment, though now, for obvious reasons, the proportions are reversed: after a series of brief laments interrupting the initial headlines of the bitter news (the disaster at Salamis, the uselessness of the Persian bows, the hated name of the Athenians), the rest of this movement is taken up with the vivid and detailed narration of the events themselves. It has been suggested that this initial prominence of the Chorus in the Messenger Scene shows that Aeschylus has not yet shaken himself free of the conventions of one-actor tragedy.[27] But surely

---

us that this use of wealth from the Laureion silver mines was an important part of Themistocles' policy (Herod vii.144) and so uses this reference in the *Persae* (237–8, transposed by Trendelenburg to follow 240) in support of his thesis that much of the play's motivation lies in Aeschylus' desire to vindicate Themistocles and his policies. On this view, see below, n 31.

26 The Queen has asked (235) whether the Athenians have a large army. The Chorus replies: καὶ στρατὸς τοιοῦτος, ἔρξας πολλὰ δὴ Μήδους κακά: 'such an army, indeed, as has (already) wrought many woes on the Persians' (236). The Chorus is referring to the defeat inflicted on the Persians at Marathon ten years earlier but there is, perhaps, an ironical ambiguity in the explanatory participial expression, for the audience knows that even as the Chorus speaks the Athenians have already inflicted another, far greater, defeat upon the Persians. (The syntactical difficulties of v 236 have, however, led to various different interpretations and explanations: see Broadhead's note *ad loc*)

27 Cf Kitto *Greek Tragedy* p 44; Broadhead pp xli–xlii, though he also believes that Aeschylus puts the traditional convention to good dramatic effect ('the feelings of the Chorus find fitting expression in the *amoibaion*,' while Atossa's 'queenly dignity would have been diminished by the lament'). (The formal question which arises here and later in the play has recently been discussed in more general terms by Ann Michelini; see below p 27 and nn 45 and 46.) This would appear to be also the view

it is appropriate that, at the first bleak announcement of the disaster, the emotional effect upon the Persian people should be expressed at once – and this only the Chorus can do. When the Queen Mother speaks, *her* concern must be personal ('Who is *not* dead?' she asks at 296 – and the Messenger, whose tactful understanding at this juncture has been praised ad nauseam by the critics, assures her that Xerxes lives), and such personal concern for the life of Xerxes must lead away from the central issue of the play, had not the Chorus already sounded the note of national mourning. Once again, the dramatic priorities and not the dramatist's fumbling with unfamiliar counters provide the sounder explanations of procedures which strike the modern reader as unusual.

The Messenger Speeches have a formal structure of their own. First, as introduction, the stark and vivid roll-call of dead heroes drowned or slain ('The noble Tenagon now comes and goes [πολεῖ: a terrible word in the context!] along the sea-washed shores of Ajax' isle,' 306–7; 'Metallus in death has changed to red the colour of his thick and shaggy beard,' 314 ff),[28] then the trilogy of disaster (Salamis, Psyttalea, and the River Strymon), each incident complete with its divine temptation, tragic overreaching, and catastrophe.[29] 'Guileful deception of god,' the Chorus has warned (93 ff); so, too, the Messenger explains the whole incredible defeat at Salamis ('Were we outnumbered? No, some god [δαίμων τις] destroyed our host,' 337–8, 345) and, in particular, the fatal deception which lured Xerxes to block the straits (φανεὶς ἀλάστωρ ἢ κακὸς δαίμων ποθέν·, 354). A series of brilliant pictures (364 ff) suggestive at once of lively action and of divine design describes the fatal sequence at Salamis.[30] Night ('*aithêr*'s darkened grove') deceives King Xerxes; day,

---

of Taplin (*Stagecraft* pp 85–6), who adds good reasons for believing that the kind of epirrhematic structure (such as we have here, between the Messenger and the Chorus) is particularly characteristic of early tragedy.

28 Cf Lattimore's comments (*The Poetry of Greek Tragedy* pp 35 ff): 'What would it [the *Persae*] be without the poetry?' In particular he speaks of the great series of catalogues in the *Persae* as opening 'splendours to ear and eye,' and (p 38) of the 'eye-witness report of battle and retreat where Aeschylus, using the language of poetry, is still as tough and bitter as the best prose writer could be.'

29 Cf Croiset *Eschyle* p 90, who speaks of the three Messenger Speeches as providing 'presqu'une tragédie en soi, avec son commencement, son milieu, son dénouement,' and of the three successive phases of the Persian disaster as joined together by a common bond.

30 Of the many tactical and technical studies of the Battle of Salamis and its treatment in the *Persae*, see in particular Hammond 'The Battle of Salamis,' and bibliography

returning, reveals the scope of that deception; then night again, at the end of the day's battle, quenches forever the false hopes of the night before.

> Groans swept the deep with lamentation, Till night's dark face erased the scene from view. (426–8)

Earlier in the play, Atossa has wondered how a people 'subject to no man' could ever stand firm against the Persian host. In the event, it is the democratic Greeks from their first cry, 'Now is the struggle on behalf of all' (405), who act as a single man throughout.[31] The descriptions of Persians in battle (the babble of Persian tongues, 406; the flight in mad disorder, 'φυγῇ δ' ἀκόσμως,' 422; the 'mob' [πλῆθος, 432] of Persians likened in defeat to 'a haul of fish,' 424) all contrast grimly with the earlier descriptions of one splendid, ordered army under one great King.

'There is an island fronting Salamis ...' (447 ff). Again, the false hope born of overconfidence begets the action of this second catastrophe, at Psyttalea.[32] Xerxes, κακῶς τὸ μέλλον ἱστορῶν, dispatches a picked band

---

there given, and Podlecki *The Political Background of Aeschylean Tragedy* appendix A, pp 131–41. The subject is beyond the scope of this study of the *Persae*. On the celebrated reference to the ruse of Themistocles at 355 ff, see the following note.

31 The marked anonymity of the Greek host in Aeschylus' treatment of the battle of Salamis has long been noted; cf, for example, Patin *Études sur les tragiques grecs* p 214, who thinks that this feature puts the emphasis on national rather than individual pride on the part of the Athenians. However, simply in dramatic terms, it is natural that, in a play presented through Persian eyes, Persians should be named and Greeks should remain as the anonymous agents of divine nemesis. That is not to say, of course, that the Athenian audience would not thrill with pride at this treatment of their exploits, or that supporters of Themistocles would not be justifiably gratified at the clear reference to Themistocles' successful ruse (if ruse it was) in persuading Xerxes that the Greek fleet was about to flee (see *Persae* 355 ff; cf Herod VIII.75). Against the suggestion that Aeschylus' emphasis on the *daimōn* would somehow diminish in the Greek mind the credit due to Themistocles, see Podlecki's arguments (*Background of Aeschylean Tragedy* pp 22–3). However, I would not go as far as this critic when he suggests (12–15) that the vindication of Themistocles was one of the main motivating forces in the composition of the play.

32 Aeschylus develops the Psyttalea incident rather more than Herodotus does at VIII.76 and 95. Some think that his particular purpose is to honour Aristeides (cf Herod VIII.95), while champions of Aeschylus as the champion of Themistocles are at pains to play down the significance of *this* particular historical reference. (See Podlecki *Background of Aeschylean Tragedy* pp 23–5, and references there given.) Here we see, perhaps, some of the dangers surrounding 'historical critics' who burden the playwright with specific political causes.

to slaughter 'those Greeks, an easy prey,' who might take refuge there after defeat at Salamis, and again, with the god's help (454–5), the move results in fresh disaster for the Persians. Apparently incidental touches in the dramatic narrative heighten the tragic effect by ironic anticipations and contrasts: the lovely strand 'where Pan is wont to walk' is the one which bodies of shipwrecked Persian sailors soon will nudge; the single shout (ἐξ ἑνὸς ῥόθου, 462) of the Greeks echoes their triumphant cry (κέλαδος ... μολπηδόν, 388–9) before Salamis, and contrasts with the babble of Persian fear (406); and again the action ends with the same disordered flight of the Persians (ἤιξ᾽ ἀκόσμῳ ξὺν φυγῇ, 470) as did the larger engagement (φυλῇ δ᾽ ἀκόσμως πᾶσα ναῦς ἠρέσσετο, 422).

It is in the third and final episode of our little trilogy that we have the clearest demonstration of divine temptation and human overstepping. The scene is laid at the penultimate stage of the long march of Persian survivors back to Asia, and this time no human power shares with the gods the agency of retribution.

> That very night, θεός raised a wintry storm all out of season and froze the whole stream of sacred Strymon. Any man who had thought before that the gods were nowhere then assailed them with their prayers worshipping earth and heaven ... And whoever of us set off to cross before the sun's bright rays [θεοῦ / ἀκτῖνας] were sent abroad hit upon lucky safety. For soon the orb of the sun with blazing countenance melted the middle passage. In a heap men fell and lucky then was he who quickly breathed his last. (495–507)

With the word θεός Aeschylus exploits the traditionally 'religious' weather language of the Greeks[33] to express in a single description the idea of Persian destruction by natural phenomena and by divine nemesis. Nor should we miss the overtone in 'sacred Strymon' (ἁγνοῦ Στρυμόνος, 497); the Bosporos which Xerxes yokes is also sacred (Βόσπορον ῥόον θεοῦ, 746): Xerxes' crime against the sea (like Agamemnon's treading on the purple) may be merely symbolic of his hybristic ambition but it is fitting that the sufferings of his host should begin in a battle at sea (where, as bowmen, 147, Persians are out of their element) and end in other sacred waters which freeze and melt with a very special vindictiveness.[34] The ambiguities of 'god' and 'weather'

---

33 See *LSJ* θεός, *s.v.*, I.1.d.

34 Cf Wardman 'Tactics and Tradition in the Persian Wars' pp 52–3, who notes the first but not the second of these ironically apt reversals. With regard to the 'sacred

(or 'the skies,' 'the sun') are finally resolved (if they need resolving) in the lines with which the Messenger concludes his tale of Persian woe.

> All this is true. Yet many things I have left out of my account in telling of the evils descending on the Persians from the hand of god [θεός, 514: the Messenger ends his account as he began it, 353 ff, with the god].

The first stasimon (532–97) provides a splendid transition between the actual and retrospective views of Xerxes' catastrophe. Three major themes stand out: Zeus the avenger ('King Zeus, now you have destroyed ...,' 532 ff); Xerxes the guilty leader ('Xerxes led them, alas; Xerxes ruined them, o woe! For Xerxes ordered all unwisely ...,' 550 ff); and the death-knell of Persian power ('No longer will there be Persian-ruling [περσονομοῦνται is the verb in the original] throughout Asia ...,' 584 ff). Interwoven with these themes are the chants of suffering and lamentation as the Chorus reflects the grief of Persian wives, 'rending their clothes with their soft hands' (537–8), of brides, 'abandoning the soft, rich beds of young delight' (541–4), and of the old, parents now childless, bewailing total woe (580 ff).

The language and imagery of the mourning-brides passage (541–5) in this Chorus remind us that Aeschylus, far from being merely the poet of 'chariots heaped on chariots and corpses piled pell mell' (as Aristophanes, *Frogs* 403, would have him), could, when he wished, be as effective in a soft, feminine, even sensual mode. Once, in anticipation, this softly mourning note has already been sounded (133–9) at the end of the parodos. In both instances, the contrast provided by the confident and strongly masculine descriptions of the glorious army departing for the war makes the soft passages the more beguiling and the grief they express more poignant. It may be that such passages are indicative of Aeschylus' attitude to the Persians and of the light in which he wishes to cast them; one critic, for example, has noted the unusual number of *habro*- compounds in the play.[35] Nevertheless, effects and contrasts of this kind are not limited to the *Persae*; one

---

Strymon' it is not enough to note, as Broadhead does in his note *ad loc*, that 'the Persians regarded rivers as sacred and that the Greeks too applied the epithet to rivers, water and other elements'; the point is, rather, Aeschylus' exploitation of such epithets to underline the ironic justice of Xerxes' fate.

35 Stanford *Aeschylus in His Style* p 113 counts five *habro*- compounds in the *Persae*: at vv 41, 135, 541, 543, 1073.

thinks, for example, of the second stasimon of the *Agamemnon* with the sensuous description of fatal Helen slipping out of 'her softly-woven (ἀβροπήνων) curtained bower' (*Ag* 690–1) to sail with Paris, 'a gentle adornment of wealth, a soft weapon of loving-glance, a heart-piercing flower of passion' (*Ag* 741–3) by which Priam and the seed of Priam would be destroyed. And here too we have an ironic contrast with the martial vigour of the parodos, for the confident Greeks and their King are also to suffer in the end, in this war waged 'for another man's wife' (*Ag* 447–8).

The contrast provided by the last strophic pair (584–97), with its muted note of triumph, is truly remarkable. For the first time the Chorus deserts its role as loyal guardians of the Persian court: it hints at the good which is to come of all this suffering but the good no longer concerns the glory of Xerxes and Persia but the freedom of Asia now saved from despotism.

> Now Persian sway through Asia's lands exists no longer ... No longer will men grovel on the ground in worship, for the power of the King is destroyed. No longer will the tongues of men be held in bitter constraint, for the people are freed and free will be their speech, since the yoke of armed might has been destroyed. (584–94, in part)

... λέλυται γὰρ / λαὸς ἐλεύθερα βάζειν, / ὡς ἐλύθη ζυγὸν ἀλκᾶς (592–4): a nice play (and a neat Aeschylean jingle: λέλυται ... ἐλεύθερα ... ἐλύθη) on λύω in its positive and negative senses of 'free' and 'destroy': still more significant is ζυγόν, for here we celebrate the final destruction of that Persian yoke which has already appeared in various ambiguous and sinister contexts throughout the play.

Tragic expectation and tragic fulfilment have now been expressed. The third movement of the play is retrospective: through the wisdom of the ghostly Darius the full significance of the catastrophe will be revealed. The summoning of Darius' ghost by ritual and by choral incantation (609 ff, 628 ff) anticipates the less literal evocation of Agamemnon's spirit in the *Choephori* (315 ff). In the present instance, the poet's purpose is more complex and it is this complexity which accounts for certain mild inconsistencies in the presentation of Darius. Darius' utterances have two functions: first (and most important) to make explicit the tragic meaning of Xerxes' fall; second, to warn the Persians against the folly of further attacks on mainland Greece – and in so doing to complete the play's debt to history by prophecies of what will happen at

Plataea.[36] Both these functions require of Darius a special degree of knowledge, as well as of wisdom, beyond that of all living Persians, and no one would baulk at such attributes of a ghostly king who, even in life, was regarded almost as a god (... Πέρσαις ὡς θεός, 711). Why, then does the poet limit Darius to the somewhat piecemeal and even inconsistent knowledge provided by certain convenient oracles? Darius knows, for example, that Persia was doomed to defeat at the hands of the Greeks (739, 787–92, 796–7, 800 ff), but not that this fate would fall on Xerxes; he is unaware, until he is told, of Xerxes' expedition against Greece, yet later (800 ff) his oracles appear to have supplied him with detailed information about the Persian land army and its final discomfiture at Plataea. The advantages of thus circumscribing Darius' knowledge are twofold and outweigh the inconsistencies.[37] In the first place, the device allows Darius to ask the right questions, that is, the questions whose answers will provide the cues for the sort of comment here required of him. Second, the oracle about the Persian defeat, combined with the uncertainty as to the time and circumstance of that defeat, provide, as we shall see, just the right proportion of freedom and necessity that Xerxes' tragedy requires. Even so, it should be admitted that for once the requirements of history, of the poet's need to mention at least the major events which actually happened, tend slightly to exacerbate the sensitive areas of Darius' piecemeal knowledge. Salamis, in the poet's presentation, is the central catastrophe for Xerxes and nothing must be allowed to distract from that. Yet in the picture, however exaggerated, of total Persian ruin, someone must be made to mention Plataea. Darius is the obvious one to do so: obviously it cannot be the Messenger, and Darius can place Plataea in the future, outside of Xerxes' personal tragedy and yet a part of the total picture of Persian *hybris* (808 ff) and Persian ruin.

36 Cf *supra* p 4 f and n 3.

37 Editors and critics from Blomfield (1814) on have worried about the inconsistencies and *lacunae* in Darius' knowledge in the *Persae*. It is, I think, misguided, to try to explain them away as do, for example, Patin *Études* 214 and Broadhead in his note to 739 ff, by pontificating on the sort of knowledge that Darius may, and may not, be expected to have. True, Aeschylus makes a gesture at explaining the inconsistency in Darius' two references to oracles at 739 and at 800 ff, for oracles are notoriously incomplete in their information. But the real reason for Darius' piecemeal knowledge is, of course, that the poet wants him to have just as much and as little as is convenient (as we shall see) for his (the poet's) dramatic purposes. This is substantially the view of Alexanderson 'Darius and the Persians' pp 3 ff and (in less detail) of Dawe 'Inconsistency' pp 30–1.

Darius' questions, once he has heard of Xerxes' defeat, go right to the crucial point: 'The reckless one, was it by land or sea he made his mad attempt?' (719), and then: 'How did so great a *land army* succeed in crossing over?' (721). And so we come to the symbolic nub of the matter. The poet chooses the Queen's words with care: 'By man-made contrivances (μηχαναῖς) he yoked the strait of Hellê' (722). Even before Darius pounces, the Queen is aware of the sinister aspect of her revelation. 'Surely [she hazards] some god settled himself (ξυνήψατο) upon his mind' (724). 'Alas, some mighty god,' (the Ghost assures her) 'and so he lost all judgment' (725).[38]

In expounding the necessary fulfilment of the oracle, Darius makes the personal guilt of Xerxes crystal clear:

> I for my part prayed that only after much time would the gods bring these things to pass. But when a man himself is eager, then the god fastens on him. (740–2)

Nowhere do we have a clearer statement of Aeschylus' tragic theology – of the double motivation of the hybristic transgressor and of the god who leads him on, once he has shown his hand; of the doom or the curse which hangs over a royal house and of the tragic individual who reaches up, as it were, and pulls the cloud down on himself. Thus (as in the celebrated 'yoke of necessity' passage at *Ag* 218 ff) does Aeschylus provide both for 'dooms,' oracle-or-curse-fulfilments, and for the free (if any man is free) and fatal decisions of the doomed one.[39]

38 Darius' shocked reaction, here and later in this scene, to Xerxes' yoking of the Hellespont (which Darius here calls the Bosporos) is perhaps the first egregiously 'ahistorical' passage in the play, for we know that the historical Darius himself had a bridge of ships built across the Thracian Bosporos by one Mandocles (Herodotus IV.87–8), and there would appear to be little difference between the two deeds as far as offence to the gods (cf Darius at vv 745–50), whether literally or symbolically understood, is concerned. Quincey 'Notes on the *Persae*' pp 182–6, suggests that 'some convenient oracles' (presumably the ones mentioned by Darius at 739) warning against such bridging are to be thought of as occurring in the meantime – an ingenious suggestion which one would prefer to see supported by clearer indications in the text. Nevertheless, Herodotus (VII.6) does tell us of the oracle of Onomacritus, used to encourage Xerxes in his expedition, that it was fated that a Persian should build a bridge across the Hellespont and march an army into Greece; it is possible that Aeschylus chooses here to give this oracle a sinister twist for the Persians.

39 It has become fashionable in much Aeschylean criticism to reduce, sometimes almost to the vanishing point, the element of human responsibility, of fault (however

The egregious quality of Xerxes' mad career stands out, in the speeches of Darius, against the whole tapestry of wise and prosperous Persian rule. Here at last the symbol, the yoking of the Hellespont, is allowed to dissolve into the real *hybris* for which it stands. The former is treated briefly, in the first of two speeches on Xerxes (739–52), and is surrounded by all the characteristics (lack of judgment, boldness, ignorance [744], delusive hope [745–6], sickness of mind [750]) associated with major affronts against the divine scheme of things. But the real significance of what Xerxes has done is reserved for the second and longer of the two speeches (759–86). Here the disaster which Xerxes has brought to his people is contrasted with the ever-increasing prosperity of Persia 'from that time when Zeus laid it down that one man was to rule all Asia, nurse of sheep' (763–4). Xerxes alone 'being young, thought fresh young thoughts' (782); disobeying his father's injunctions to him, he sought to go beyond the *moira* of Zeus and to attack mainland Greece as well. (The lesson is brought home still more explicitly at the end of Darius' next speech, with its summary of Xerxes' career,

ὕβρις γὰρ ἐξανθοῦσ' ἐκάρπωσε στάχυν
ἄτης, ὅθεν πάγκλαυτον ἐξαμᾷ θέρος [821–2]

For *hybris* when it has blossomed produces a crop of Atê [Destruction] whence it reaps a harvest fraught with tears.

and the warning that Ζεὺς κολαστής is the harsh corrector of the man who, despising τὸν παρόντα δαίμονα, lusts after other things.) This, then,

___

qualified), in Aeschylus' tragic sufferers. This tendency has, of course, gone hand in hand with the tendency to question the justice of Zeus in Aeschylus, at least in any sense which might provide some measure of meaning, some hint of an ethical pattern in human suffering, from which man might be said to learn, and to find some consolation in the tragic catastrophes presented by the poet. (See above, n 7.) Perhaps the best which can be said for the more extreme form of this approach is that it has overthrown the oversimplified, pietistic interpretations of Aeschylus which presented him more as a theologian, particularly as a theological champion of Zeus, and a moral philosopher, than as a tragic poet. It is curious, however, that the two most eloquent and learned spokesmen for the god-doomed tragic sufferer in Aeschylus, Page and Lloyd-Jones in the works cited above (n 7), make no use at all of this passage in the *Persae* (739 ff) in their estimate of Aeschylus' treatment of the role of Zeus, and of human guilt, in tragic suffering. And yet this passage surely sheds light on the subtler and more vexed problem of the guilt of Agamemnon (also under a curse or 'doom' from the past) in the sacrifice of Iphigenia.

is the real offence of Xerxes: the crossing from Asia to Europe against the ordinance of Zeus.[40] No Greek (as Professor Kitto has pointed out)[41] would normally regard a bridge of ships as an impiety but Aeschylus has managed to play it up as such to secure a powerful visual symbol (comparable to Agamemnon's walking on the purple) to convey with the immediacy of drama the essential nature of Xerxes' overreaching *hybris*.

Like the Messenger's account, the utterances of Darius fall into three parts (Aeschylus' fondness for sets of three is well attested).[42] The third speech prophesies the fate at Plataea of the picked band of the Persian army left to fight on in Greece. Once again, as in each of Darius' speeches and in the Messenger's accounts of disasters at Salamis, Psyttalea, and the Strymon, the tale begins with references to delusive hope (κεναῖσιν ἐλπίσιν πεπεισμένος, 804) and to violence and outrage (the ravaging of Greek temples, 807–12), on the part of Xerxes and his army:

Here [in Boeotia] there awaits them to suffer the last and greatest of their woes, in payment for their outrage [ὕβρεως ἄποινα, 808] and their impious designs. (807–8)

Wherefore, for evil deeds, they suffer evils no less themselves, and will suffer. (813–14)[43]

40 This is the traditional view of the 'real' offence of Xerxes, symbolized by his bridging of the Hellespont, though some critics have expressed it more explicitly than others. See, for example, Murray *Aeschylus* p 125, Kitto *Greek Tragedy* pp 38–41, Mazon *Les Perses, Notice* p 57, Winnington-Ingram *Studies* pp 10–11, Deichgräber *Die Persentetralogie* pp 196–7, and Broadhead p xxix, cf pp xvii–xviii. (The latter two are less explicit in their statements; Broadhead, for example, describes the *hybris* of Xerxes in more general terms as that of a man 'who, not content with his inherited prosperity, sought to rival the gods themselves and to overstep the limits beyond which mere mortals might not go.' Garvie, on the other hand ('Aeschylus' Simple Plots' p 70) strenuously resists this interpretation (see below, n 53) and finds the basic contrast of the play (and the one which, presumably, provides its tragic meaning) to be between the 'former splendour and present ruin' (p 70) of Darius and the Persians. In this speech (759–86), Aeschylus lets the ghostly Darius 'forget' the extra-Asiatic expeditions by his own generals and, in at least one case (Herod IV.88), by himself.
41 Kitto *Greek Tragedy* p 38.
42 Cf Solmsen *Hesiod and Aeschylus* pp 127 ff and 157 ff.
43 The whole passage (807–15) in which Darius, with his special knowledge, describes the Persian outrage to the temples of the gods, and the sure reprisal it will bring, provides another clear anticipation of a passage in the *Agamemnon*: Clytemnestra's almost psychic 'fears' (*Ag* 338 ff) lest the Greek army desecrate Trojan temples and bring ruin on themselves, are also disastrously fulfilled, as we learn from the Herald's speeches, at 527 ff and 648 ff

The heaps of Persian dead at Plataea will make known even to the third generation the lesson 'that man, being mortal, must not think more than mortal thoughts' (818–20).

Just before his return to the nether world, Darius adds a minor but thematically significant instruction to Atossa: she is to go to meet Xerxes with 'whatever raiment is suitable,' since all his rich clothing is torn to shreds in grief at his disaster (832–6). And she should comfort him as well: 'For to you alone, I know, he will endure to listen' (838). To the Chorus of elders he adds the (mildly sardonic?) advice: 'Take pleasure, even amid trouble, while you can: wealth profits not the dead!' (840–2).

The ghost of Darius now descends to Hades.[44] The Queen, after a brief speech accepting Darius' instructions, also makes her departure. Since, contrary to expectations aroused by Darius and herself, this completes her role, its several interesting and, in places, puzzling, features may now be reviewed in the context of the play as a whole.

In the first episode, we have seen that the dream and the portent experienced by Atossa complement in dramatic form the premonitions already expressed in lyrics by the Chorus. We have noted, too, that the motif of 'dangerous wealth,' suggested, perhaps unconsciously, in the Chorus's descriptions of Persian power, is given more specific formulation by the Queen (see vv 162–4). Nevertheless, the Queen herself, on this her first appearance, is splendidly dressed, for the Chorus describe her as 'dazzling to the eyes, like a god' (150–1).

On the arrival of the Messenger, the Chorus first serves as the recipient of his news but is replaced by the Queen before the Messenger gives his detailed report. The same sequence is followed when the ghost of Darius appears: when the Chorus twice professes too much fear to speak in his presence, Darius repeats to Atossa his request for information about the troubles which have caused their invocations. Is this repeated 'replacement' merely a 'formal matter,' the second actor being used (perhaps clumsily) to usurp what is frequently in Aeschylus a choral function? Or is there, in each case, a sound dramatic reason for this alternation of interlocutors? Critical opinion is divided on the matter. Ann Michelini, in a recent, subtle discussion, has indicated that there may be truth in both explanations, though she gives more emphasis than most to the 'historical' explanation, that is, that this use of the second actor as 'a surrogate for the chorus is a natural and

---

44 For interesting suggestions as to how the whole 'ghost of Darius scene' might have been staged, see Taplin *Stagecraft* pp 116 ff; cf pp 103–7.

obvious first solution' to the problem of adapting the old 'actor-chorus dialogue' to the relatively new development of 'two-actor' tragedy.[45] Nevertheless, Michelini credits Aeschylus with dramatic reasons as well for this procedure: 'In both cases, the switch [that is, from Chorus to actor or interlocutor] is associated with the kind of communication required, a change from the wails that typify mourning ritual – and the lyric emotionalism of the chorus – to a clearer and less passionate speaker.[46]

The sequences just observed repeat, at least in formal terms, the sequence consisting of the parodos and the first scene between the Queen and the Chorus-Leader. There similar material (anxious premonitions about the absent army) was treated first in lyric and then in dramatic terms. In the latter sequences, however (that is, in the 'Messenger' and 'Darius' scenes), the take-over by an actor from the Chorus involves much more than a switch to rational discourse. It is necessary that the Queen be drawn into the action, particularly in connection with the detailed news of the catastrophe, for it is she who will pass on the information to Darius. And this in turn is necessary because (though this may not be the only reason) the instructions from Darius at the end of the scene can be given only to her.[47]

The second entry of the Queen at the beginning of the Second Episode, 'without my chariot, without my former luxury' (as she tells us at vv 607–8) provides one of the most striking visual symbols of the play. The Queen's drab appearance contrasts significantly with the glamour (remarked by the Chorus) of her earlier entry and it is this contrast which gives point, as Taplin has observed, to this 'mirror scene.'[48] We

45 Michelini *Tradition* p 29. (Cf Taplin *Stagecraft* p 87, who gives less emphasis to 'the historical explanation' for Aeschylus' use of Chorus and actors in this play.) She comments further on the Queen's initial silence during the Messenger's report, that it 'conveys both her aloofness and her even greater suffering.' Cf also Smethurst *Artistry* p 133, who has noted the structural similarity between these initial exchanges between actor and Chorus in the two passages under consideration.
46 Michelini *Tradition* pp 32–3. For her full discussion of these passages and the critical issues raised by them, see her section 'The Chorus and the Actor' in chap. 1, pp 16–26.
47 On the problems raised by Atossa's two exits, and especially her "exit lines," see the appendix to this chapter: 'Atossa's "exit lines" at vv 529–31 and 849–51: "devices of false preparation"?'
48 Cf Taplin *Stagecraft* p 100: '... nearly always the similarity [between the two situations in 'mirror scenes'] is there in order to bring out the contrast between them.'

have noted in the Queen's earlier speeches her worries, in advance of the catastrophic news, about Xerxes' excessive wealth '... lest it overturn the prosperity (ὄλβος) won by Darius, not without the help of some god' (163–4). Now (as Taplin paraphrases the Queen's present mood), she realizes that 'a thoughtless overconfidence in these externals (of prosperity) leads to their destruction,'[49] and her unadorned appearance illustrates her bitter discovery (601 ff) of the transient nature of the good fortune which the *daimōn* bestows.

Atossa's modest appearance as she returns, unadorned, for the evocation of Darius' ghost provides a sort of symbolic bridge between the initial emphasis on Persian magnificence and the final ghastly manifestation of Persian ruin by the Persian king himself. The Queen, as she sets about obeying Darius' commands that she meet Xerxes with replacements of his tattered raiment, rent in grief, declares that of all their woes, the dishonour attaching to Xerxes' ragged attire is the one which most oppresses her:

> O *daimōn*! How many bitter griefs assail me! But this one gnaws the worst: to hear of the disgrace to the raiment of my son, to the very garments which he wears. (845–8)

This brilliant oriental touch (which has been misunderstood by some editors) – and indeed the whole 'appearance sequence' which we have noted – reminds us to what degree the *Persae* is concerned with symbols, with 'externals,' and, in the last tragic analysis, with loss of face. Thus, we should regard Atossa's unfulfilled intention of restoring Xerxes' garments (849–51) not merely as a device for concentrating attention on the final scene but more particularly as a means of accentuating, and even adding to, an essential aspect of Xerxes' ruin.[50]

---

49 Ibid.
50 This whole passage (vv 845–51) has been variously interpreted. Broadhead, for example (in his note to vv 847–8), approves of Schutz's comment, '*in his verbis et matrem et mulierem facile agnoscas,*' etc. But this concern for appearance and shame at its loss is a Persian, not merely a maternal, characteristic. (See Sidgwick's more sensible note *ad loc*) Smethurst, *Artistry* p 125, views both exit lines of the Queen (at vv 529–31 as well as at vv 849–51) as devices for focusing attention on Xerxes and his eventual return. (Elsewhere, p 132, Smethurst rightly stresses the visual effect and thematic importance of Xerxes' ragged appearance in that final scene.) Thalmann, 'Xerxes' Rags' p 267 ff, regards (as I do) the point of the Queen's lines at vv 845–51 to be to 'renew and focus the question, raised on the Queen's first exit, of what the nature of Xerxes' return will be' ... a return which, after the earlier emphasis on

The role of Darius in the play (in addition to his hierophantic, didactic contribution) is to provide contrast with the ruinous Xerxes, as the wise, temperate Persian king who waged successful wars but knew his *moira*, and who sought without success to impose this restraint upon his son.[51] Darius himself has already established his position (especially at vv 779 ff) to a considerable degree; it is now the function of the Chorus to develop (in the third stasimon, 852–906) this picture of Darius, with the greater expansiveness available to lyric treatment. The first strophic pair (852–63) gives a litany of Darius' kingly virtues and of the prosperous attributes of the kingdom he ruled; the remaining three strophic pairs provide, in the sweepingly vague style of Aeschylean geography, a panorama of Darius' exploits and of his mighty empire. (Dramatic, as opposed to historical, considerations, dictate, of course, suppression of all mention, at this point, of the defeat of Darius' generals at Marathon, though the conquest, in Darius' reign, of Thracian towns from the Propontis to the Strymonian gulf, and of Aegean islands, both eastern and western, are included without demur. The land expeditions [which, like the Cycladic islands, admittedly stretch well beyond the Asiatic domain which Darius has declared bestowed by Zeus] are treated somewhat ambiguously: in the case of those specifically mentioned, such as 'the Acheloian cities of the Strymonic Lake' [867], the Chorus makes clear that the victories must have been achieved by Darius' commanders, without Darius' presence; no specific mention seems to be made of the Scythian expedition at which we know from Herodotus that Darius was indeed present.[52] Thus does the poet reduce to the minimum, at least as far as expeditions into mainland Greece are concerned, any suggestion

---

Persian concern for appearance, robes, and wealth, will imply 'the complete ruin of their Persian supremacy, the destruction of their empire' (p 270).

For further consideration of the problems raised by the Queen's exit lines at both 529 ff and 849 ff, see appendix to this chapter.

51 It is true that Darius limited his statements about the results of his many expeditions to the claim (781, cf 785–6) that *he* did not cause so great woes as Xerxes. (Note also that in the expression ἀπεστράτευσα πολλά [780] he tacitly excludes Marathon, where he was not personally the commander.) It is left to the Chorus to extol Darius' exploits in more positive terms.

52 Vv 858–70, esp 864–70, have been subject to various interpretations; see references in Broadhead's note *ad loc.* At 864 ff, the Chorus exclaims, 'How many cities did he [Darius] capture without crossing the River Halys, without even leaving his own hearth ...!'; since the Chorus then goes on to mention various conquests *beyond* Darius' Asiatic borders (cf Herod v. 14–16), the implication is that these conquests were achieved by Darius' generals.

of Darius himself committing the extra-Asiatic follies of his son.)[53] Not till the last few verses of this ode is the contrast with Xerxes' exploits – the purpose of this whole paean of praise of Darius – made explicit:

> But now, sorely defeated by dreadful blows at sea, we suffer all too surely a change of fortune from the gods. (904–7)

Unlike most tragedies, the *Persae* does not present its catastrophe as evolving from the action presented on the stage. Rather, we have viewed the inevitable fall of the hybristic Xerxes from three aspects: through the foreboding of the Chorus, through the eyewitness account of the Messenger and through the wise retrospection of the Ghost of King Darius.[54] Now at last we see the thing in itself in the ragged and moaning person of King Xerxes, whose power and magnificence have been so firmly established in the opening passages of the play. The effect is all the more powerful for its long postponement: indeed, after all that has gone before, the mere presentation of the King, ragged and lamenting with the Persian elders, is sufficient to effect the tragic catharsis. This effect is further enriched, and the various strands of the actions drawn together, by the fulfilment, in this final kommos, of various tragic expectations previously provided.[55]

53 Garvie has remarked ('Aeschylus' Simple Plots' p 70; cf nn 22, 23) that this whole ode ought to embarrass 'those who think that Aeschylus wrote the play to teach the audience that Xerxes' *hybris* is punished.' This may be a possible view but the ode seems to me to provide difficulty of a rather different kind, namely, that it praises the military career of Darius which, in 'historical' terms was not much less 'overweening' than that of the son whose folly and *hybris* Darius (though not, or at least not explicitly, the Chorus) has criticized. It is true that the only passages in which Darius has used the word *hybris* (808 ff and 821–2) refer to the Persian army in general, but in view of the previous emphasis on Xerxes' responsibility for the expedition it would seem unwise to distinguish too sharply between the two.

54 The role of Darius provides us with one of the most striking anticipations of the *Agamemnon*'s dramaturgy in the use of a prophetic character to relate, in a single scene, the significant moments in the past, present, and future of tragic themes. Cassandra in the *Agamemnon* is by far the most brilliant example of this device, which could not, indeed, be fully exploited till its use in a trilogy like the *Oresteia*, where the past and future are so fully, and dreadfully, furnished. But the ghost of Darius is, dramatically speaking, Cassandra's ancestor.

55 This would appear to be a widely accepted view of the exodus. (Cf Belloni's bibliographical discussion of the passage, *I Persiani* pp 233–4.) Holtsmark, for

First must come the shock of Xerxes' physical appearance. Far from seeing a restored or a rehabilitated Xerxes such as the Queen Mother had hoped she might present, we gaze on a king in tatters and one who, moreover, draws attention to his rags of defeat and desolation by his directions ('Tear your hair and rend your robes!' 1056 ff) to his grieving Elders.[56] Thus, in this instance at least, spectacle, the rags of Xerxes, must contribute powerfully to the tragic effect.

To the earlier description of Xerxes' mighty armament, the 'resistless wave' of men with their chariots, lances, javelins, and bows (especially bows), this brief exchange provides a grim antithesis:

XERXES   You see this arrow-bearing –
CHORUS   What's this you say you've saved?
XERXES   this treasury for shafts?
CHORUS   Slim saving from such might![57] (1020–3)

So, too, the fearsome list of chieftains is answered by a dread roll-call of the drowned, now nosing the shores of Salamis, as Xerxes, once the King of Kings, is forced, like a criminal at the bar of justice, to answer the relentless questions of the Chorus (956–1001).

---

example, 'Ring Composition in the *Persae* of Aeschylus,' regards the exodus as providing the culmination and fulfilment of the fears and anxieties expressed at the beginning of the play, ie, as the completion of the 'ring composition' (the largest of many which he finds in the play) introduced in the parodos.

56   Belloni, by contrast (both in his introduction, lix ff, and in his notes on this passage), finds a strongly rehabilitating element in Xerxes' return and in his shared lamentation with the Chorus of Elders. It may be that Xerxes' self-humiliation frees him (rather belatedly!) of his *hybris*, as this critic argues, but it is difficult to find in this tragic finale quite the promise of revival, even of restored royal authority, which Belloni finds in the support shown by the Elders for the King. Other critics have also remarked on this support, on this impression of solidarity between Chorus and King, at least in the latter part of this final *kommos*, without, however, taking quite such a positive view of this effect as Belloni does. See, for example, Garvie 'Aeschylus' Simple Plots' p 71 and Avery (whom Garvie cites here) 'Dramatic Devices in Aeschylus' *Persae*' p 181. Cf more recently Schenker, 'The Queen and the Chorus in Aeschylus' *Persae*' pp 291–3, whose view of the final *kommos* seems, however, closer to that of Belloni in that he, too, finds a strongly rehabilitating element in Xerxes' shared lamentation with the Chorus.

57   Wardman, 'Tactics and Tradition in the Persian Wars' 49–52, observes the sequences of references in the play to Persian arrow-power (86, 147, 556, 926); this passage completes the motif with nice irony.

But of all the fulfilments of this dreadful scene, the final emphasis lies on the unnamed *daimōn* who, throughout, has hovered over the spectacle of Xerxes' *hybris*:

Woe for my fate which without warning fell,
How savagely the god [δαίμων] has fallen on the Persian race! (908–12).

... and alas for that proud array of men [κόσμου τ᾽ ἀνδρῶν][58] whom the god [δαίμων] has now shorn. (920–1)

Alas, you gods [δαίμονες] you have set on us a woe unlooked-for and far-shining, like to the glance of Atê![59] (1005–7)

58 κόσμου τ᾽ ἀνδρῶν (920): an ironic term for the Persian host, for the Messenger has described the Persians as fleeing in wild disorder (ἀκόσμως, 422) in contrast to the surprising discipline (οἱ δ᾽ οὐκ ἀκόσμως ἀλλὰ πειθάρχῳ φρενί, 374) of the democratic Athenians and their allies (cf vv 241–3).

59 Cf Winnington-Ingram's observations (*Studies* pp 4–8) on the Chorus's mistrust of the *daimōn* (at vv 157 f.); on the blame of the *daimōn* by the Messenger (at 345 ff, 353 ff), by Atossa (at 472 f) and by the Chorus-Leader (at 515 f). These observations should be related to Winnington-Ingram's view (cf n 21, above) that in the earlier part of the play it is divine *phthonos* (rather than divine punishment of human *hybris*, later noted by Darius) which is treated (by Chorus and characters) as responsible for human disasters. Even at the end, Winnington-Ingram suggests (ibid pp 13–14) the Chorus fails to profit by Darius' interpretation of events 'upon the highest moral and religious level' and to advise Xerxes accordingly (cf v 830). And so, Winnington-Ingram concludes, for the Chorus and for Xerxes it is still only the *daimōn* and Xerxes' hateful *moira* which has caused the disaster.

APPENDIX

Atossa's 'exit lines' at vv 529–31 and vv 849–51: 'devices of false preparation'?

The Queen's two departures (at the end of 'the Messenger Scene' and of 'the Darius Scene,' respectively) and more particularly the speeches which precede them have occasioned considerable fuss among the critics, and for similar reasons.[1] Before her first departure, Atossa bids the Chorus (at vv 529–31) comfort her son and conduct him to the palace if he should return before she does, but in the event she returns to the scene *before* Xerxes' arrival. At the end of 'the Darius Scene' Atossa declares her intention (849–51), following Darius' instructions, of bringing Xerxes fresh clothes to replace the torn ones before he arrives home, and this 'dramatic expectation' (if that is what it is) is also not fulfilled. Most critics tend to regard these passages as 'devices of false preparation' (the expression is Sidgwick's) intended to concentrate attention on Xerxes' return at the end of the play.[2] This is perhaps a true, if only partial, explanation of the *second* passage, for here Atossa's stated mission occasioning her exit is specifically directed toward the return of the King. But in the case of the other 'exit-lines' (at 529–31), no motive connected with Xerxes' return is given to Atossa for her departure. The passage may indeed have the effect of making the audience think for the moment of that return, but if that is its purpose it would seem to be a peculiarly gratuitous and acontextual way of achieving what could be just as easily achieved without any arousal of false expectations. Therefore, those critics who argue that Atossa's instructions to the Chorus at 529–31 would better fit the context at

1 For an interesting discussion, with generous bibliographical references, of these two passages (among others) in relation to the structure of the play, see Garvie 'Aeschylus' Simple Plots' pp 66 ff. (Some differences from his conclusion will, however, be ventured below.) Cf also Taplin's full treatment (and further references to other views) which will also be considered below. Thalmann, by contrast (whose view of the point of these passages has been mentioned in n 50 above), argues, from a close scrutiny of the passages in relation to what follows them, that neither is an example of inconsistency or of false preparation.

2 See, for example, Sidgwick *Persae* p 60; Wilamowitz *Aischylos Interpretationen* p 44; Dawe 'Inconsistency' p 27 f; all cited by Taplin, p 93 n 2.

851 (where Jocasta's fear of missing Xerxes on his return is actually about to be fulfilled) are surely on the right track, and Taplin and others may be justified in actually transferring the lines to precede Atossa's second and final exit.[3] However, while agreeing with Taplin as to where these instructions of Atossa might better be placed, there is perhaps another way of explaining their actual positioning in our texts.

Atossa's first departure from the stage, which is almost unmotivated, is actually a matter of dramatic convenience provided mainly to make possible the powerful visual effect of her re-entry divested of her regal finery (at 588), but also to enable the poet to mark (by her exit and later re-entry) the division between 'the Messenger Scene' and 'the Ghost of Darius Scene.' The artificial nature of Atossa's exit and re-entry appears also in another minor yet significant detail. Atossa explains her departure by saying, without any reference to Darius' ghost, that she must fetch a sacrificial cake for the dead (523 ff) and adding the vague hope that 'something better might eventuate thereby.' When she returns, however, she brings quite different and more elaborate offerings which are clearly intended, since she accompanies her libations with directions to the Chorus, to complement the lyrical invocation and arousal of Darius' ghost, which now ensues.

Now if Atossa, for reasons of dramatic convenience, is required to leave the scene at v 531, before the first stasimon, it is just as appropriate that she should at this point make some preparation for Xerxes' possible return in her absence as it is that she should do so before her later (and final) departure. This circumstance, rather than any intentional arousal of 'false expectation' by the poet, would seem to be the reason for having Atossa give her directions about Xerxes at vv 529–31. And the directions themselves (that the Chorus should comfort Xerxes and escort him to the palace) are surely normal enough, since 'normally' the Queen might be expected to be present herself to greet her son in such bitter circumstances. They need not, surely, be regarded as an attempt at 'maternal characterization' on the poet's part (a suggestion which has been rejected as alien to Greek tragedy).[4] At any rate they require of the

3 See ibid pp 96–7 and references given, p 97 n 1. Taplin believes that the dramatic purpose of Atossa's request at vv 529–31 (when transferred to follow vv 849–51) is to explain in advance Atossa's absence from the stage when Xerxes arrives.
4 Such suggestions by, eg, Broadhead p xxxvii and Kitto p 44 have been rejected by Taplin p 93 and n 1. However, it seems a shade doctrinaire to deny the poet

poet no greater concern for 'psychology' than does Darius' later advice to Atossa *as a mother* (at vv 837–8) concerning her soothing of Xerxes on his return.

---

any consideration of maternal concern on the part of Atossa. Cf also Broadhead's reasonable defence (p 143, in his note on vv 529–31) of Mazon's view (p 80 n 1) that the Queen fears suicide on Xerxes' part.

CHAPTER TWO

Septem (*The Seven against Thebes*) and its trilogy

1 The myth and the tetralogy

The Seven against Thebes (or the *Septem*, as it may conveniently be called) is the third play in its trilogy. A papyrus fragment (P Oxy 2256 fr 2) supplies the names of the preceding two plays (*Laius* and *Oedipus*) in the trilogy, along with the date of production (467 BC) and the fact that it won the first prize.[1] As far as we can tell from the one fully extant Aeschylean trilogy (the *Oresteia*), although the individual plays of a trilogy can make dramatic sense on their own, their full force and meaning can only be realized from seeing them in their total trilogic context. Therefore, in studying the *Septem* we should seek to recapture what little can be known of the preceding two plays.

The meagre fragments of the first two plays tell us little of their content; fortunately, the main outlines of the legend are known from Sophocles' *Oedipus Tyrannus* and *Oedipus Coloneus*, and from Euripides' *Phoenissae*, though one must always remember that individual trage-dians adapted their treatments of a myth to suit their own dramatic themes. The legend goes back at least to the cyclic epic, the *Thebais*, and possibly to the still more shadowy *Oidipodeia*. Of the *Thebais*, a few details from the siege of Thebes by 'The Seven' are preserved; of the legend relevant to the earlier two plays of our trilogy, we learn that Oedipus cursed his sons, Polyneices and Eteocles, for offering him a cup (probably one which had belonged to Laius) whose use he had forbidden, and (the occasion of a *second* curse?) for failing to serve him

---

1 useful discussion, of these fragments, see Hutchinson *Septem contra Thebas* Intro. 1, pp xvii–xxx. References to this excellent edition, of which much use has been made in this chapter, will be by author's name alone.

the choicest portion of meat; we learn also that the curse took the form of declaring that the sons would divide their patrimony not in love but in reciprocal and fatal bloodshed.[2] As we shall see, both the circumstances and the wording of the curse in Aeschylus' trilogy may be different from the epic version.

The *Septem* itself provides some information about the content of the first two plays. We learn from *Septem* 745 ff that Laius, the father of Oedipus, was thrice warned by Apollo that he could save the city only by dying without issue; that, ruled by his own ill-counsel, he begat doom for himself in the form of father-slaying Oedipus; and that Oedipus, in turn, mated with his own mother to produce 'a bloody brood' (*Septem* 755). We know from Sophocles' *Oedipus Tyrannus*, of course, that these dread deeds of parricide and incest were committed in ignorance by Oedipus, who blinded himself when he discovered what he had done. It can be guessed from one of our fragments,[3] that in the *Laius* of Aeschylus, Oedipus had already been born and was exposed as an infant to die (and so, that Apollo's warning was only reported in that play); presumably, also, the murder of Laius by Oedipus also occurred in the first play of the trilogy.

Oedipus' discovery of his guilt, his self-blinding, and his cursing of his sons would naturally all have occurred in the *Oedipus*, the second play of Aeschylus' tragedy. What is more significant, it would appear at least possible, from *Septem* 778–90, that these three events (discovery, self-blinding, son-cursing) all happened in fairly rapid sequence. Indeed it has been argued (though not, perhaps, conclusively) from vv 785–6, that the cause of Oedipus' cursing his sons in Aeschylus' *Oedipus* was his horror at their incestuous origin – a change of motivation which would keep the doom-laden, familial theme, reviewed in the third play, constantly before our minds.[4]

Knowledge of the actual *wording* of Oedipus' curse would, no doubt, prove helpful to a full understanding of Eteocles' attitudes at various points in the *Septem*, though the degree of importance to be attached to this tends to vary with critics' assessment of the relevance of Eteocles' motives to the tragic meaning of the play. In any case, we can only make reasonable guesses, based mainly on snatches of choral song just

---

2 See *Thebais* fr 2.9 f and fr 3.4 (quoted in Hutchinson p xxix).
3 See fr 171M (= 122 Nauck) and Hutchinson's comment, pp xxiii–iv.
4 This view depends in part on the interpretation of τροφᾶς (786) which Hutchinson (p xxv) takes to refer, in this context, to 'origin,' not 'nurture.' See n 45 below. Cf also Baldry 'The Dramatization of the Theban Legend' for discussion of this and other possible Aeschylean innovations on the myth.

before and just after the catastrophe, about the wording of this curse. As Eteocles rushes forth to do battle with his brother, the Chorus reminds us, in terror, of his father's curse upon his brothers, 'that with sword-deciding [lit., 'iron-distributing,' σιδαρονόμῳ] hand they would divide the property' (788–90). On the basis of this and similar passages (for instance, at 727 ff and 941–6), one editor suggests, reasonably, that the curse in Aeschylus' version might simply have taken much the same form as in the *Thebais*, except that 'it was very likely to have mentioned iron,' since this is mentioned in all the relevant passages of our play. Other scholars, however, believe that the language used for Oedipus' curse in several passages of the *Septem* suggests that, in the usual manner of oracles and sometimes of curses, Oedipus' curse was cryptically phrased, so that the Chorus and even Eteocles might not have been fully aware of its true meaning until the moment of its fulfilment arrived.[5] Certainly the two passages cited in this connection do rather support this latter view. Readers must, however, choose for themselves, from these and other indications of the final play, whether or not to believe that Eteocles is aware from the beginning that he and Polyneices are doomed, if Oedipus' curse avails, to mutual fratricide.

When the *Septem* opens, Thebes is about to be defended by its king, Eteocles, against the assault of Polyneices (with Argive allies) who, as we learn later in the play (637–8), has been exiled by Eteocles. How this situation came about in our trilogy we do not know; presumably there has been some information about this background, possibly in a Messenger Speech, in the latter part of the *Oedipus*. It seems clear, as at least one scholar has pointed out,[6] that the version followed in Euripides' *Phoenissae* (69 ff) has not been followed in Aeschylus' trilogy. In the *Phoenissae*, Eteocles, reneging on an agreement to rule alternately with his brother, is presented as unjustly keeping Polyneices from assuming the kingship. The Aeschylean Eteocles (as we shall see) is consistently presented as the noble defender of the city against a rebel prince leading foreign foes against his native land (see especially 580–6). We are not, perhaps, justified in believing also that our trilogy

---

5 For the first view cited, see Hutchinson p xxix. The latter view is, perhaps, the majority one; see, for example, Tucker *The Seven against Thebes* pp xxviii–ix and Cameron *Studies in the Seven against Thebes of Aeschylus* pp 24–5. Tucker suggests that the enigmatic language of Oedipus' actual curse was (approximately): πικρὸς ἔσται χρηματοδαίτης ξένος πόντιος πυριγενής ('bitter will be the property-dividing, fire-born stranger from across the sea'); see Tucker p xxix.

6 Cameron *Studies* p 26.

followed the version given in Hellanicus, according to which Polyneices chose possessions and exile, rather than kingship, and then presumably reneged on his choice.[7] All that we are justified in concluding is that by the beginning of the *Septem* we are meant to accept Eteocles as the king and legitimate defender of Thebes against his rebel brother, Polyneices, and his Argive allies.[8]

The satyr play following this trilogy was, according to the *Hypothesis* to the *Septem*, the *Sphinx*. Though little can be guessed of its content from the three brief extant fragments[9] and one (possible) vase representation, it presumably celebrated, in the absurd terms suitable to the satyr play, Oedipus' victory over the monster named in the title.

2 Structure of the *Septem*

The *Septem* is one of the great 'battle plays' in Western literature, yet no actual battle action, on stage or reported, disrupts the gradual and relentless resolution of its personal tragic theme. In each of its parts we find the tensions, so essential to tragic structure, between conflicting claims, values, and interests; yet this is done without recourse to any formal *agon* (such as, inevitably, we find in Euripides' version of this conflict), for at no point does any antagonist to the central tragic figure make his appearance. Battles concern the fates of armies, of nations, of cities, and the *Septem*'s battle over Thebes is no exception, yet the city's destiny is decided by a single moment in the tragic action of the play. Some critics have remarked on a swing from civic to personal

---

7 So Cameron argues, ibid pp 27 ff. Nor need we believe with this critic (ibid pp 26–8) that the two brothers originally understood the Curse quite literally as requiring them to submit the question of their inheritance to a Scythian arbitrator and were then pleased to be able to follow the method described in the Hellanicus instead! See also Cameron 'Epigoni and the Law of Inheritance in Aeschylus' *Septem*,' where this critic develops this interpretation rather further.

8 Even this conclusion requires, perhaps, a mild caveat, as far as the play preceding the *Septem* is concerned. In Aeschylean trilogies (at least to judge from the *Oresteia* and from indications in the Danaid trilogy) the injuring and the injured parties do not always remain the same from play to play.

9 These fragments are all quoted in Hutchinson's introduction pp xx–xxi: 182M (= 236 Nauck), 181M (= 235 Nauck), 183M (= 237 Nauck). The first of them (182M) does, to be sure, contribute to Aristophanes' satire of Aeschylean hexameters in the passage of Aristophanes' *Frogs* 1264–95 in which it is quoted (at *Frogs* 1287) as an Aeschylean tag. See also Hutchinson's comments, pp xxi–ii, on a vase-painting from the mid-460s representing the Sphinx and four satyrs (wearing robes and holding sceptres) which he believes may represent this play.

emphasis (from concentration on the fate of the city to that of the family and the central tragic figure),[10] yet even that observation, true as it is, tends to obscure the view of personal and civic destinies as inseparably intertwined in their progress and resolution.

The third play of a trilogy enjoys certain structural advantages. The situation has, by this time, been thoroughly presented and the audience is already aware of some of the expectations to be fulfilled, of the issues to be resolved. In this, it will be aware of the armed threat hovering over Thebes and of the fratricidal curse which will in some way bring the brothers' struggle over their inheritance to its fatal resolution. Thus, the dramatist can plunge directly into the action of his play and can exploit the audience's knowledge by injecting, often with ironic effect, hints of one element or another of the situation (be it past dooms or horrors prophesied) at whatever moment it may have the greatest impact.

The structure of the *Septem* falls into four clearly discernible parts. The first part (vv 1–368, that is, to the end of the first stasimon) deals with the anticipation of the coming battle. Here the King's personal situation receives only the merest hint,[11] while the driving force of the passage resides in the tension between the furious discipline of the commander-in-chief and the hysteria of the Chorus of Women, whose songs reflect the plight of the city and the terrors of the siege.

The second part, the 'Shield Scene' (369–676), is concerned entirely with the Theban Scout's report of the attacking chieftains at the seven gates and with Eteocles' posting of seven champions to lead the defence

---

10 This is a recurrent and well-demonstrated theme in William Thalmann's treatment of the play in his *Dramatic Art in Aeschylus' Seven against Thebes*; see, for example, chap. 2, esp pp 31 ff, and chap. 5, pp 105 ff. See also Hutchinson p xxxix on the alleged 'discontinuity,' occasioned by this duality of themes, between the two parts of the play: 'The battle for Thebes is subordinated and grows ever less significant; the destruction of the family is the centre of concern.'

Some critics (eg, Cameron *Studies* p 29) relate the danger to the city to the original, 'familial' curse on Laius, the personal danger to Eteocles almost exclusively to the curse of Oedipus. (Cf also Flintoff 'The Ending of *The Seven against Thebes*' pp 270–1.) With this alleged division of the play's concerns into the fate of the city and of the individual and his royal house, one should mention, at least for historical interest, Wilamowitz's (perhaps fanciful) explanation: that the first part of the play is based on the older, saga version of the *Thebais*, in which Eteocles (illustrating his name) appears as the glorious defender of his native city, while the second part is based on a later epic in which Eteocles was the bearer of an inherited curse. See Wilamowitz *Aischylos Interpretationen* pp 56 ff, discussed by von Fritz *Antike und Moderne Tragödie* pp 194–5.

11 See below, p 42 and n 14 on vv 69 ff.

against them. It is clear that these seven sets of adversaries represent, in a sense, the whole attacking and defending forces,[12] but by thus isolating the leaders the poet is enabled gradually to individualize the conflict and so to bring it to its expected climax. This time, the scene's tension lies in the contrasts between the hybristic attackers and the valorous, virtuous defenders appropriately posted, in each case, to face them. By this device (as the number of remaining gates diminish), the likelihood gradually increases, with the growing excitement of the scene, that the seventh gate will see the two brothers meeting in the most 'appropriate' (and inevitable) confrontation.

The third and penultimate part of the play (677–791) again pits Eteocles against the Chorus (and again in a partly epirrhematic passage), but this time it is the women who seek, with even less success than Eteocles in his attempt to calm *them*, to restrain the King from playing his destined role. This panel of the play ends with a splendid transitional ode (the second stasimon) reflecting on the past follies, woes, and curses of Laius and Oedipus, portending (the Chorus fear) more horrors still to come. The emphasis is now on the individual and familial theme, yet even as Eteocles embraces the Curse, he still acts, as we shall see, as the Commander, the defender of the realm.

In the fourth and final section of the play (792–end), the Messenger's reports of the battle (the saving of the city and the fratricidal death of Eteocles and Polyneices) are followed by retrospective comments and lamentations from the Chorus (and, at least according to the received text, from Antigone and Ismene, the sisters of the slain princes).[13] Inevitably (for the catastrophic event concerns the brothers and tragedy deals in the fate of individuals), lamentation predominates in the exodus, but we shall find that 'the City theme' is still not quite forgotten.

3 Prologue, parodos, first episode, and first stasimon (1–368)

Citizens of Cadmus, whoever guards the city's safety like the helmsman at the rudder of a ship, should say what must be said, not close his eyes in slumber. For if we should fare well, the god's alleged to be the cause. But

---

12 This is evident from the Scout's description (55–6), in his brief appearance in the Prologue, of the seven attacking chieftains casting lots to see against which gate each of them is to lead his company of men.

13 There is considerable doubt about the authenticity of certain parts of the exodos as we have it, as well as concerning the ascription of various verses in it. See below, pp 61 ff and appendix 3 to this chapter.

if (and may it not happen thus) misfortune should fall on us, then Eteocles'
name would men keep crying through the city, in lamentation and prelude
to disaster. From such may Zeus the Averter, true to his name, defend us!
(1–9)

Thus does Eteocles, in his opening words, characterize his responsibil-
ities as defender of the realm.[14] In keeping with this view, he calls on
every degree of Theban manhood, those in their youth, in their prime,
and in their full maturity

... to defend their city, the altars of their native gods, their children, and
Mother Earth herself, their most beloved Nurse. (14–16)

The list is significant. Eteocles is a commander who believes that he
should defend his native gods as well as they him. The inclusion, too,
of Mother Earth in this list of what must be defended has, perhaps, an
ironic overtone, particularly in view of the parenthetical description
which follows it ('hospitable receiver of all our childhood ills, who
nourished you [Thebes' citizens] to be shield-bearing householders ...'
(18–19). Oedipus' curse (of which the audience would be well aware) is
to involve the brothers, bitterly, in their share of Theban soil.[15]
    Despite the apparent touch of cynicism in his opening words, Eteo-
cles' piety (and cautious confidence in the gods) is real: god will provide
good endings (εὖ τελεῖ θεός, 35) provided that man does his part. So,
too, it is in obedience to his prophet's advice that Eteocles has sent his
Scout to report on the enemy's battle plans. For the rest, all is business
('Man the battlements ... rush to the gates! Take arms and hurry! To the
towers, to the gates! – and be of good heart as you wait there!' 30–4).
The Scout's report that even now the seven enemy chiefs are drawing

14 There is, of course, nothing impious about the attitude expressed toward the gods in
    this passage, nor in the hero's later prayers (eg, at 69–77) based on the self-interest
    imputed to the gods. Both are in accordance with traditional archaic views; cf W.H.
    Adkins 'Divine and Human Values in Aeschylus' *Seven against Thebes*' pp 32–68.
15 One should, however, guard against 'over-personalizing' or otherwise over-
    interpreting these and subsequent references to 'Mother Earth.' One critic goes so
    far as to suggest that Eteocles' desire to possess Thebes exclusively (dispossessing
    Polyneices) recapitulates Oedipus' incestuous possession of Jocasta. See Helen
    Bacon and Anthony Hecht, Aeschylus, *Seven against Thebes*, translation with intro.
    and notes, p 9, and Bacon 'The Shield of Eteocles' p 31. Cf also R. Caldwell 'The
    Misogyny of Eteocles' pp 217–18, who suggests a similar application of the 'incest
    theme' in this connection.

lots for the seven gates provides the first sinister anticipation of the climactic scene soon to come. Eteocles, however, betrays no concern for the personal threat which, in view of the Curse, these preparations may involve. Far from it: the Curse itself (*Ara*), and the Spirit of his father's vengeance (*Erinys*) are, with anticipatory irony, included with Zeus, Earth, and the city's gods in Eteocles' prayers for the city's protection (69 ff),[16] and the prayer ends with the typically heroic reminder to the gods of their own interests:

For a city honours its gods when it fares well! (77)[17]

The parodos and the first stasimon of the *Septem* provide us with the most splendid and vivid impression, first, of a city besieged and, second (in the terrified imaginings of the Chorus), of a city captured. In between comes the highly dramatic, epirrhematic episode (181–286) in which Eteocles berates the women's dangerous panic and the Chorus sing their replies. Thus we achieve, vicariously, the total experience of a siege: the initial panic at the sights and sounds of coming battle: the slaughter, rape, and devastation of (imagined) defeat, and, in marked contrast to the Chorus's hysteria, the furious control of the Commander who, as the action of the play progresses, is to frustrate that calamity.

In the opening dochmiacs (78–108) of the parodos all is confusion. Oddly assorted images – a flood of horsemen, a towering cloud of dust, horses' hoof-beats, now flying, now 'roaring' like a breaking wave; jumbled reports of sights, sounds, and fears; prayers, wildly interjected, to unnamed gods – all crowd together with the disorder of raw experience. When the formal ode begins at v 109,[18] the imagery is more powerfully marshalled ('A wave of high-crested heroes, driven by Ares' blast, breaks against the city,' 112–15; '... the sky rages with brandished spears!' 155) and the descriptions become more specific as reports from the field become more coherent ... and more signifi-cant ('Seven shining captains stand before their seven gates, where the

16 Eteocles prays not merely that these supernatural powers should not destroy (μή ... ἐκθαμνίσητε, 71–2) the city, but also that they should be a defence (ἀλκή, 76) for it. It is possible that there is dramatic irony involved here: the fulfilment of the Curse in the fratricidal struggle will, in effect, save the city. However, this may be suggesting an over-subtle meaning in these lines which an audience could not be expected to grasp at this point in the drama.

17 Cf *Choeph* 255–61.

18 Not all editors agree, however, on the strophic arrangement of vv 109–50; see Hutchinson's arguments against this in his note *ad loc.*

lots have chosen them.' 124–6). So, too, the gods are now addressed by name, in due order and in manner appropriate to their particular prerogatives. Ares and Aphrodite, for example, are called on to honour their special relationship with Thebes (135–42);[19] Apollo *Lykeios* is asked (with an Aeschylean pun) to be a very wolf in battle (145–6); and Artemis is asked to bring her bow (149). The holy goddess Ogka is remembered (164–5) with a special prayer, to recall the Phoenician origins of Thebes;[20] even Argive Hera, addressed more curtly (*o potni' Hera*, 152), Argive warriors being numbered among the attackers,[21] is included in this careful catalogue. But even in the midst of these well-ordered prayers, the beginnings of battle panic keep intruding ('Aaaaah! I hear the rattle of chariots about the city!' 151; 'Aaaaah! Even now the sling-tossed stones assail the battlements!' 158) and the ode ends with a solid cascade of hysterical supplication to all the gods, *en masse* (166–80).

A striking feature of this parodos is its effective use of sounds and images[22] which help the audience share with the Chorus something of the terror of the off-stage battle preparations. Wind and water images, often favoured by Aeschylus at moments of high excitement, predominate. The enemy host 'streams' ($\acute{\rho}\epsilon\hat{\iota}$, 80) from their camp, 'thunders like a mountain torrent' (85–6), and 'surges, as a wave driven by Ares' blasts, around the city' (114–15). By way of contrast, the dust raised by the approaching army (which is probably all that can actually be seen from within the city) rises to the heavens 'As a silent [$\mathring{a}\nu\alpha\nu\delta os$], clear and certain messenger' (82).[23] But the most arresting device for bringing the battle preparations onstage, as it were, is the use of often onomatopoeic *sound*-words: it is the sounds of the approaching army which most affright the Chorus and it is this effect which the audience too can share most readily. The army, as we have heard, 'thunders' (85) as it approaches. The Chorus shudders as it hears the beating ($\kappa\tau\acute{\upsilon}\pi o\nu$), the din ($\pi\acute{a}\tau\alpha\gamma os$) of the shields (103). Bridles 'ring murderously' ($\kappa\iota\nu\acute{\upsilon}\rho o\nu\tau\alpha\iota$ $\phi\acute{o}\nu o\nu$, 123) about the horses' jaws as the Chorus now hears the actual 'clatter of the chariots' ($\mathring{o}\tau o\beta o\nu$ $\mathring{a}\rho\mu\acute{a}\tau\omega\nu$, 151) and the 'loud creaking of

19 Cadmus, founder of Thebes, married Harmonia, daughter of Ares and Aphrodite.
20 Ogka was the Phoenician goddess equivalent to Athena; see *scholia ad loc.*
21 Hera could hardly be expected to favour the Thebans in this battle; see Tucker's note *ad loc.*
22 On imagery in the *Septem*, see, among others, Thalmann *Dramatic Art in Aeschylus' Seven against Thebes*, chap 2.
23 Compare *Ag* 494–7, although there it is the Herald himself, in contrast with the dust which he raises, who is described as $o\mathring{\upsilon}\tau'$ $\mathring{a}\nu\alpha\nu\delta os$ ('not silent').

laden axles' (153) right around the city. Seldom has an audience been more brutally assaulted by a barrage of battle clamour!

Into this confusion strides Eteocles and the first confrontation between the Chorus and the warrior King begins.

ETEOCLES   I ask you, you insufferable creatures [θρέμματ' οὐκ ἀνεσχετά], do you think that this is best for the city's safety and for the confidence of an army under siege, that you should fall weeping and wailing on the statues of the city's gods, the sort of behaviour that sickens those with any self-control? Never, in disastrous or in happy circumstances, may I have to deal with the female tribe! In command, a woman's unbearably bold and brash but when she's terrified, she only adds to the danger to house and city! (181–90)
CHORUS   Dear son of Oedipus, I fear the beating clatter (ὄτοβον, ὄτοβον) of the chariots' din ...
ET.   What, then? When the ship labours in the surging wave, does a sailor find safety by racing stem to stern?
CHOR.   Headlong to the ancient statues of the gods I rush, when the storm of murderous stones comes sleeting on the gates.
ET.   Pray, rather, that the towers may stem the hostile tide. Gods quit a captured city, so the story goes. (203–18, in part)

The first episode follows a standard archaic form: opening *rhesis* (speech) from the central character (181–202); an epirrhematic passage between protagonist and Chorus (203–44); a brief iambic exchange, repeating in dialogue form the main issues of the epirrhematic passage (245–63); a final *rhesis* from the protagonist (264–86) summing up in strongest terms his original position.

Eteocles' initial tirade against the Chorus ends with a threat of death against all who disobey his commands, and a further order to keep indoors and leave 'the external crisis' to men. In the epirrhematic passage which follows, the terror of the Chorus, again singing in excited dochmiacs, contrasts sharply with the continued stern admonitions of Eteocles. While the Chorus scream their fears at the sounds of the approaching war-chariots (203–7) and the rattle of stones beating at the gates (212–13), Eteocles suggests rather that cool heads and stout defences are needed in stormy seas (208–10; 216–17). The constant terrified prayers of the women continue to infuriate the King, who insists that pre-battle sacrifices to the gods are the concern of *men*; the women should keep quiet, not create panic, and remain indoors (230–2; 236–8). The scene ends with Eteocles' enunciation of a proper soldier's prayer, 'May the gods fight on our side!' (266), and with a promise to the gods (consonant with his former cautious attitude to their beneficence) of bounteous sacrifices if the city be preserved.

One of the main effects of this little scene must surely be its theatrical power: the contrast it presents between the strength and masculinity of the protagonist and the terror of the female Chorus. It is the sort of theatrical contrast in which Aeschylus indulges elsewhere, in the *Prometheus Vinctus*, for example (if that play *is* by Aeschylus), and, with considerable variations, in *The Suppliant Women*. The device is particularly effective and dramatically relevant in this play, since it is essential to the presentation of Eteocles as, above all, the dedicated soldier, the defender of the realm, without a thought of personal danger. Eteocles' apparent misogynism is, perhaps, intended only to emphasize this contrast (for commanders of the heroic age, battles and prayers about battles *were* the affairs of men). Thus, it is not as significant as a character trait (and perhaps a culpable one) as it might be taken to be in more 'psychological' drama.[24] The contrast between the Chorus's and the Commander's views of what constitute proper prayers is, of course, part and parcel of this major contrast between them, but it provides as well a touch of anticipatory irony to be fulfilled when we see how the gods do, actually, answer their respective prayers.

Between this scene contrasting the attitudes of Eteocles and the women whom he is defending and the central 'Seven Gates' exchange between the Herald and Eteocles comes the magnificent first stasimon. Its placing, as we shall see, is significant.

The first strophe and antistrophe recapitulate, with sharper imagery, the earlier themes of civic terror and desperate prayer. Panic still distracts the Chorus ('... fear will not let my spirit rest,' 287) from complete obedience to Eteocles' admonitions. Images of terror (the fearful dove covering her young before the deadly snake, 291–4) give way to actual descriptions (jagged rocks being hurled upon helpless citizens, 298–300) of the attack which is beginning. The strophe ends

---

24 It should also be noted that Eteocles' objections to the women's taking part in public rituals (though expressed in rather extreme terms!) is soundly based on Greek practice. For a contrary view of the emphasis and significance of these scenes, see Caldwell 'The Misogyny of Eteocles' pp 193–231. Caldwell, quoting Barthes's view that 'language defines the man,' and regarding Eteocles' language here as a reflection of his 'unconscious,' believes what he regards as Eteocles' misogynism here to have its source in the hero's own incestuous origins. Readers will also find a good bibliographical summary of conflicting views on this passage in Caldwell's article.

with a prayer 'to all the Zeus-sired gods'; as the prayer is developed in the antistrophe, it contains reminders to us of the glories of the threatened realm ('deep-soiled land, all nourishing stream of Dirce ...,' 306–8) and to the gods of the *kudos* they will gain if they inflict weapon-grounding disaster (ῥίψοπλον ἄταν, 315; a fine untranslatable phrase) upon the enemy.[25]

The rest of the ode (321–68, two strophic pairs) consists of a series of brilliant images of the lot of the victims as a city is being sacked. The great word-tapestry of this passage provides perhaps our most vivid picture from the ancient world of this piteous spectacle: women, young and old, clothes torn, dragged off, like horses, by their manes (326–9); maids still unwed torn from the breasts of wounded, shrieking mothers; rape and pillaging as the towering net of ruin and the din of battle encompass the city. Depiction of the utter wastage of the earth's rich bounty gives way, at the end of the ode, to that of the captive women's grim prospect: the 'nightly rite' which will be their only relief from days of woe (345–68).

Impressed as we may be by these vivid cameos, we must also look for their dramatic point. These prophetic visions describe precisely what is *not* to happen in this play. Instead, the city will be saved but one great horror which the audience know *will* come to pass is not here touched upon. It is the *polis* which will survive, the brothers who are to die, in unspeakable bloodshed. Thus, by this bold and splendid piece of irony, the audience is forced to do its work: to replace the dreadful (but not unprecedented) scenes of horror with one in a sense more dreadful, which stands outside the familiar sequence of human woes; and to realize, perhaps, that the life (women, children, crops, as they have been enumerated) of the community is to depend on the fratricidal death of the cursed sons of the cursed Oedipus.[26]

4   Second episode ('The Shield Scene') (vv 369–685)

While the early choral odes of this play have provided most vivid, if generalized, impressions of the siege and (in the Chorus's terrified imaginings) the capture of a city, the great central episode (369–685)

25 On the attitudes imputed to the gods, cf vv 76–7 and nn 14 and 17, above.
26 These observations need not, however, lead inevitably to the so-called 'Opfertod' or 'sacrificial death' view of the action to which we are soon to see Eteocles commit himself. On this question, and debate thereon, see below pp 53–4 and appendix 2 to this chapter.

paints, with equal vividness, a series of cameo-portraits of the individual heroes soon to be involved. As such, it cannot fail to remind us of the *teichoskopia* of *Iliad* 3.161 ff. However, unlike the more specific imitation of the Homeric passage in Euripides' *Phoenissae* 88–201, the present scene goes far beyond a review of heroic personnel in its relevance to the play's dramatic themes.

In this scene, Eteocles' Scout reports the enemy chieftains chosen by lot to attack each of the seven gates of Thebes, and Eteocles announces, in answer, the appointment of an appropriate Theban defender at each gate. Here, as before (with one brief exception), Eteocles makes no mention of the Curse in his defence arrangements until the climax of the scene. The spectre of the dread confrontation with Polyneices has, however, been well suggested by the poet and must, by this time, be in everybody's mind.[27] The Scout, in his Prologue appearance, has already told of seven furious chieftains (42) casting lots for the gate which each will attack (55–6); the Chorus, in the parodos, has repeated this information; most significantly, Eteocles, at the end of the first episode, has informed the Chorus that he will now go and post six men, with himself as the seventh, to oppose the attackers at the seven gates. Thus, though Eteocles describes each of the assigned defenders strictly in terms of his moral and military suitability to meet his declared opponent, we, the audience, experience a mounting sense of the inevitability, and indeed (in a singularly shocking sense) the appropriateness, of the final confrontation at the seventh gate. With each successive assignment (some, apparently, already made, some only now decided,[28] but each with the objective judgment of the military commander), Eteocles brings himself closer, and with no hint of awareness, to his own personal catastrophe. As the King pronounces each of his choices for the first six gates with cool and measured judgment, we become aware again of the irony of his earlier advice to the Chorus: 'not by frenzied outcry will you escape

---

27 Not all critics, however, agree on this point; see, for example, Shepherd 'The Plot of the *Septem contra Thebas*' pp 73–4. Shepherd comments, 'Eteocles has no reason to expect that his brother will be one of the seven leaders of the assault.' He adds, surprisingly, 'I do not believe that ... the recital, *seriatim*, of the names of the seven champions was felt by the audience to be a part of the fatal workings of the Curse' – a very different view from that to be taken of this passage in this chapter.

28 This, at any rate, is the obvious (or naive?) interpretation of the fact that Eteocles uses a variety of tenses (three future, one present, two perfect, and one aorist!) in announcing his postings of the defending captains who will meet the seven chieftains whom the Scout identifies. Again, not all critics agree; the subject has been much debated, though it is not, perhaps, quite as crucial to the interpretation of the play as some have thought. See appendix 1 to this chapter.

your fate!' (τὸ μόρσιμον, 280–1). Nor, apparently, by rational military decisions will Eteocles himself avoid *his* fate.

While it is the increasing sense of inevitability which provides the main excitement in this series of exchanges between the Scout and the King, various additional features in the description of the seven attackers combine with this effect to render the passage unique among the battle scenes of Greek tragedy. As before, even before the battle is joined, the *noises* of battle – the clangour of bells beneath a shield (385–6), the nose-pipe snortings of the horses (461–4) – are already heard. Snake-images, reminiscent of the Chorus's fears at 291–4, abound: Tydeus' savage utterance is likened to a serpent's hiss (380–1); Hippomedon must be warded off 'like a chill snake from nestlings' (503), and 'writhing snakes' encircle the image of Typho on that hero's shield (495–6). Finally (and it is this feature which has given the scene its name among the critics), each attacking chieftain is characterized both directly and by the emblem emblazoned on his shield. By this device, the poet can illustrate the hybristic qualities of the attackers, just as Eteocles, by his ingenious interpretations of these shield-emblazonings, can use them as prognostications of their bearers' overthrow.[29]

The shields of Tydeus and of Hippomedon (and Eteocles' reading of them) provide, perhaps, the best examples of this particular form of threat and its reversal. On Tydeus' shield

the heavens [are] emblazoned 'neath the luminous stars and at their centre shines the brilliant moon, the night's bright eye, effacing all the starry firmament. (387 ff)[30]

29 The devices on the attackers' shields are used as symbols which Eteocles then interprets; however, as Hutchinson observes, '... the meanings with which they [the devices] are invested are all, for Greek spectators, natural and direct' (p 106). This editor is justly sceptical about the 'complex and devious structures' which recent critics have sought to impose on 'the Shield sequence.'; he gives as an example Vidal-Naquet's 'anthropological' interpretation of the device on Polyneices' shield (vv 644–7). Other examples of 'complex' interpretations of this scene are to be found in Bacon 'The Shield of Achilles,' in Lupas and Petrie *Commentaire aux Sept contre Thebes* and in Froma Zeitlin's book-length study, *Under the Sign of the Shield*, which contains full biographical references to other studies of this scene. Valuable as such interpretations may be (especially Zeitlin's, for those adopting her approach), the treatments of Hutchinson and of Thalmann (in *Seven against Thebes* chap. 5) are, perhaps, more congenial with the present discussion.

30 The pictorial effects (here and elsewhere in this scene) are, of course, much more vivid than could actually be achieved on a shield's emblazoning: an interesting example of the need for 'the willing suspension of disbelief.'

This image of Night (with its brilliant eye, the moon, presumably representing Tydeus) is soon turned against its bearer by Eteocles:

> for if the night of death should fall upon his eyes, then ... that boastful crest would, to its bearer, prove too true a prophet! (403 ff)

The shield of Hippomedon shows Zeus' monstrous enemy, Typho, 'spewing black, flame-shot smoke, fire's flickering sister.' But the shield of Hyperbius, whom Eteocles sends against Hippomedon (and who is the only defending champion whose shield-emblazoning is described), bears Zeus himself and Zeus' thunderbolt ... 'and no one yet has witnessed Zeus defeated!' (514).

Shield and its bearer, particularly in the case of the hybristic assailants, are closely identified: sometimes it is the figures, sometimes the scenes depicted on the shield-emblazonings, which provide the material for Eteocles' triumphant prophecies. Thus Megareus, one of the Theban defenders, is imagined displaying as victory-spoils not only the arms of the assailant Eteoclus but also those of the warrior on his shield and even the fortress which that warrior is pictured, all too confidently, as assailing! (478–9). But perhaps the most elaborate example of this conceit (if one may call it that) occurs in the case of Parthenopaeus, who carries on his shield an image of the flesh-devouring Sphinx pinning beneath her a Theban warrior, 'so that many a weapon might at him [the Theban warrior] be hurled!' (544). Eteocles, in his rejoinder, reverses the optimistic application of this shield's device: the bearer of that especially hated beast, the Sphinx, will never be allowed to pass within Thebes' gates! (558–9).

In addition to these devices affecting the style and content of individual passages in 'the Shield Scene,' certain structural features affecting the scene as a whole have been noted by various critics. Thus, the incident reported at the first gate, where the prophet Amphiaraus restrains Tydeus (and presumably the rest of the host) from attacking because the omens are not fair (377 ff) balances, in a sort of ring composition, the incident at the sixth gate, where the same prophet, after rebukes to both Tydeus and Polyneices himself, nevertheless ends by uttering a battle-cry as one going willingly to his inevitable doom (587–9); the latter passage, in turn, seems to provide an ironic anticipation of the similarly fatal decision soon to be taken, this time by the Theban king, at the seventh gate.[31] It has been further suggested

---

31 Cf Hutchinson pp 103–4; on the second point, cf also Thalmann pp 118–19.

that the whole 'seven gates sequence' mirrors a shift, significant for the action of the play as a whole, from the fate of the city to the fate of the brothers.[32] Here the crucial moment is found to occur in the preparations at the fourth gate: as we have seen, the shield emblems (involving Typhon and Zeus, respectively, 511–13) 'determine,' according to Eteocles' prophecy, *Thebes'* victory, while the fact that two *personal* enemies, Hippomedon and Hyperbius, are to meet at this gate turns our concern toward *personal* confrontation and ultimately, of course, toward the fratricidal one.

By such devices, the poet succeeds in introducing considerable variety into his preview of the coming battle while still conveying a sense of mounting tension as we approach the seventh gate. So, too, the sudden announcement of a wise and moderate attacker (Amphiaraus, ἄνδρα σωφρονέστατον, 568) at the sixth gate, followed by Eteocles' suitably moderate reply (597 ff) to this very different sort of challenge, gives the audience a momentary respite, a lull in outrage, before the announcement of the most violent and impious attacker next to come.

'The seventh attacker at the seven gates, I'll tell you now ...' (631–2). Thus, to Eteocles, the only remaining defender of the city, does the Scout begin his announcement of Polyneices as the last, and longest-awaited, of the enemy champions. In Polyneices' battle-prayer (as the Scout reports it) one notes a savage irony in his intentions toward the city, combined with a curious sense of reciprocity in his intentions toward his brother Eteocles. The prayer opens with a furious city-sacker's vaunt (ἀλώσιμον παιᾶν', 635), yet closes with a pious appeal to the native gods of his paternal land to aid his cause (640–1). As for his brother, Polyneices prays that he may slay him, but, *if he does, that he may die beside him*, or else that he may drive him into exile, *as he himself was banished* in similar disgrace (636–8).[33] Polyneices' shield-emblazon complements the irony of its bearer's appeal to his ancestral gods: Justice, advancing with due modesty (σωφρόνως ἡγουμένη, 645), is there shown leading this would-be city-sacker to take possession of his ancestral halls (642–8).[34]

---

32 See Thalmann pp 105–6 and, for the following point, p 112.

33 These verses indicate that Polyneices, at least, has no certain expectation of death at his brother's hands, in fulfilment of Oedipus' curse.

34 There have, however, been several able defences of the validity of Polyneices' claim to Justice (*Dikē*) as at least equal to that of Eteocles. See, for example, Gagarin *Aeschylean Drama* p 121, who observes that Polyneices' intention to wrong his brother for wrong done to himself 'conforms to the traditional pattern of retribution which we saw [ie, earlier in Gagarin's book] soften in the *Oresteia*.' See also the interesting comments of Adkins ('Divine and Human Values in Aeschylus *Seven against Thebes*' pp 53–5) on this matter. He observes that Polyneices is ἀτίμητος (deprived of τιμή,

The first three verses of Eteocles' reply provide the only example, in his answers to the seven announcements of the Scout, of a departure from the impersonal considerations of a military commander-in-chief.

O god-maddened, god-hated, tear-drenched [πανδάκρυτον] house of mine – and Oedipus! Alas! now truly are the curses of my father being fulfilled! (653–5)

But hardly is this heart-cry uttered when Eteocles stifles it:

It is not meet to wail and make complaint, lest woes should thereby only wax the more! (656–7)

The commander-in-chief is again in charge: Eteocles' self-abjuration is precisely the same, and to the same purpose, as his earlier rebuke to the disruptive, panic-stricken Chorus. For the rest, Eteocles' answer to this last announcement from the Scout parallels the answers sent to each of the other hybristic assailants: rebuttal of the apparent promise of the enemy's shield-device (in this case, rebuttal of Polyneices' claim to Justice it implies) and the posting once again of the most suitable defender of the gate.

Trusting in Justice,[35] I'll go and will myself take issue with him. For who else has more right? [τίς ἄλλος μᾶλλον ἐνδικώτερος;] Leader against leader, brother against brother, enemy against enemy, I'll set myself. Come, with all speed, my armour ...! (672–6)

---

honour) by Eteocles, just as Eteocles is, as Polyneices claims, 636 ff, ἀτιμαστήρ (the one who has deprived *him* of honour). Comparing Polyneices' attitude in this regard to that of Achilles, Adkins argues that the latter's claim on *Dikē* (Justice) and the θεοὶ γενέθλιοι (the familial gods) are in accordance with traditional, firmly established early Greek values.

Both these views are, I feel, true as an objective view of the mythical situation rather than of the way in which Aeschylus has chosen to direct our sympathies in this play. Amphiaraus (as Adkins himself points out) has refuted in advance Polyneices' claim to justice on the grounds that he is attacking his motherland (see vv 580–6). Adkins admits that Aeschylus would probably agree with Amphiaraus but feels that attitudes to such questions in Aeschylus' day were by no means clear.

35 v 672, lit. 'Trusting in these arguments [ie, his foregoing arguments, that Justice repudiates Polyneices] ...'

The Chorus-Leader, seeking to restrain Eteocles from the danger of kin-bloodshed, warns the King not to be seized with a passion like his brother's. Eteocles (again showing little such passion) replies by declaring honour and reputation to be his primary concern:

> If one should suffer evil, let it be without disgrace, for this alone, among the dead, brings gain [κέρδος]. Never will fair reputation [εὐκλεία] be based on evil, shameful deeds! (683–5)

Until his passionate cry at the Scout's seventh and last report, Eteocles has acted (toward the Chorus, toward the gods, and toward the military situation) as a commander-in-chief whose sole concern has been the defence of his beleaguered city. No thought of his personal fate has been allowed to distract from this concern, for no mention of his father's Curse – save that with the other divine powers it may protect and not destroy the city – has passed his lips. It is, then, the combination of Eteocles' military decisions and the lot which determined the posting of the attacking chieftains which has brought him to the final and fateful decision. After the single outburst, the single admission of the working of the Curse, he returns to his military role and declares his final inevitable choice. Aeschylus' constant concern with the tragic blend of free choice and of divinely imposed Necessity which that choice itself fulfils can have no clearer expression than in this great sequence of decisions and their tragic consequences.

This treatment of Eteocles' decision may sound like the (currently unfashionable) 'Opfertod view,' according to which Eteocles 'chooses' the fulfilment of his father's Curse, by the fratricidal encounter now embarked on, in order to save the City. It is perhaps close to that view (of which there have, to be sure, been several formulations), but differs from it in that it sees Eteocles' final decision as primarily the consistent finale of all his previous choices, as commander-in-chief, in appointing suitable defenders at the city's gates. As the audience has no doubt foreseen (and as Eteocles *may* have foreseen but refused to consider) that final decision coincides with the fulfilment of the Curse, which suddenly makes its presence felt to the horrified ears of the King. Nevertheless, Eteocles has (as he tells us) no real choice but (once again) to make the appropriate assignment at the seventh gate. The 'Opfertod view,' by contrast, tends to oversimplify the matter, making Eteocles say, in effect, 'I will, by this decision, accept my fate, fulfil the Curse and experience mutual fratricide in order to save the city.' It tends, that is, to see only one track of action instead of the inevitable convergence of two tracks, which is essential to the tragic element in this culmination.[36]

5 Second episode (*epirrhema*) and second stasimon (686–791)

The passage (686–719) following Eteocles' dread decision provides both striking parallels with, and striking contrasts to, the exchange between Chorus and King in the first episode (203–63).[37] In structure, the scenes are very similar (an epirrhematic passage followed by a stichomythic conclusion), but now, in contrast to the earlier scene, it is the Chorus who seek, unsuccessfully, to restrain Eteocles. It is a commonly accepted view that from the moment Eteocles recognizes the working of the Curse (that is, at 653 ff) and especially in this altercation with the Chorus, Eteocles is in the grip of an eager, fratricidal madness. Curiously enough, however, the vividly passionate expressions in which the scene abounds are to be found, for the most part, in the excited, dochmiac utterances of the Chorus rather than in the King's controlled, iambic replies. A closer look at the actual exchanges between them may serve to illustrate this paradox.

To the King's stern insistence on εὐκλεία (fair reputation) as the basis of his decision, the whole Chorus now replies in song (in what looks like a clear case of overreaction):

> Why are you raving, dear youth? [τί μέμονας τέκνον;] Let soul-smiting, spear-raging madness not carry you away ... (686–7)

Eteocles answers (689–91) more with resignation to the family's fate than with fratricidal fury, but, once again, it is the Chorus who indulge in blood-curdling imagery in their warnings:

> It is the savage bite of passion urges you to murderous harvest of forbidden blood! (692–4)

And once again the King intones an answer more fatalistic than impassioned:

---

36 For various views on this essential point of interpretation in the *Septem* see appendix 2 to this chapter.

37 The similarity and contrast have, of course, been noted by critics; see, for example, Winnington-Ingram *Studies in Aeschylus* pp 33–4 (and references there given) for this and the following point.

There hovers near my father's bitter, unremorseful Curse, urging 'gain'
[κέδρος, ie, the winning of renown][38] before death follows fast. (695–7)

By the end of this epirrhematic passage, the Curse is felt as an almost
physical presence on-stage. The Chorus argue that, if resisted with
prayers to the gods, it may decline in power, 'though *now* it rages still!'
(νῦν δ' ἔτι ζεῖ, 708). For Eteocles, however, this raging presence (ἐξέζεσεν
γὰρ Οἰδίπου κατεύγματα, 709) is the dread fulfilment of expectations till
now suppressed in dreams:

Too true those apparitions of nightly dreams, the fell dividers of our fathers'
realm! (710–11)[39]

The Chorus now cease their singing, but the Chorus-Leader (in the
brief passage of stichomythia) makes her final appeals that Eteocles
must not at any cost go to the seventh gate:

For god honours even an ignoble victory! (716)

Eteocles' last two responses to such urgings sum up the heroic and
the fatalistic reasons, respectively, for scorning them:

A soldier must not heed a plea like this! (717)

and

38 There has been some disagreement about what Eteocles means by κέρδος (gain) at 697.
I agree with Hutchinson in taking the sense from 683–5, where Eteocles has spoken
of avoidance of dishonour, or of 'a fair reputation' (εὐκλεία) as the only gain (κέρδος)
to be found among the dead. Hermann and Smythe (cited here by Hutchinson),
however, take 697 to refer simply to the 'gain' of slaying Polyneices before being
slain himself. Cf also Winnington-Ingram's somewhat different view (pp 38–9). He
believes (in the context of his fuller discussion, pp 31–40, of Eteocles' motivation)
that for Eteocles κέρδος here means 'inflicting on his enemy the ultimate harm,'
in return, in accordance with heroic standards, for the harm which Polyneices is
seeking to inflict on him.

39 I see no reason for believing with Anne Burnett that Eteocles had previously thought
that the dreams boded a *peaceful* division of the realm, 'and that the dream, like
the Curse, had just now taken on a new and sinister meaning for Eteocles.' What
evidence is there that either Dream (here referred to for the first time) *or* Curse had
ever had anything but 'a sinister meaning' for Eteocles? See Burnett 'Curse and
Dream in Aeschylus' *Septem*' p 357; however, the whole article (pp 343–68) needs to
be studied to judge Burnett's argument in its full context.

When the gods send ills, there's no escaping them! (719)

In the second stasimon (720–91)[40] which follows the great dramatic climax just described, the poet provides the central generalizing ode (comparable to the second stasimon of *Agamemnon*, especially to its coda at *Ag* 750–81) which looks back at the whole mythical sequence of disaster on the House of Laius and then relates these troubles (somewhat surprisingly) to the Solonian-Aeschylean theme (expressed in modified form in both *Persae* and *Agamemnon*) of the dangers of too great prosperity. There is a marked change in tone and perspective between the Chorus's utterances here and in the earlier lyric passages. Gone are the terrified women of the parodos and the first stasimon; gone, too, are the desperate females beseeching Eteocles to avoid the horror of kin-bloodshed, no matter what the cost in honour. The Chorus now sing in their other voice,[41] looking back in sombre reflection on the remote and less remote causes of the present danger and picturing in terrifyingly accurate terms the imminent horror soon to be described in its actuality. Only at the very beginning and at the very end of the ode is the note of personal terror allowed (in a sort of ring composition at variance with the tone of the ode as a whole) to intrude upon this sombre, almost fatalistic recounting of the way things have been, are, and will be, in the House of Laius.

Three themes are developed in the three almost equal parts of the ode (720–41, 742–65, 766–91), save that the final theme is allowed an extra stanza – a reasonable extension since, as we shall see, the third or 'summing-up' theme may be said to imply the previous two. As one critic has well observed, of the subject, and its treatment, of this ode: 'The history of the Labdacids is an organic whole.[42]

40 For various interesting comments concerning the imagery and interpretation of this ode, see Manton 'The Second Stasimon of *The Seven against Thebes*' pp 77–84.

41 This contrast might be expressed, though in oversimplified terms, as 'Chorus as commentator' as distinguished from 'Chorus as character,' or, as T.G. Rosenmeyer has expressed it, the Chorus as 'narrator, as enunciator of wisdom,' and the Chorus 'as potential agent.' See Rosenmeyer *The Art of Aeschylus* chap. 6. These and other related points are discussed in more detail in chapter 5 (below).

42 Hutchinson p 161. In his long note on vv 720–91, Hutchinson offers a somewhat different analysis of this ode from the one to be suggested here. Neither analysis, it should be noted, adheres to the *strophic* arrangement in the thematic divisions suggested. As Hutchinson observes, the strophic pairs themselves are sharply distinguished from one another in metre so that he is able to say of the ode's *content*

The first theme (720–41) is concerned with the house-destroying, evilly prophetic, father-invoked Fury (or Erinys) fulfilling mad Oedipus' Curse by means of the Chalybian stranger's (that is, the sword's) apportioning[43] and the mutual slaughter of the brothers. The theme is developed in three parts. The first part (720–6) sketches the fear of Oedipus' deadly Curse, which is to destroy the House and sons alike. The second part (727–33) provides a detailed description of the content of Oedipus' Curse: the prophecy of the sword's apportioning and an ironic description of the shared inheritance. In the third part (734–41) the Chorus mourns in advance the inevitable results of fratricide: the pollution of the land with brothers' blood. This melancholy sequence is then capped by a backward glance (which also serves as a transition to the second theme) at the House's ancient woes of which the present ills are but a newer version. The language in each of these three sections of the ode's first (or 'Curse of Oedipus') theme is precisely and marvellously apposite. ὀλεσίοικος ('house-destroying,' 720) is the first modifier of the Erinys, that god 'not like to other gods'; κακόμαντις ('evilly prophetic,' 722) is the last – an expression which carries, perhaps, an overtone of the first prophetic warning of Apollo to Laius. Oedipus, the imprecator, is βλαψίφρων ('maddened,' 'touched in the head,' 725), whereas the sword, the Chalybian stranger evoked to fulfil his Curse is πικρός and ὠμόφρων ('bitter' and 'savage-minded,' 730). The land of Thebes – or part of it – is mentioned first as the inheritance of the brothers: just so much as will cover them in death after the division by the sword. This in turn provides a suitably grim introduction to the theme's finale: the land's *pollution*, as the brothers die by one another's hand (αὐκτόνως αὐτοδάϊκτοι, 734–5) and the same Theban soil (γαῖα κόνις, 735) drinks the black blood of slaughter (734–41).

The second theme (developed in vv 742–65) takes the curse on the house back to its origins in Laius' offence after Apollo's 'triple warnings' that he *save the city* by dying without issue (742–9). This theme covers

---

(as analysed by him) that it is arranged in a form 'which deliberately conflicts with the metrical [form] ...' (p 161).

43 Hutchinson p 163 (in his note on vv 727–33), draws attention to the variety of ways in which the prophesied division of the Theban land by the sword is described in the play. Sometimes the image of the lot is used (ironically), as here, in connection with this division, sometimes not. (The other passages concerned are 788–90, 816 f, 833 f, 906–10, and 941–6). Hutchinson also discusses the possible (again ironic) relation of these descriptions to actual (somewhat conjectural) practices (eg, lot, arbitration) of distributing property inheritance, disputed and otherwise, in Aeschylus' day and earlier.

the whole sequence of woes from Laius' folly: Oedipus as parricide and mother-marrier (750–7) and the third wave of woe which now surges about the city (758 ff). The terrible metaphors for Oedipus' incestuous marriage ('sowing the sacred field which was his mother, field whence he was sprung,' 752–3), revive again the 'land motif,' reminiscent of the Theban soil which described the brothers' shroud (731 ff, 736 f). The motif of the city's safety reappears in the final section of this theme, as the third wave of disaster (that is, the clash of the accursed brothers) 'breaks around the city's hull' (760–1) and Chorus fear lest the city be destroyed amid the slaughter of its princes (758–65).

The ode's third and final theme provides the ethical coda (766–91). This time the transition to the new theme is effected by the completion, in the new context, of the image of the storm-beleaguered ship with which the preceding stanza ended. The grievous changes of fortune arising from the ancient curses are now connected (somewhat strangely, perhaps) with too great a weight of wealth which demands (for safety) to be cast from the ship's hold. That it is Oedipus' dangerous prosperity which the Chorus mean becomes clear in the next stanza, which celebrates the honour paid to Oedipus by citizens and city-gods for saving Thebes from the Sphinx:

> For what man have the gods and the citizens and the wide-ranging throng of humankind honoured as greatly as they honoured Oedipus ... ? (772–5)[44]

This final theme develops in detail the effects of Oedipus' curse upon *his* sons, just as the second theme dealt in detail with the woes of Oedipus, following from Laius' folly:

> With heart maddened by the horror of his marriage, learned too late, Oedipus accomplished twofold evils: with his father-slaying hands, he tore his eyes out and against his own children, angered at their wretched origin,[45]

---

44 For the sentiment and even, to some degree, the expression, cf Sophocles *OT* 1089 ff, of which the present passage is a striking anticipation.

45 I read ἀθλίας ... ἐπίκοτος τροφᾶς, as in Hutchinson's text, for ἀραίας ... ἐπικότους τροφᾶς of the MSS, at vv 785–6. However, the main difficulty for the interpretation of the passage is provided by τροφᾶς, the genitive of cause explaining Oedipus' angry cursing of his sons. Does it refer to the sons' 'wretched *nourishing*' of their father (according to one version of the legend, Oedipus was displeased at not receiving the best portion of meat at table) or to their own 'wretched [ie, incestuous] *origin*'? Hutchinson, arguing (I think rightly) for the latter version (Intro pp xxv–vi), suggests that the whole run of the sentence indicates that both evils (the self-blinding and

he uttered curses, that by sword-deciding might the brothers should get
their share of their inheritance. (778–90)

Thus, the ode ends with the first explicit account of the Curse itself,
the last verse (790–1) echoing the Chorus's initial fear that the Erinys is
now bringing the Curse to its accomplishment.

It will be clear from the analysis of this ode, with its parallel treatment
of the woes resulting from Laius' transgression and from Oedipus'
curse, and from the explicit intermingling of these woes at vv 740–1,
that, as the trilogy nears its close, the poet wishes us to see the whole
sequence of disaster as a sort of blight upon the family, stemming from
Laius' transgression (παραβασίαν, 743), then renewed by the curse of
Oedipus of which it was, if indirectly, itself the cause.

Several critics have, as we have already noted, stressed the change
of emphasis from the civic to the personal in the action of the *Septem*.[46]
In broad outline this observation is, no doubt, true; as we have seen,
Eteocles suppresses almost entirely any hint of his personal danger or
personal fate in connection with the Curse which he knows is hanging
over him, and, until the terrible 'recognition' at the Scout's seventh
announcement, has concentrated exclusively on the defence of the city.
Even then, after the first brief outburst, his soldierly duty remains
his paramount consideration. It is true, also, that from this point on,
particularly during the Chorus's attempts to dissuade Eteocles, the
dramatic interest is inevitably concentrated on the fulfilment of the
Curse, and so on the personal fate of the brothers, particularly Eteocles.
Nevertheless, there is, perhaps, a danger that in concentrating on the
obvious, critics may fail to notice the degree to which 'the civic theme'
is also kept quietly before the audience's mind, even in passages
where one might expect almost exclusive emphasis on the threat and,
eventually, the actuality of the fratricide.[47]

---

the son-cursing) wrought by Oedipus stemmed from anger at the discovery of his
incestuous marriage and progeny. But certainty on this rather crucial point in the
text seems impossible.

46 Cf. above, p 40 and n 10.

47 Cf Winnington-Ingram *Studies in Aeschylus* 20 ff, who notes the various ways
(including the recurrence of the 'Ship of State' metaphor) in which we are reminded
of the civic theme, despite the climax in individual, fratricidal combat. Cf also
Sheppard ('The Plot of the *Septem contra Thebas*') who makes an interesting
comparison between the *Septem* and the *Oresteia* with regard to the shared interest
between individual, family, and city which both works manifest; he finds that these
three themes are better integrated in the *Septem*.

Thus, in the ode which we have just discussed, while the immediate circumstances require that the Chorus's major concern should be the fortunes of the house of Laius and especially the doomed sons of Oedipus, the theme of the city's safety still arises repeatedly at certain significant moments in their treatment of the myth. Long ago, we hear, Apollo's original warnings to Laius were directed to the saving of the city (745–9). Even before that reminder, two references to the Theban land have been slipped into the Chorus's song: first, their reference to the brothers' inheritance ('... just so much of that land as will cover them in death,' 731–3) and again (after the fine image of the ship of state beset by the triple wave of disaster) in their expression of fear lest the city be destroyed along with the princes (758–65). With the arrival of the Messenger in the next episode, this emphasis on the theme of the hero and family over the civic theme is to be temporarily reversed.

6 Third episode, third stasimon, kommos [?], and exodos [?] (792–1078)

Take heart good daughters! This city has escaped the yoke of slavery! (792–3)

With his initial words, the Messenger sets the Chorus's hearts at rest as far as the fate of their city is concerned. Here and for the next six verses (794–9) his talk is all of the city's safety and the successful defence of six of the seven gates. Only in the last three verses (800–2) of his speech does the Messenger allude, and then somewhat cryptically, to the fate of the brothers, and the stichomythic passage which follows (803–10) deals mainly with the elucidation of this event through the Chorus's questioning.[48] Finally, the second Messenger speech (811–21) 'balances' the first by dealing mainly with *the brothers'* fate. Here, too, however, the city's safety is again mentioned (815) and the Messenger himself sums up the balance which the poet has suggested by these structural devices: 'Such things as have happened call for rejoicing ... and for tears!' (814).

---

48 The Messenger's statement, πόλις σέσωσται ('The city has been saved') occurs at both 804 and 820. Thus, at least one of these occurrences has been deleted by various editors (and both of them by Hutchinson, since the verse provides difficulties in both contexts). However, the fate both of the brothers and the city is well established in other verses of the Messenger's report.

As we have noted, the personal catastrophe, the fulfilment of the curse of Oedipus and of the doom inherited from Laius' folly is, of course, the tragic climax of the play. What, then, are we to make of the fact that, even in the midst of these climactic passages, the minor theme, the city's safety, still keeps surfacing? The conclusion, surely, that from Eteocles' dedication and the curse-fulfilling fate which it has triggered, some larger good has been achieved. Eteocles has initiated the action with exclusive emphasis upon the safety of the city. It is fitting that, in the fulfilment of his individual doom and that of his brother, the achievement of his initial goal should not be forgotten.

In the anapaests (822–31)[49] preceding the final stasimon, the Chorus express their ambivalent emotions (πότερον χαίρω ... ἢ ... κλαύσω, 'Am I to rejoice ... or weep? 825 ff) over the saving of the city and the death of the brothers. At the end of the passage, however, both brothers are blamed as ones who, 'full of strife' (πολυνεικεῖς, 830), have perished through their own impious policies. By contrast, the strophic pair of stanzas (832–47) which follows deals primarily with the more remote causes of the tragic fratricide: the dark, accomplishing curse of Oedipus (832–3) and the disobedient counsels (βουλαὶ δ' ἄπιστοι, 842) of Laius. (It is interesting that both 'causes' are given in sequence at 832–42: a point which strengthens the general impression, never clearly stated, that Oedipus' cursing of his sons is itself a sort of continuation of the curse on the family due to the disobedience of Laius.)[50]

During the next (astrophic) stanza (848–60), the bodies of the slain brothers are carried on-stage, as the opening verse ('Now is the Messenger's report made manifest!' 848) clearly indicates. Thus, the stanza serves as a sort of lyric prelude to the formal dirge (875 ff) which will be sung in alternation by the two halves of the Chorus. With the approach of the funeral cortège, the tone of the Chorus becomes more conventional in their lamentation of the twin fates, the twofold woes mutually inflicted on the brothers. With hands beating their heads, the singers 'will speed the funeral barque across the Acheron, to that sunless yet hospitable shore where Apollo never treads' (855–60).

As the corpses of the slain brothers are displayed on-stage, the play ends with an impressive song of lamentation, sung in alternating stanzas by the two halves of the Chorus (875–960), and a brief final passage

49 The anapaests at vv 822–31 have been doubted by both Page and Dawe and deleted, I think unreasonably, by Page. See, however, Dawe's arguments in 'The End of the *Seven against Thebes* Yet Again' pp 88 ff.
50 Cf the theme of the second stasimon, vv 720 ff, esp at vv 740–4.

(961–1004) in which this alternation is broken into single-verse or else half-verse exchanges sung by the two leaders of the semi-Choruses, respectively.[51] As one editor has observed, this whole sung finale approaches very closely to ritual mourning, 'lamentation' being 'the chief vehicle through which death in Tragedy stirred up the emotion of the audience.'[52] Thus the play is, in a sense, over at this point and one may not, perhaps, expect any fresh thematic developments in these lyrical lamentations. Several themes are, to be sure, repeated from earlier passages, though in slightly different terms. Here the most striking examples are the recurrent lament for the destruction of the House by the brothers' lethal 'reconciliation' (879–85, 933–6); the brothers' sharing of their bitter patrimony (of their native earth) in death (911–14, 937–50);[53] and the repeated blaming by the Chorus of the Curse invoked on the brothers by their father Oedipus (886–7, 945–6, 953–5).

There are, however, two features of these lyrical lamentations which do, perhaps, modify our final impression of the tragic meaning of this play. One is the disappearance of a previously recurrent theme, the saving of the city; the other is the disappearance of any distinction between the brothers' actions or characters, heroic or culpable, in the Chorus's mournful reviews of the tragic events just consummated. The grief of the city and of the land is declared for both brothers equally (900 ff);[54] equal, too, and equally ironic in the Chorus's expression of it,

---

51 Problems concerning the authenticity and the attribution of various verses from v 860 to the end of the play will be considered in appendix 3 to this chapter. See also the excellent discussion and bibliography in Hutchinson's edition, pp 190–1 (on vv 861–74) and 209 ff (on vv 1005–75). For the purposes of the present study, the anapaestic passage, 861–74, introducing Antigone and Ismene as new arrivals on-stage, may be regarded as deleted; so too may the passage at 1005–53, between a Herald and Antigone, and the Chorus's anapaestic tail-piece (1054–78), which is dependent for its sense upon it.

52 Hutchinson p 178. (See also his whole note on vv 822–1004, pp 178–81.)

53 Cf the earlier reference, at vv 727–30 (with marked verbal similarities to vv 941–6) to the sword as 'bitter apportioner.' Note also Winnington-Ingram's comments, in connection with Oedipus' curse, on the double aspect (as 'kindly mother' and as receiver of the dead) which Earth presents in this play. (See Winnington-Ingram Studies in Aeschylus p 25, n 23, and his references to Cameron and Dawson ad loc.)

54 Several critics have commented on this even-handed treatment of both brothers in the Chorus's lamentations after their death. But this should not, I think, be taken (as Gagarin, for example, takes it, Aeschylean Drama p 23) as indicative of the attitude to be taken toward the respective rights and wrongs of the two brothers in the total action of the play.

is the share which each brother will inherit, in death, of the patrimony for which he fought (911–14, 944–6, 947–50). Perhaps most significant in this connection is a little passage which in *form* is reminiscent of a conventional eulogy for the slain warriors but which actually turns out to have the opposite effect:

> One may say of these two in their striving and suffering that they have wrought many woes both on citizens and on enemy strangers alike. (922–5)

Both citizens *and* attackers have suffered from this internecine strife; once again, no distinction seems to be made between what one brother or the other has done in this regard. Again, a little later, one hemi-Chorus sings, 'O you who have crowned this race with woes!', with again no distinction between the brothers. Immediately after this, however, the same singers conclude this passage of choral exchanges with their final (and perhaps more just) assessment:

> The all-accomplishing Curses [from Oedipus] shriek their bitter Victory-songs ... Atê's trophy is raised over the gates, those gates where the brothers perished, and the avenging family spirit [*daimôn*], now that it has conquered both of them, now takes its leave. (953–60)

The new attitude expressed toward the brothers, now represented as equal in doing and suffering, and in the mourning accorded to each, becomes yet more marked in the more equally balanced and formally symmetrical exchanges (961–1004) between the individual singers with which the play concludes.[55] This equality of treatment is, no doubt, occasioned by the presence of both corpses onstage: in death, both princes are equally royal, both corpses are there to be mourned, and it would be difficult, in the circumstances, for the Chorus to make distinctions between them. This conclusion need not, I think, erase the impression created earlier of an Eteocles who achieves some measure of heroic *aretê* in the defence of the city, in spite of, if even in the fulfilment of, the curse of Oedipus. But it does put this element of human achievement, and of human responsibility, in its place, as it were, so that at the end of the trilogy the suffering of the third generation can be seen in its supernatural perspective of the working out of the family doom initiated by Laius' ἀβουλία ('folly') with regard to Apollo's oracle,

---

55 Note, especially, among several examples of this 'reciprocal symmetry,' vv 962–3 and 989–90.

and perpetuated by the curses of the accursed Oedipus. In this respect, Aeschylus' Theban trilogy manifests that blend of freedom with an inevitable doom, supernaturally imposed, which we may observe as present, to some degree at least, in all the poet's extant work.

APPENDIX 1

The timing of Eteocles' assignments at the seven gates

Few points in the interpretation of the *Septem* have been as strenuously debated as that which concerns the timing of Eteocles' appointments of the seven leaders to defend each of the seven gates of Thebes. At the end of the first episode, the King has told the Chorus that he will make these assignments ($\tau\acute{\alpha}\xi\omega$), 'before the hurrying messengers with their rush of words arrive and inflame us with urgent necessity' (282–6). The first stasimon intervenes between Eteocles' departure on this mission and 'the Shield Scene,' in which Eteocles answers the Scout's report of the attacking chieftains (and their shield-emblazonings) with his own announcements of the heroes who will oppose them. It is, of course, a well-established convention of Greek tragedy that a choral ode can be understood to fill any gap in time which the action of the play requires. So far, then, there would seem to be no compelling reason why Eteocles should not have completed his assignments for the defences of the seven gates *before* he returns to the scene and hears the Scout's report. This view has been strenuously urged by Wolff (followed by several other critics),[1] who then asserts that, since all seven defenders including Eteocles himself have *already* been assigned to their respective gates, Eteocles does not willingly or consciously assign himself as his brother's antagonist. (In the end, Wolff makes the gods entirely responsible for the fraternal confrontation, as for all others, in that it is they, he alleges, who determine the lots by which the *attacking* chieftains have been posted.)

Major uncertainties concerning this view arise, however, from two features of 'the Shield Scene,' both of which have been stressed, by von Fritz and others,[2] in rebuttal of Wolff's views. One of these is the fact that three future tenses (at 408, 621, 672), as well as one

---

1 Wolff 'Die Entscheidung des Eteokles.' Cf also Otis 'The Unity of *The Seven against Thebes*' pp 159–60 and Burnett 'Curse and Dream in Aeschylus' *Septem*' pp 347 ff.
2 Von Fritz *Antike und Moderne Tragodie* 200 ff. See also Kirkwood 'Eteokles Oiakostrophos' pp 12 ff. Cf Taplin *Stagecraft* p 152, whose views on the timing of Eteocles' appointments are similar to those of von Fritz and Kirkwood.

present tense (at 553), two perfect tenses (at 448 and 473), and one aorist (at 505) are used in Eteocles' declaration of *his* assignments, in answer to the Scout's announcements of the attacking chieftains. The second and even more arresting feature is the fact that, as we have seen, Eteocles, in each case, describes his choice of defender in terms of his *appropriateness* (in one way or another) as defender against the particular attacker (and his shield emblazoning) whom he is assigned to confront. It is this feature which the adversaries of Wolff's view, with some justice, urge most strongly as far outweighing the alleged indication of prior appointments by Eteocles in his statement of intention at vv 282–6. Von Fritz, for example, argues that spectators could hardly be expected to retain this information during the long intervening choral ode, especially when the appropriateness of Eteocles' appointments in relation to the Scout's announcements leads us to think otherwise. So, too, Kirkwood's best argument here is that 'the matching assignment [by Eteocles] is always put in terms of the particular opponent [announced by the Scout].'[3] It is this emphasis on the *appropriateness* of Eteocles' assignments (the indications that in each case he is choosing his defending chieftains to confront specific features of the attackers) which has led several critics (again von Fritz, Kirkwood, and Taplin will serve as representative examples) to argue that *all* Eteocles' postings are made during the scene with the Scout. This position, however, runs into difficulty with the tenses of Eteocles' appointments similar to 'the tenses difficulty' faced by Wolff. Just as the three future tenses tell against Wolff's argument (and have been used in refuting it), so, too, the three past tenses tell against those arguing for the opposite view. Though one sympathizes with this understanding of the total dramatic impact of this scene,[4] none of the defenders of *all* of Eteocles' appointments being made 'on the spot,' as it were, really gets around this considerable difficulty. Von Fritz provides the most ingenious of various attempts to do so but as Hutchinson comments: 'Wolff's view that the futures denote a past action is untenable;

---

3 Kirkwood 'Eteokles *Oiakostrophos*' p 12. Less convincing, however, is Kirkwood's argument that, even if we accept, as he doesn't, that Eteocles made his *choices* of defenders before hearing the Scout's announcements, 'there is nothing in vv 282–7 to suggest that Eteocles proposes to *station* his champions before he knows the disposition of the attacking leaders.' Eteocles does, after all, use the verb τάξω ('I will *station*,' 284) in the passage (282–6) cited at the beginning of this appendix.

4 Cf Taplin *Stagecraft* p 152: 'The entire construction of the *Redepaare* is symmetrical ...' Therefore, Taplin argues, since some of Eteocles' choices seem to be made in answer to the Scout's announcements, all of them must be.

no less so the view of von Fritz that the pasts can denote a present choice.'[5]

We are left finally with the view that Eteocles 'means' the tenses that he uses, that is, that some of his appointments were already made before the scene with the Scout (that is, those of Polyphontes, Megareus, and Hyperbius, of whose postings past tenses are used at 448, 473, and 505, respectively), while the others are made 'on the spot,' in response to the Scout's announcements. This was Wilamowitz's view[6] and I think that it is correct, even though it seems 'unsatisfactory' as spoiling the 'symmetrical construction' of the scene, as Taplin has described it. (Hutchinson, among others, also regards this view of Wilamowitz's as 'most unattractive,' though, along with other recent editors of the *Septem*, Lupas and Petre, he seems to accept it, since he denies that the tenses can mean other than what they say.)[7]

If we accept, as I think we must, that three of Eteocles' 'assignments' have been made before the scene with the Scout, the others in response to the Scout's announcements, then clearly Eteocles must have been interrupted in this procedure by hearing of the Scout's arrival, and there are indeed indications of haste and urgency in the Chorus's descriptions (369–74), first of the Scout's and then of Eteocles' hurried return (σπουδή is used in both cases) to the scene to engage in this exchange.

The issue involved in this debate is, of course, more than academic. The more responsible Eteocles' choices are made to appear (that is, the more of them appear as sound military responses to the attacking chieftains announced), then the more the Commander's all-too-appropriate choosing of himself for the last gate will appear not simply as the outburst of furious passion but as the final and inevitable climax to a series of consistent decisions.

Such a view of the matter provides us with an excellent example of what many would regard as the classic tragic situation: the inevitable fulfilment of a supernaturally ordained catastrophe (or, at this stage, 'catastrophic situation') through a series of free decisions made in accordance with the 'character' (or at least the dominant characteristic

---

5 Hutchinson p 105.

6 Wilamowitz *Aischylos Interpretationen* pp 61–2.

7 Hutchinson p 105; see also his complete note on vv 369–652 (pp 103–6). Cf. also Lupas and Petre *Commentaire* p 120, who compare (rather oddly) the temporal spread implied by the different tenses with the spatial spread implied by what is going on outside the gates.

displayed in the drama) of the tragic figure. The extreme opposite view, that each of Eteocles' choices of defenders at each of the seven gates was made *before* he heard the Scout's account of the various attackers at those gates, would, of course, mean that the *appropriateness* of those choices was a matter of coincidence, or chance – or rather of what appears to be the chance decisions of the commander-in-chief. Such an interpretation reduces, though it does not destroy, the characteristic aspect of Eteocles decisions as, throughout, those of an ideal and eminent commander, for in that case he has made his choices unaware of the identity of the attackers against whom he is posting his leaders. It introduces, however, another ingredient often observable in tragedy (one dear to the heart of Aristotle and most conspicuous in Sophocles' *Oedipus Tyrannus*), namely, the element of ignorance, or of *unawareness*, in the characteristic and fatal decisions of the tragic sufferer-to-be.

If, as seems reasonable, the timing of Eteocles' choices of defenders (that is, whether before, or in answer to, the Scout's accounts of the attacking chieftains) is essential to the relation between character and action in the *Septem*, then it is surely unlikely that Aeschylus' choice of tenses to indicate that timing would be casual or accidental.

The only conclusion which one can safely draw from Aeschylus' subtle mixture of tenses in this crucial sequence of confrontations is that the poet does not wish us to draw definite conclusions. Rather, the catastrophic event is to appear (in tragedy as in life) as the result of a combination of 'chance' and of significant choices, a combination in which one is challenged, without hope of certainty, to determine the deciding factor.

APPENDIX 2

'Eteocles' fateful decision': various views

The view which I have defended, in the foregoing chapter, of Eteocles' fateful decision at vv 653 ff is similar to the views expressed by von Fritz and Kirkwood.[1] Both these critics reject what is perhaps the majority view that Eteocles undergoes a transformation with the onset of the Curse at v 653, and both provide excellent summaries of previous scholarly opinion on the subject. Von Fritz's discussion, beginning with an account of the older 'naive' form of the 'Opfertod view' and continuing with various refinements, criticisms, and rebuttals of it, culminates with his own excellent arguments[2] for a consistent '*Gestalt*' of Eteocles which, he believes, informs the whole action of the tragedy. (Kirkwood's similar discussion[3] is, perhaps, preferable with regard to the slightly greater emphasis which he places on the power of the Curse in bringing about the tragic catastrophe.)

In view of these and other detailed reviews of this scholarly controversy, it will suffice here to suggest a few prominent features of its history. Wilamowitz's attack on the 'Opfertod interpretation' introduced the view (somewhat ill-supported by his reference to *Sept* 274 ff, but accepted by several subsequent scholars) that Eteocles had no expectation of being doomed to die in the coming battle.[4] Solmsen's later emphasis on the Erinyes as the all-important feature of the play introduced the still popular belief in the transformation of Eteocles and his motivation after v 652. Solmsen also emphasized the complete separation (in his view) between Eteocles' fate and the saving of the city.[5]

Wolff introduced a more fatalistic twist to Solmsen's view of the play with his argument[6] that all of Eteocles' 'gate-assignments,' including that of himself at the seventh gate, had been made before the Scout's

---

1 Von Fritz *Antike und Moderne Tragödie* pp 193 ff and Kirkwood 'Eteokles *Oiakostrophos*' pp 9–25.
2 Von Fritz pp 205 ff.
3 See esp Kirkwood pp 12–13.
4 See Von Wilamowitz-Moellendorff *Aischylos Interpretationen* pp 56 ff and 67; cf von Fritz p 194.
5 Solmsen 'The Erinyes in Aeschylus' *Septem*'; see esp pp 197–200 and 206–8.
6 See above, appendix 1 to this chapter.

report of the seven attacking chieftains. Thus, like Solmsen, Wolff regards Eteocles' recognition of the power and meaning of the Curse to be the turning-point of the play, but, unlike Solmsen, Wolff has Eteocles recognize the working of that power upon himself as a *fait accompli* about which he can do nothing.[7] Patzer also follows Solmsen in stressing the 'frightful awakening' of Eteocles at v 653, when he suddenly realizes the working of the *Erinys* (the deified personification of the Curse) and gives himself up to it. Patzer's own contribution (based on a somewhat dubious reconstruction of the wording of the Curse) is the argument that Eteocles had previously misunderstood the Curse to mean simply that the possession and rule of the Kingdom would be decided by the outcome of the battle over Thebes. (Like Wilamowitz, Patzer argues that nowhere does Eteocles show expectation of his own death.)[8] In this connection we should note also the curious 'conversion,' as it were, of the 'Opfertod view' by Brooks Otis, who believes that the Olympian gods make use of the destructive Erinyes to save the city of Thebes at the expense of Eteocles as an unwilling scape-goat. Otis compares unfavourably the moral incompleteness of this compromise between the two divine orders, with the resolution in the *Oresteia*, where the Erinyes are frustrated by the Olympians, and the *dikê* of the *polis* reflects the rights of the individual.[9] But the comparison is surely a somewhat limping one.

Winnington-Ingram[10] is in agreement with most recent critics in believing that the Curse dominates Eteocles' fatal decision but argues further that it works through a fraternal hatred that is already there. While admitting that the distinction between the Curse and the mind of Eteocles is hard to draw, he does see Eteocles' decision more in personal than in 'city-defender' terms. This emphasis on the personal, 'family-feud' element in the climax of the play leads Winnington-Ingram to believe that Aeschylus may be using the Theban legend to dramatize the conflict between archaic, *genos*-privilege, endangering the city-state by its feuds, and the preservation of the *polis* which, he seems to believe, Eteocles saves almost by accident in the fury of his fratricidal strife. Again, as with Brooks Otis's argument, one feels that the play is being overloaded with political philosophy.

7 Wolff 'Die Entscheidung des Eteocles' pp 89–95, esp pp 91–3.
8 Patzer 'Die dramatische Handlung der *Sieben gegen Theben*' pp 97–119, esp pp 101–4 and, for the last point, 109–10.
9 Otis 'The Unity of the Seven against Thebes,' esp pp 156–7 and 168–72.
10 Winnington-Ingram *Studies in Aeschylus* pp 31–40, 52.

APPENDIX 3

Some problems concerning the end of the *Septem*

The authenticity of certain passages at the end of the *Septem* has been hotly debated by classical scholars and a consensus has not yet been reached. Since the issue has been discussed in numerous studies of the *Septem*, only the main points will be reviewed here, with reference to a few leading proponents of one side or the other of the debate.

After a lyrical passage (848–60) which looks like a prelude to the formal lament at 875 ff, the manuscripts have a passage of anapaests (861–74) in which the Chorus announce the arrival of Antigone and Ismene to join in the funeral dirge over their slain brothers' bodies. Then, after a long ode (875–960) lamenting the brothers,[1] there follows an antiphonal dirge (961–1004) ascribed by many editors, following some indications in the manuscripts, to Antigone and Ismene. At 1005, a Herald enters and proclaims (1005–25) that by decree of the city Eteocles is to receive honourable burial but Polyneices 'unhonoured burial by winged birds.' A confrontation ensues between the Guard and Antigone, who declares her intention to bury Polyneices. The manuscripts end with the Chorus pondering this altercation in anapaests (1054–78), probably (but see Page's *apparatus*) breaking into hemi-choruses at 1066 ff and 1072 ff, one siding with the official edict, the other with Antigone.

The principal disagreement concerning these passages has been between those who would accept the parts concerning the burial of Polyneices and those who would reject them as an interpolation influenced by Sophocles' *Antigone*.[2] Thus scholars subscribing to the

---

1 This passage was probably sung antiphonally by the two halves of the Chorus; see, however, Page's *apparatus criticus* for the manuscript ascriptions and editorial comment; see also his reference to Lloyd-Jones *ad loc.*
2 The most celebrated defence of the passage involved is that of Hugh Lloyd-Jones, in an important article (both for its discussion of the passages in question and for the total view of the play and the trilogy there suggested), 'The End of *The Seven against Thebes.*' Lloyd-Jones provides a good summary of leading arguments against the authenticity of the passages which he defends. On the other side of the question, see Dawe's attempted rebuttal of Lloyd-Jones 'The End of *The Seven against Thebes.*' See also Taplin *Stagecraft* pp 170–80, on vv 822–1004, and pp 180–6, on what he describes

latter view reject 1005–78 (end). Some (such as Hutchinson) would also
reject 861–74 (since the main reason for introducing the sisters at this
stage in the play would seem to be for Antigone's role in the burial
issue) and ascribe the antiphonal dirge at 961–1004 to the leaders of the
two halves of the Chorus, without the participation (indicated in the
manuscript) of Antigone and Ismene.[3]

Against the objection that the confrontation between the Guard and
Antigone looks forward to a new issue beyond the action of the play
(namely, Antigone's burial of Polyneices and its results), Lloyd-Jones
points to other plays, Sophocles' *Oedipus at Colonus*, for example, where
such anticipations occur, and argues further that, even in the *Septem*,
other passages relating to the fate of the family and the city point to
such future events.[4]

With regard to the first of these points, Dawe has argued, with
some justice, that, unlike Lloyd-Jones's other examples of allusions to
the future in other plays, the present instance concerns a substantial
portion of the play and concerns, moreover, an individual who has not
even been one of the play's *dramatis personae*.[5]

Lloyd-Jones's second and more wide-ranging argument – that even
in the *Septem* there are other passages relating to the future – is bound

---

as 'the false ending' at 1005 ff. (Taplin, as usual, provides valuable 'theatrical' insights
on these passages, together with useful comparisons with other tragedies.) For a
brief, general but useful summary of the problem, see Christopher Dawson *The Seven
against Thebes, a translation with commentary* pp 22–5.

3 The textual decisions involved here also help answer the 'theatrical' question,
'When were the corpses of Eteocles and Polyneices carried on-stage?' This action
would appear to have taken place at v 848 ('These events are now made manifest,
even as the words of the Messenger previously expressed them'), except for one
difficulty which is now removed. The matter is clearly explained in Taplin's excellent
discussion (*Stagecraft* 170–6). Such an entry (of characters or corpses) Taplin shows us
(by comparisons with other Aeschylean plays, most notably the *Persae*, whose final
sequence most resembles that of the *Septem*) might normally be expected at the *end*
of the act-dividing lyric, not, as appears to be the case here, thirteen verses (848–60)
before its end. However, once 861–74 are seen as an interpolation, preparing for the
(interpolated) entry of Ismene and Antigone, then (as Taplin was perhaps the first to
remark) 848–60 could be regarded as 'an astrophic prelude to the main lament' at
vv 875 ff, the act-dividing lyric of vv 822 ff would end at v 847, and the arrival of
the corpses at this point would conform to normal Aeschylean practice. (We should
note also, in addition to his elucidation of this particular theatrical point, Taplin's
interesting discussion (pp 170 ff) of the structural parallels between final sequences
of the *Persae* and of the *Septem*.)

4 Lloyd-Jones 'The End of *The Seven*' p 83.

5 Dawe 'The End of *The Seven*' p 18.

up with his insistence (against arguments of Wilamowitz and Solmsen)[6] on the continuation of the family-curse theme as it affects both family *and* city throughout the action of the play and even, by implication, beyond it. The passages cited in support of this argument are 745 ff, 840–4 and 902–3. At 745 ff, the Chorus quotes Apollo's oracle to Laius as saying that Laius could save the city only by dying without issue; from this it is argued that Thebes continues to be in danger as long as the descendants of Laius survive. Lloyd-Jones finds evidence that the poet regarded this danger to the city as continuing beyond the action of the play. At 902–3, the Chorus sing that the lands for which the whole struggle of the doomed brothers came about 'remain for those born after' (μένει ... τοῖς ἐπιγόνοις). Lloyd-Jones (with other critics) takes this to be an allusion to the myth of the Epigoni, according to which the sons of the defeated Seven, including Thersandrus, son of Polyneices, wreaked vengeance on Thebes. Consonant with this interpretation, the

6 See Lloyd-Jones 'The End of *The Seven*' pp 87–92 (and references there given to Wilamowitz, Solmsen, and others). Lloyd-Jones rejects Wilamowitz's view that *The Septem* unsuccessfully combines two disparate traditions, 'the family curse theme' (allegedly ending with the death of the brothers) and 'the destruction of Thebes' (ie, by the Epigoni, cf vv 902–3, 840–4); he also rejects 'the Opfertod view,' defended by Robert and Klotz (see his references) and others. Lloyd-Jones approves of Solmsen's emphasis on the power of the Curse in its effect on Eteocles' decision, but criticizes Solmsen's further argument that '... in the end ... Aeschylus felt that the Curse, when coming to a head, should be confined to the family and not affect the City' (see Lloyd-Jones p 89, quoting Solmsen p 207).

None of the answers to this problem of the *Septem* is completely free from difficulties. However (as I shall argue below), since Lloyd-Jones's emphasis on the future destruction of the city (and so of the continuing power of the Curse) depends on the uncertain interpretation of but a few words towards the end of the play, I think it is safer to reject it. On this point, we may accept as more reasonable the view that Aeschylus was willing (for the sake of the play's and the trilogy's climax, rather than for the somewhat 'pietistic' reasons alleged by Solmsen) to forget the emphasis on the city in Apollo's original warning to Laius.

Among more recent defenders of the doubted passage at the end of the play, E. Flintoff, 'The Ending of *The Seven against Thebes*' pp 344–71, tends to support Lloyd-Jones's conclusions. He too believes that issues beyond the trilogy, including the fate of the City, 'the Epigoni episode,' and the issue of Polyneices' burial, achieve real (and in his view justifiable) prominence at the end of the play. He also refers to Pausanias IX, 5.11 to argue that Antigone and Ismene (whose existence at this period Dawe questions) are mentioned in the epic *Oidipodia*. (Less impressive, among arguments favouring the retention of the Guard-Antigone scene, is Clifford Orwin's emphasis on the rightness of Polyneices' claims on Justice and familial support; see Clifford Orwin 'Feminine Justice: The End of *The Seven against Thebes*' pp 187–96.

Chorus's somewhat ambiguous expression μέριμνα δ'ἀμφὶ πτόλιν (843), which can mean 'worry [looking to the future] concerning the city,' is taken to be another reference to the still possible future fulfilment (even with the brothers dead) of Apollo's warning to Laius about the city.

Two of the three key passages mentioned above are, it is generally recognized, open to other interpretations. Dawe[7] understands the sentence at v 843 (as Klotz, cited by both Lloyd-Jones and Dawe, did before him) as referring simply to present lamentation *around* the city *for the brothers,* and takes ἐπιγόνοις at 903 to refer simply to 'those born after' (again as Klotz also did). In further rebuttal of the idea that the Epigoni are mentioned or even thought of in this play Dawe also insists, against Lloyd-Jones's rather unconvincing argument to the contrary, that the adjective ἀτέκνους applied to the brothers at 828 must indeed have its usual meaning of 'childless' here (and therefore, of course, that Polyneices' son Thersandrus, in the legend of the Epigoni, is not, in this play, thought of as existing). Dawe also quotes seven other passages in the *Septem* (of which, perhaps, 742–5, 951–60 and 1054–6 are the most relevant), which he claims indicate Aeschylus' exclusion of the Epigoni form his treatment of the legend in this play.

In fairness to Lloyd-Jones, it should be pointed out that the above-mentioned alternatives to his arguments have already been considered by him; with the exception of ἀτέκνους (which does, I think, provide a real difficulty to his interpretation), the passages mentioned (ie, at 843 and 902–3) can, perhaps, be taken either way. Lloyd-Jones's interpretation really stems from his total reading of how Aeschylus might be expected to have treated the myth in this trilogy, that is, from his belief that the family curse must be thought of as still operative after the death of the brothers, and his total rejection of any interpretation of the play (most of all the so-called Opfertod view) which suggests that Eteocles, intentionally or otherwise, 'saved the city' by his death.

My own view is that the evidence for these alleged anticipations of civic and family fortunes beyond the action of the play is too uncertain to stand as a defence of the 'burial of Polyneices' passage, and that, considered by itself, an apparently irrelevant intrusion of this magnitude is more likely than otherwise to have been due to an interpolation influenced by Sophocles' *Antigone.*

---

7 For the following arguments, see Dawe 'The End of *The Seven*' pp 19–21.

CHAPTER THREE

Supplices (*The Suppliants*)
and its trilogy

Preliminary comments

For many years, Aeschylus' *Supplices* was regarded by the great majority of classicists as the earliest extant Aeschylean play. The main basis for this view was the prominence of its Chorus, due not only to the high proportion of the play devoted to its songs but also to its central importance, as a group personality, to the dramatic situation with which the play is concerned. This feature (when treated without further discrimination), together with the limited degree of characterization involved in the roles assigned to the first and especially to the second actor, fitted the general awareness that Greek tragedy had, in some way, evolved from a predominantly lyrical to an increasingly dramatic structure, and sufficed to convince scholars, in the lack of any firm external evidence concerning its date, that the *Supplices* was indeed the earliest Greek tragedy which we possess. (Kitto, for example, treated the *Supplices* as something very close to 'lyrical tragedy' as he described what he regarded as the earliest form of tragedy, that is, tragedy with one actor and the Chorus: '... we can ... see in the *Supplices* an example of a drama otherwise lost to us.')[1]

The publication of Oxyrhinchus Papyrus 2256, fragment 3, in 1952, changed not only the 'dating' of the *Supplices* but also our understanding

---

1 Kitto *Greek Tragedy* p 1. That there was development in Greek tragedy from a predominantly lyrical to an increasingly dramatic structure, and that this development was connected with the introduction of a second, then of a third actor, is not, of course, to be denied. However, it was the probable role of the Chorus in the earliest form of tragedy which was (understandably) misunderstood when it was thought that the *Supplices* was our earliest extant play.

of its structure. This fragment of a *Hypothesis* to one of the plays in the Danaid trilogy (to which our play belongs) established beyond reasonable doubt that the trilogy was produced after 467 BC and provided at least a possible indication that its production date was 463.[2] Majority opinion based on this evidence, considered with certain political circumstances (to be mentioned later), now favours a date in the later 460s for the *Supplices*.

These facts about the dating of the *Supplices* are well known but are worth repeating here if only to provide a point of reference for recent and instructive criticism, helpful to our understanding of what actually influenced the peculiar structure of this play, of the kind of 'dating arguments' advanced before the discovery of the papyrus fragment. Of particular relevance is A.F. Garvie's observation that the use of the Chorus as protagonist in the *Supplices* really provided no grounds at all for the early dating since there is no indication, or even likelihood, that the Chorus had ever normally been used in this way. Garvie rightly regards this feature as an individual one dictated by the myth and by the poet's treatment of it – and a feature, moreover, which would be more likely to appear at a more sophisticated rather than at an early stage of tragedy, since it runs counter to the usual use of the Chorus as 'commentator' on the tragic action or perhaps, in early tragedy, as provider of a lyric threnody to accompany that action.[3]

A second (and related) point worth citing from Garvie concerns the treatment of the central character in the play, the Argive king Pelasgus, which also had once been regarded as a sign of an early Aeschylean tragedy: 'The determining factor is not the date of the play but the dramatic necessity ... In the *Supplices* we are interested not in the character of Pelasgus but in his dilemma.'[4]

If Kitto and Garvie disagree concerning the probable nature of 'lyrical tragedy,' they are in agreement, at any rate, about the centrality and the

---

2 See Smythe and Lloyd-Jones eds *Aeschylus*, Loeb edition, vol II, appendix, no 288, pp 595–8, for the papyrus fragment and discussion thereon. See also Garvie *Aeschylus' Supplices, Play and Trilogy* chap 1, and Johansen and Whittle eds *Aeschylus: The Suppliants* vol I. (Subsequent references in this chapter to the latter two works will be made by authors' name[s] alone.)

3 See Garvie pp 113–15, and chap 3, passim, for other relevant points.

4 Ibid p 132. Cf the similar criticisms by Lloyd-Jones of those who treated the allegedly dull and prosy characterization of Danaus as a sign of the early date of the *Supplices* (Lloyd-Jones 'The *Supplices* of Aeschylus: The New Date and Old Problems' p 370).

impressive treatment of the dilemma in which Pelasgus, the protagonist (at least 'in the purely technical sense,' as Garvie adds), is placed in the action of the play. In other passages besides the one quoted above, Garvie concentrates on this feature of the play, and also on the *agon* between two hostile parties which develops toward the end of the play, as signs of the relatively 'advanced dramatic technique' of the *Supplices*.[5] Kitto, too, is eloquent about the dilemma of King Pelasgus as 'the centre of his [Aeschylus'] tragic idea.'[6]

This view of the tragic centrality of the King's dilemma would certainly seem to make Pelasgus the protagonist in more than 'the purely technical sense,' and yet this role has been assigned to the Chorus by both the critics whom we have quoted. Is it possible for a play to have more than one 'protagonist,' in the sense of that dramatic personality (whether of an individual or of a group) with which the dramatic action of the tragedy is most concerned? This is a point to be kept in mind when we turn to a detailed study of the play, for only one's own analysis of its action can decide for each reader where he will place 'the centre of the playwright's idea.'

The situation and the plot of the *Supplices*, as well as what little is known of the subsequent action of the trilogy, may be briefly stated. The fifty daughters of Danaus of Egypt (represented by the Chorus in the play)[7] arrive in Argos in flight from their cousin-suitors, the fifty sons of King Aegyptus, who would impose marriage on them against their own and their father's will. Their specific claim to sanctuary at Argos, in addition to the claims of any suppliant appealing in the name of Zeus, 'guardian of suppliants,' is that they are descendants of Io, the Argive maid pursued by Zeus to Egypt: Epaphus, the touch-conceived son of Zeus and Io, was the founder of the royal family to which the Danaids and the sons of Aegyptus belong. The supplication of Argos (its mode and manner, the issues it involves, its ultimate success) provides the central action of the play; this action ends with the arrival of the violent Egyptian suitors (represented by their Herald) and the Argive king's acceptance of war with the Egyptians as the price of his pious defence of the suppliant Danaids.

5 See Garvie pp 131–5.
6 Kitto *Greek Tragedy* p 9.
7 It is now generally agreed that a Chorus of twelve (or possibly of fifteen) represent the fifty daughters of King Danaus; cf Pickard-Cambridge *The Dramatic Festivals of Athens* pp 234 ff

Details (hypothetical and otherwise) of the trilogy development (the succeeding plays, the *Aegyptii* and the *Danaides*, are lost)[8] may be postponed, but a brief outline of the more relevant parts of the Danaid myth should perhaps be indicated here: it seems likely that some of the playwright's effects in the first play exploit such knowledge on the audience's part. The Egyptians prevail in their battle with the Argives (whose king, Pelasgus, is slain) and force marriage (in Argos) on the Danaids. Obeying a command from their father, the Danaid brides swear to slay their Egyptian bridegrooms on their wedding night. Only Hypermestra (whose union proves to be a gentle rather than a violent one) spares her bridegroom, Lynceus. So this royal couple, on the one hand, and the murderous widows, on the other, now represent, as it were, rival solutions to the Danaids' problem: each side may be expected, depending on the circumstances, to bring the other to 'justice' (as each side sees it), and indeed this is precisely what one finds in different strands of the tradition. We know, however, who prevails in the end, for Lynceus and Hypermestra are known from other sources to have established a new dynasty in Argos.[9]

Several partial versions of, or references to, the Danaid myth in various post-Aeschylean sources[10] supply information on various other aspects of it, particularly concerning the fear of the Egyptian suitors and the original motivation of the Danaids' flight from them. These versions differ in several important respects but they agree in indicating that the original trouble arose not between the Danaids and their cousin-suitors but between Danaus and Aegyptus in rivalry over the kingship (of Egypt, in some versions, of Argos, in others). Again, according to several accounts, it is *Danaus'* fear of the sons of Aegyptus as prospective bridegrooms (urged on by Aegyptus) which is paramount,

---

8 These are the titles, and the sequence, of the other plays of the trilogy which are accepted by the majority of scholars. Both, however, have been debated: for a discussion of the arguments, see Garvie chap 5, esp pp 183 ff. See also the appendix to this chapter, on the trilogy, pp 104 ff.

9 See, for example, Aesch *PV* 865–9.

10 For detailed information and comments on the material concerned, see Garvie pp 163 ff, Johansen and Whittle vol I, pp 40–55, esp pp 47 ff; see also Bonner 'A Study in the Danaid Myth' and the more recent study of Sicherl, 'Die Tragik der Danaiden,' which we shall be considering later, in the appendix to this chapter, on the trilogy. Some of the ancient references considered in the more contentious parts of these discussions include *schol* Homer *Il* 1.42, *schol* Aesch *PV* 853, *schol* Eur *Or* 872, *schol* Statius *Theb* II.222 and VI.269, Hyginus *fab* 168. It is, of course, sometimes difficult, sometimes impossible, to tell where the post-Aeschylean sources reflect versions of the Danaid myth which Aeschylus chose to employ in this trilogy.

a fear inspired by an oracle that he, Danaus, would be slain by one of these prospective sons-in-law. It was this fear (in these versions) which caused the flight from Egypt and later (when the marriage was eventually forced on them) Danaus' command to his daughters to slay their cousins on their wedding night. This may or may not have been also the motivation of Danaus' murder-command in our trilogy (in the lost play following the *Supplices*). More important for our play and for the trilogy which (at least in the opinion of most scholars) it introduced, is the question whether in the matter of the Danaids' flight from their suitors the poet also followed what appears to have been the traditional version. Indeed, this question of the Danaids' motivation may prove to be one of the main interpretative problems of our play, and possibly (depending on how we answer it) one of the keys to the new meaning which Aeschylus brings to his treatment of the myth. Is the Danaids' flight due to their abhorrence of *kin*-marriage, or of *violent* marriage (without the consent of the maidens or their father), or of *any* marriage, and so of men in general? Or is it (as some have argued) fear, induced by the oracle, for their father's safety which motivates the Danaids? However, as we shall see, it is the Danaids' own aversion to the marriage which is stressed throughout the play, and it is the Danaids, rather than Danaus whom Aeschylus has chosen to make the decisive element of his treatment.[11] And another feature of the poet's treatment, the interweaving of the Danaids' supplication with the myth of Io, may also provide us with a preliminary indication of the theme which is to be developed in this trilogy.

Related to the question of the Danaids' 'motivation' is the question of their justification. How are we to regard these defenceless suppliants who, by the most lethal methods of supplication, bring war and bloodshed, and later further blood-pollution, on the land where they seek sanctuary?[12] Answers, or at least partial answers, to both these

11 Sicherl's arguments (in 'Die Tragik der Danaiden') for the *oracle* (though it is not mentioned in the *Supplices*) as providing the motivation for the Danaids' flight will be considered in the appendix to this chapter, since it has implications for one's view of the trilogy.

12 Méautis *Eschyle et la trilogie* pp 53–61 is particularly critical of the pressure which the Danaids exert as suppliants, not only on the Argive king but on Zeus himself! Cf also Garvie pp 212–15 and Johansen and Whittle, vol I, pp 37–40. On the whole question of the motivation and justification of the Danaids in this trilogy, see also Zeitlin 'The Politics of Eros in the Danaid Trilogy of Aeschylus,' esp pp 203–9. I regret that this excellent article was brought to my attention too late for adequate discussion here. Several issues raised in it (including, for example, Zeitlin's observation of the

questions must be sought from the poet's presentation, in the only extant play of the trilogy, of the Danaids and their situation, and of the language and imagery by which that presentation is effected.[13] But the full significance of that treatment cannot, of course, be grasped unless the whole tapestry of the trilogy (to the extent to which we can guess it) is at all times kept in mind.

The parodos (vv 1–175)

The prominence of the Chorus in the play is marked initially by the absence of a prologue; it is the Danaids themselves who, in the anapaestic introduction (1–39) to the parodos, reveal the dramatic situation and provide certain anticipations (conscious and otherwise) of the themes to come.[14] The first words are addressed to 'Zeus the god of suppliants,' for it is he who is to be the guardian spirit of this play. The Danaids' flight from Egypt is due to no blood-guilt of their own but to their self-chosen avoidance of 'impious marriage' with the sons of Aegyptus. Their claims on Argos are based on their descent 'from the gnat-tormented heifer' (once the Argive maiden Io) embraced by Zeus. The Chorus's prayers now extend to 'the city, the land and its bright waters' (prayers to the native spirits which we shall have occasion to remember before the play is over), to the gods above and to the chthonic gods who hold their seats below, and finally to 'Zeus sôter tritos' ('Zeus the Saviour,' regularly invoked the third in the series of libations), that they may protect the suppliants and destroy their pursuers. The chant which had begun with a picture of the Danaids' escape by sea ends with a prayer (which will also be remembered at the close of the play) that 'the violent swarm born

---

trilogy's 'central irony,' that in seeking to avoid the pollution of kin-marriage the Danaids incur the pollution of kin-bloodshed) anticipate points made more briefly in this chapter. Zeitlin, however, and several of the studies to which she refers, discuss these issues in broad social, political, and even theological (or mythical) terms, while I have limited my treatment of these issues to their resonance in the immediate dramatic context and to discussion of the devices employed in their expression. See also n 35, below.

13 For excellent treatments of the imagery of the *Supplices* in relation to its major themes, see Murray *The Motif of Io in Aeschylus' Supplices* pp 22–45, 65 ff, and Fowler 'Aeschylus' Imagery' pp 10–23.

14 As Taplin notes (*Stagecraft* p 193), 'Not only is the opening entry [of the Chorus] a crucial action [ie, the representation of the Danaids' supplication] but the choreography will have reflected the Danaids' flight and their hopes of security, both in the anapaests and in the great strophic song which follows.'

of Aegyptus' seed' may perish in storms at sea, ere they accomplish that marriage which θέμις ('custom,' 'law') forbids them (1–39).

Flight, supplication, marriage, kinship, and violence: the themes of the Chorus's prelude are the themes of the play and of the trilogy, and the language of this prelude hints (beyond the awareness of the Chorus) at certain ironies to be made more explicit and at certain ambiguities to be resolved. By their claim to have fled 'by no public ban for deed of blood' (6–7), the Danaids are giving assurance that they are bringing no pollution upon the land where they seek refuge: yet it is precisely this which their refuge in Argos *will* bring upon the Argives. They have fled, rather, 'by their own self-chosen avoidance of men'; yet the strange phrase αὐτογενῆ φυξανορίαν (8) must be meant to hint at the kinship[15] as well as the violence (cf ἑσμὸν ὑβριστήν, v 30) of the Egyptian suitors as relevant to the Danaids' abhorrence of them. But kinship has, for the Danaids, a positive function as well. It is through kinship with Io that they are to base their claims on the Argives, and the circumstances whence that kinship came about will be seen to have a certain similarity to the Danaids' own career, both now and in the future. Even in this early passage, the imagery anticipates, perhaps, something of this similarity. The Danaids' connection with Argive Io springs from Zeus' 'touch and breathing' (ἐπαφῆς κἀξ ἐπιπνοίας, 17), his gentle mating with the gadfly-driven heifer, and it is with 'reverent

---

15 αὐτογενῆ (Turnebus) φυξανορίαν (Ahrens) (for αὐτογένητον φυξάνοραν of the mss): as Johansen and Whittle put it, 'The literal meaning, "self-generated" implies here, "generated by ourselves," αὐτο- referring not to the substantive qualified by the compound adjective but to another part of the sentence, namely the subj.' Most editors and commentators agree, whether they read the dative or accusative here. Taken by itself, αὐτη might be thought to mean 'of our own race,' as George Thomson ('*The Suppliants* of Aeschylus' pp 27–8) takes it here, but in the context of the present passage (as Johansen and Whittle and others have clearly shown) the contrast is between enforced exile for blood-guilt (ἐφ' αἵματι κ.τ.λ., v 6) and the Danaids' *own voluntary exile*. Nevertheless, I believe that the poet has consciously chosen this word to keep 'the kin-element' in the abhorred marriage before our minds as well. Wilamowitz' translation '*aus angeborenen Männerfeindschaft*' ('from inborn man-hatred') though not perhaps acceptable as a literal translation (cf K. von Fritz *Antike und Moderne Tragödie* p 161), suggests yet another overtone to this subtle phrase. In addition to these and other references in Johansen and Whittle's note, see also Ireland 'The Problem of Motivation in the *Supplices* of Aeschylus' pp 14–15, who shows by his summary of various discussions that the interpretation of this expression has been very influential in critics' decisions about the basic motivation of the Danaids. Critics' errors here have (in my opinion) been due to concentration on one meaning to the exclusion of others as at least suggestive overtones in a typically Aeschylean multivalent expression.

breath of the land' (αἰδοίῳ πνεύματι χώρας, 28–9) that the Chorus pray Zeus to receive them in Argos.

A few other points relevant to later developments may be noted in this prelude. The Danaids' prayers are addressed to 'the gods below' as well as to 'the gods above': an invocation which is to acquire a somewhat grim significance during their supplication of the Argive king (and perhaps a grimmer one later in the trilogy). In their third appeal to 'Ζεὺς σωτὴρ τρίτος' (26), the Chorus are, of course, simply following the ritual convention of addressing 'Zeus the Saviour' third in succession (after Olympian Zeus, the Heroes, and Zeus of the Underworld); perhaps, however, the poet (as in the reference to 'Zeus the triple-thrower' at *Agamemnon* 171–2) is directing our hopes to solutions which Zeus may bring in the third play of the trilogy. Finally, the Chorus (and the poet) remain suitably vague about just what it is which renders marriage with the Egyptian cousins unacceptable. They do indeed pray that these suitors may perish ...

> ere they mount enforced marriage beds which *themis* ['law' or at least 'estab-
> lished custom'] forbids them, assuming kin-rights which are not theirs. (37–9)

However, the phrase which the Chorus use for their suitors' wrongful assumption of kin-rights (σφετεριξάμενοι πατραδέλφειαν, 38) is obscure in the extreme[16] and even the injustice of their suit (ὧν θέμις εἴργει, 37) will, as we shall see, be questioned by the Argive king himself.[17]

The parodos proper (40–175) may be divided thematically into four parts. The first part (40–85) develops 'the kin-theme.'[18] It begins with an invocation to Epaphos (son of Io and Zeus), whose relationship to

---

16 σφετεριξάμενοι πατραδέλφειαν: literally (perhaps), 'assuming (for themselves) their uncle's rights as represented by us'; see Johansen and Whittle's defence of this interpretation of this difficult expression. (πατραδέλφειαν is a ἅπαξ [a unique occurrence] and probably an Aeschylean coinage.)

17 See v 336 and the Chorus's reply at 337. Cf *infra* pp 87 and 89 and notes.

18 As several scholars have noted of this ode, 'The first three strophic pairs [= vv 40–85] form a coherent whole, which is both metrically and thematically unified': Rash *Metre and Language in the Lyrics of the Suppliants of Aeschylus* p 33. Rash's 'thematic divisions' of the parodos as a whole (vv 40–85, 86–111, 112–75) differ slightly from those suggested here; however, the additional thematic division which I shall suggest at vv 154 ff is supported by Rash's metrical summary, ibid 78.

    With certain specific exceptions, thematic analysis of the choral odes of the *Supplices* in this study will not be accompanied by metrical analysis. Readers interested in Aeschylean metrical technique and in observing relations between the themes and the metres of the Chorus in this play are referred to Rash's study and

themselves the Chorus promise soon to prove (40–57). It ends, by a sort of 'ring composition,' with an invocation to 'the gods of our race' (θεοὶ γενέται, 77) at whose (Argive) altars the Danaids will take refuge against the violence (ὕβρις) of their suitors (77–85). In between comes a mythological comparison: the Danaids liken themselves to Mêtis, 'Tereus' piteous wife, the hawk-chased nightingale':

> If any seer happens by and hears my plaint, he'll think he hears the cry of Tereus' piteous wife, the hawk-chased nightingale, for she, kept from her leafy river banks, mourns for her haunts of old, and and adds to her laments the death of her own child, who meeting with his wicked mother's wrath, perished by kin-murder at her hand. (58–67)

This mythological analogue (in which the exiled fugitive becomes herself a vengeful kin-slayer) provides an ambiguous note to the Chorus's appeal for sympathy, a note which is sounded again as the Chorus applies 'the piteous lot' of Mêtis to themselves (68 ff).

The final sentence in this intermediate 'lamenting' passage suggests a double meaning of a different kind (at least if the uncertain text on which it depends, and which it perhaps supports, be accepted):

> I pluck the flowers of grief, fearful (concerning) kin-friends [δειμαίνουσα φίλους] as to whether any kin-champion [κηδεμών] of our exile from the Egyptian land will here appear. (73–6)

Here the 'kin-friends' concerning whose help the Chorus are fearful are, of course, their newly found Argive kin. However, the expression δειμαίνουσα φίλους, *taken by itself*, means simply 'fearing (kin-)friends,' and could, before one hears the following clause, quite naturally be taken to refer to the Chorus's fear of their cousin-suitors.[19]

---

to Scott *Musical Design in the Aeschylean Theater,* as well as to such standard works as Kranz *Stasimon.*

19 For the use of φίλος for *kin,* ie, ones with whom one would expect friendly relations, cf Aesch *Ag* 1236; Soph *Antig* 10. The MS reading δειμαίνουσα φίλους (= M, φόλους, corrected by the διορθότης) has been corrected by some editors to δειμαίνουσ', ἀφίλου (Weil, Johansen, and Whittle), by others to δειμαίνουσα, φίλος ... (Enger, Vürtheim, Page). However, despite the uniqueness of the particular use of the 'anticipatory accusative' which it involves (see Johansen and Whittle's note *ad loc*), the MS reading has been accepted by several editors (eg, Murray, Wecklein, Mazon, Weir Smythe). Could it be that Aeschylus is willing to strain the syntax for the sake of the play on meaning suggested above?

For their second theme in the parodos, the Chorus launches into a splendid account (86–111) of the effortless power of Zeus' will. In several ways (in its generalizing style, in its placing in the ode, and, at times, in its contents), the passage suggests comparisons with the so-called Hymn to Zeus in the parodos of the *Agamemnon* (*Ag* 160–83).

> Secure and safe and not upon its back it falls, whatever the will of Zeus brings to its accomplished end. For the paths of his thought stretch dim and mysterious, hard for mortals to discern. He hurls men to utter destruction from their high-built towers of hope – and yet he needs no might of arms. Seated on his sacred throne, Zeus satisfies, as he sees fit, his will. (*Suppl* 91–103)

The Chorus apply this paradigm of the destructive power of Zeus to their own needs:

> Let Zeus look upon mortal *hybris*: how the evil shoot bursts forth anew,[20] waxing wanton in its foul plans for marriage with me. With passion for its goad, his violence will learn too late its error, when it comes to ruin. (104–11)

Nevertheless, the ambiguities remain. The Chorus have admitted that the will of Zeus is hard for mortals to discern (93–5), repeating the thought so splendidly expressed in the preceding strophe that Zeus' wish 'flares in the darkness' (89–90). Can we be certain that the ruin forecast for the suitors will actually be accomplished in accordance with the will of Zeus? Or that, if it is, the agents of that will need themselves be free of guilt in the mind of Zeus?[21]

In the third movement (112–53) of the parodos the Chorus sing, in gentler iambic rhythms, of their own plight and its hoped-for remedies. Lament alternates with supplication, first to 'the Appian land' of the Argives (in the refrains at 117–22 and 128–34), then (at 138–40 and 144–50) to the divine protectors, Zeus and Artemis. The imagery appearing in the second of these strophic pairs seems to reflect the virginal preoccupations of the Danaids, just as earlier in the ode the 'Tereus and Mêtis image' betrayed their latent violence.

---

20 Cf *Ag* 763 ff.
21 Cf *Ag* 1505 ff. Clytemnestra fulfilled the justice of Zeus on Agamemnon but, as the Chorus asks, 'Who will say that she is guiltless?' Clytemnestra in turn is to suffer for *her* deed of violence in the next play of the *Oresteia* trilogy. (In references to, and translations of, the foregoing passages of the *Supplices*, I have not followed Westphal's transposition [accepted by Page] of vv 89–90 and 93–5.)

– our ship with its robes of flaxen sails kept me safe from the stormy blasts and brought me here with favouring winds. On this score I have no complaints. Only may the all-seeing father provide in time a happy completion to my toils.

May the glorious seed of my glorious mother escape, unconquered and unwed, the embrace of men. (134–43) May Zeus' pure daughter [Artemis], who keeps safe the sacred portal walls [ἐνώπια] look on me as would a willing helper on a willing ward. May she, angered at our pursuit, come with all her power as our defender, a maiden to a maiden's aid[?] (144–50)

The significance of ἐνώπια, 'the walls' which Artemis is here (v 146) represented as protecting, has been much debated. Keeping in mind the image in the strophe of the ship protecting the virgins from the stormy sea, one is tempted to see in the second passage a more overtly sexual connotation to Artemis' protection.[22] Moreover, the language of the refrain (141–3; 151–3) rather encourages this interpretation both in its overt meaning ('May the descendant of Io escape men's embrace') and, perhaps more emphatically, in the poet's choice of words for beginning and ending the refrain, σπέρμα ... ἐκφυγεῖν.

In the final strophic pair and refrains (154–75), the mood (along with the metre) changes again. The latent violence of the Danaids (already hinted at in their self-comparison with Mêtis, 60 ff) appears in their first threats of suicide if they should fail to win protection at Argos. Here, too, we learn the grimmer significance of the Chorus's earlier invocation of the chthonic powers ('grievous avengers!' 24–5), in addition to the Olympian gods:

> Perishing by the noose, we will approach Zeus-of-the-dead with our suppliant boughs, if we don't succeed with the Olympian gods! (157–61)

22 Johansen and Whittle cite four Homeric passages as providing the only other occurrences of ἐνώπια in Greek poetry; they also cite scholiastic explanations of the word as meaning 'wall' and, more specifically, 'front walls' and, even, 'entrances' or 'entrance walls.' Garvie pp 157–8 and Vürtheim *Aischylos' Schutzflehende* 83–90 (also cited by Johansen and Whittle) have between them refuted various attempts to identify the walls in question here with various specific temples or other buildings at Athens or in Argos. Though I reached the tentative conclusion suggested above independently, I now note that Murray *The Motif of Io* p 29 (also cited by Garvie) has also suggested the possible sexual symbolism attaching to the use of ἐνώπια here. He alleges similar symbolic use, ie, with sexual connotation, of a building or its parts (viz ἐδώλια) quite plausibly at *Sept* 454 and still more justifiably at *Choeph* 71–2.

Finally, in the last strophe, the Chorus give a new and daring twist to the 'kinship theme': if their supplication fails, they declare, Zeus himself will be assailed by their just charges for abandoning the offspring of Io (168–74).

The supplication (vv 176–523)

The first long episode of the play (vv 176–417) falls into three parts: an iambic passage between Danaus and his daughters (represented by the Chorus Leader, 176–233);[23] a second iambic exchange, between the Chorus-Leader and the Argive king, Pelasgus (234–358); and an 'epirrhematic kommos' between the (singing) Chorus and Pelasgus, answering in iambics (359–417). Thus, there is a nice dramatic progression moving from the (mainly strategic) instructions of father Danaus to his daughters, through the first confrontation with the King in which the Danaids state their case in dramatic (that is, spoken) form, to the final passage, in which the whole Chorus sing their claims in the more emotional and vehement terms suitable to lyric expression. We shall note, too, a significant shift in the basis of the Chorus's appeal as they move from the dramatic to the lyric mode.

In Danaus' two speeches of advice and encouragement (176 ff, 222 ff), there are several passages in which conventional rhetoric suited to the situation is, perhaps, exploited for the sake of certain touches of dramatic irony. First of all, Danaus reminds his daughters to stress their blood-guiltless, unpolluted state (τάσδ' ἀναιμάκτους φυγάς, 196), a point which repeats the anticipatory irony which we have already noted of the Chorus's claims at vv 6–7 of the Prologue. Second, there is the paternal advice to be submissive: 'bold-speaking ill becomes the weaker ones' (203) – an admonition which we shall observe the Danaids heeding less and less. Finally, there is the striking image of Danaus' concluding peroration:

> Now take your seats on sacred ground, like doves in fear of hawks, fellow-members of the feathered tribe, enemies, though kin ones, polluters of their race. For how can birds preying on other birds be pure? (223–6)

---

23 I agree with Taplin (*Stagecraft* pp 193–4) and some others that Danaus probably enters with the Chorus at the beginning. However, Taplin does appear to have it both ways when he seeks later (ibid p 198) to mitigate the (structurally unusual) lack of an 'entry' after the first choral song by suggesting that 'the intervention of Danaus [by his speech at 176 ff] may be regarded as virtually the equivalent of an entry.'

This much-discussed passage has been used by some critics to support the view that it is the kinship of the Egyptian suitors which particularly repels the Danaids.[24] Presumably it is both the violence and the kin element in the Egyptian pursuit to which the imagery of the passage draws attention. But is the horror expressed at vv 225–6 horror at kin-*violence* or horror, as well, at the idea of kin-*marriage*? The ambiguity is, perhaps, intentional (since they do not want these kin-suitors, the Danaids themselves may not distinguish very clearly between the two ideas), but there seems to be at least a suggestion of the latter (that is, revulsion from kin-marriage) in the expression ἐχθρῶν ὁμαίμων καὶ μιαινόντων γένος: 'enemies who are kin and pollutors of the race' (225).

The 'doves and hawks image' is both striking and strange. It reminds us of the 'hawk-pursued nightingale' to which the Danaids compared themselves earlier, at vv 59 ff. (It reminds us also of the similar image used for the Danaids and their suitors at *Prometheus Vinctus*, 857 ff.)[25] Will the dove-like Danaids also turn, like Mêtis in the earlier comparison (58 ff), to violent vengeance against their own kin? Such anticipations, however unconscious on Danaus' part, are reinforced by the prophetic utterances which follow, that even in Hades 'another Zeus' will hold a final judgment on the unjust kin-predator, who would marry 'an unwilling bride against her father's will' (227–31). Thus, are the infernal

24 See, for example, Fowler 'Aeschylus' Imagery' pp 14–15. See also Smethurst's subtle discussion (*Artistry* pp 215–16) of vv 226–8, concerning the stylistic devices, involving both verbal and syntactical repetition, employed in the comparison of the birds (hawks and doves) with the humans (the cousin-suitors and the fleeing maidens) in this passage. Cf Dumortier, *Les images dans la poésie d'Eschyle* p 7, who compares this passage (vv 223–4) with various other 'bird of prey images' (eg, at vv 30–3, 60–2) which he regards as providing the principal metaphor of the play. The simile suits the 'predator-prey' aspect of the dramatic situation better than it does the 'kin-aspect,' in that hawks and doves share the same species but not the same genus. Cf also Johansen and Whittle *ad loc*, who also comment (in somewhat more complex terms!) on the imperfection of the comparison here involved.

25 Cf Sommerstein 'Notes on Aeschylus' *Supplices*' p 68, who makes both the same comparisons and who thinks (as I do) that the mention of Tereus as a hawk, instead of, traditionally, as a hoopoe, at vv 60–2, is intended to prepare us for the present simile.

The use of parallel imagery for the same subjects as *Suppl* 223 ff and *PV* 857 ff seems to me to have some bearing on the question of the authenticity of *Prometheus Vinctus*; so, too, does the extensive treatment at *PV* 853–73 of material which belongs mainly to the Danaid trilogy but which has a sort of overlapping relevance to the theme and action of the *Prometheus* trilogy as well.

powers (already twice-invoked by the Chorus, at vv 24–5, 154–61) kept constantly before our minds.

The Argive king (Pelasgus) now enters, demanding to know the identity of the stranger suppliants. However, as in much of the ensuing scene, the Danaids take the initiative from him and require first that the King identify himself. This he does in a speech (249–73) which includes a little mythological background about the land ('this plain of Apia,' 260 ff) on which the Suppliants are now standing. Apis, we learn, had purified this land of many man-destroying monsters which the earth had caused to spring up when defiled by the pollution of many deeds of blood. Before we put this mythological 'digression' down to mere Aeschylean expansiveness, we should ask, perhaps, whether the King's reference to ancient 'blood pollution [265], surgeries and deliverances' (τομαῖα καὶ λυτήρια, 268) performed on this land may not be an ironic anticipation of similar events to come.[26] His rights to interrogation thus established, the King returns to the question of the Danaids' identity. The Chorus-Leader now sets about proving the Danaids' Argive stock as their special claim to protection; this she does by answering the King's knowledgeable questions about their gadfly-driven ancestress, Io, to his satisfaction.[27] (The distribution of verses in this stichomythic exchange is not made clear in the MSS, but this last point is established by what is obviously the King's statement at v 310: 'You have told all these matters in accordance with my own knowledge of them.') When the tale of Io's wanderings reaches Egypt, however, the Chorus-Leader is able to supply the King with new information, particularly concerning Io's

26 This suggestion of a dramatically ironic allusion to the later murder of the Egyptian suitors (and to subsequent purifications) may seem fanciful, but there are other passages in Aeschylus where cognates of τέμνω are used with just such sinister 'anticipations.' Cf Agamemnon's mention (at Ag 849–50) of cautery and surgery for clearing the land of treason and (at Cho 539) the Chorus's curious expression ἄκος τομαῖον (cf ἄκη τομαῖα of the present passage) for the 'magical cures' (or 'cures by shredding') which Clytemnestra hopes to achieve by the libations over Agamemnon's tomb. In neither case have scholars found difficulty in seeing ironic and sinister suggestions of other surgery or cures, involving Agamemnon and Clytemnestra respectively. (Cf Johansen and Whittle's reference in their note to Suppl 268; curiously, they do not suggest such an ironic reference for this passage in the Supplices.)

27 Here we should note an interesting difference from the tale of Io's wanderings as told in the Prometheus Vinctus. In the Supplices, Hera's jealousy alone is made responsible for Io's troubles (her transformation into a heifer and her later gadfly-driven wanderings from Argos until she eventually reaches Egypt) and nothing is made (as it is in Prometheus Vinctus) of Zeus' erotic persecution as the cause of all her anguish.

deliverance by Zeus and the birth of Epaphos, her 'touch-conceived' son by Zeus (313, 315).

The King now sets about questioning the Chorus (326 ff) about the reasons for their flight and supplication and, when he has discovered this, the particular grounds (justifying their supplication) for their rejection of marriage with their suitors. In their opening statement (vv 1–39) we have already learned of the Danaids' 'self-chosen avoidance of men' (8) arising, it would appear, from the impious nature of the marriage being thrust upon them, the violence (30), and possibly the relationship, of their suitors.[28] The Chorus-Leader now repeats their 'hatred of the marriage-bed' (332) and makes more specific their particular rejection of 'Aegyptus' race' (335). To the King's more pressing questions as to whether it is personal dislike or the contravention of law or social custom which is the basis of their rejection, the Chorus-Leader prevaricates: 'Who would buy one's kinsmen as one's owners?'[29] This answer leads to an exchange typifying, perhaps, male and female attitudes to kin-marriage, the King arguing that such unions lead to an increase in familial power, the Chorus-Leader, that in such marriages the wife can too easily be put aside, if things go badly (339).[30]

---

28 This view of the Danaids' attitude is also substantially the view of von Fritz *Antike und Moderne Tragödie* pp 183–9, who believes, further, that the amelioration of this attitude of the Danaids provides the secret mainspring of the ensuing plays of the trilogy.

    Among the many articles specifically devoted to the question of 'the motivation of the Danaids' see Ireland 'The Problem of Motivation in the *Supplices* of Aeschylus' and MacKinnon 'The Reason for the Danaids' Flight,' both of which also contain good summaries of various views on the matter. See also Garvie pp 215–24 and Johansen and Whittle, vol 1, p 34. Macurdy in 'Had the Danaid Trilogy a Social Problem?' is particularly helpful on the legal aspects of the Danaids' position. The view of Thomson *Aeschylus and Athens* chap 16 that the main issue at stake in the Danaids' rejection of their cousin-suitors is 'exogamy vs endogamy' (and the socio-political corollaries of these positions) has, I think, been successfully refuted by several of the scholars mentioned above. Cf also Vürtheim *Aischylos' Schutzflehende* pp 21 ff, who also deprecates the view that this trilogy was primarily concerned with the obligations and rights of heiresses.

29 Editors have differed concerning the text and interpretation of v 337; for a full discussion (and a rendering different from that given above), see Johansen and Whittle's note *ad loc*. I have followed the reading of the MSS (except for Turnebus's correction of the accent on ὠνοῖτο). Some editors read ὄνοιτο (Robortello), 'criticize,' and φιλοῦσ' as a conditional participle instead of φίλους, with the meaning 'Who would criticize their lords if they loved them?'

30 Again, as at v 337, not all editors and translators agree about the meaning of this verse (339). Some take it to be a sarcastic comment from the Chorus-Leader to the effect that the King is seeking an easy way to be rid of the Suppliants, ie, by

The King still hesitates to grant his protection, partly in fear of war with the Egyptians (342), partly because he is still unconvinced of the intrinsic justice of the Danaids' cause (344). Immediately, the Chorus-Leader, having failed to win her case on its own terms, so to speak, changes her approach and bids the King to respect the suppliant wreaths about the city's gods.

With the emotional tone thus raised (the King cowers, 346, at the mention of the suppliant wreaths), the appeal moves into its second phase. The whole Chorus now takes over, invoking Themis of the suppliants (360) and threatening pollution of the city (375), in terrifying bursts of song, as the King, in iambic passages, continues to express his hesitation: fear of pollution on the one hand, and of war with the Egyptians on the other, compounded by uncertainty about the Danaids' legal right (which they fail to assert) against their cousins' claim. At any rate, as the King asserts (365–9), it is the people who must decide. He ends the epirrhematic passage by declaring his need for 'deep and solitary counsel' (we may note the ring composition of this repeated phrase, at 407 and 417, with which this little speech is framed) to resolve his dread dilemma and, presumably, to advise his people rightly.

As the King ponders, the Chorus now complete their lyrics (two final strophic pairs, 418–37) without interruption. In each stanza, their tone becomes more urgent and compelling. Reminders of the duties of pious hosts are followed (in the two central stanzas, 423–32) by fresh images of the violence of the suitors, now pictured as dragging the suppliants away from the altars ('like a horse by the fetlock!') and finally by warnings that the King's descendants will reap the appropriate 'rewards' of his decision.

When the King's 'ponderings' finally result in the disappointingly negative statement, 'I shall let this quarrel pass me by!' (452),[31] the

---

arguing himself out of obligations to defend them. So Vürtheim in his note *ad loc*, quoting Wilamowitz to the same effect, and Macurdy, 'Had the Danaid Trilogy a Social Problem?' p 97, who strenuously rejects the technical meaning 'divorce' for ἀπαλλαγή here.

31 ἦ κάρτα νείκους τοῦδ' ἐγὼ παροίχομαι: the text and sense of v 452 (and particularly of the verb παροίχομαι in this context) are admittedly uncertain. I have followed the version defended in Johansen and Whittle's note *ad loc*. Though the statement sounds rather a weak one after the King has spent so much time deliberating, it seems the best of several suggestions which have been made (better, for example, than Johansen's earlier version, in his 1970 translation, 'Assuredly I am at a loss about this quarrel'), especially in that it provides a cue for the Chorus-Leader's final 'assault' on the King.

Chorus-Leader, in a final dialogue with the King, plays their last and
most lethal card:

- I have breast-bands and girdles ...
- Quite proper for women-folk ...
- They provide a fine contrivance ...
- A contrivance of what sort?
- To adorn these holy images ...
- Speak clearly! This is riddling talk!
- To hang us from these statues of the gods! (457–65, in part)

It is a passage of thrilling and sinister theatricality, well suited to the
riddling delays of stichomythic style. At its end, the King bursts forth in
a passionate acceptance of his lot. Despite the blood-price ('men's lives
for women's sake,' 477) he must pay, he must bow down before the
wrath of Zeus, the suppliants' god: 'Among mortals, that is the greatest
fear of all!' (479). King Pelasgus, then, will be the Danaids' advocate
before the Argive *demos*.

Thus ends the first part of our play. The Danaids have eventually won
their victory over King Pelasgus, but paradoxically our sympathy for
the beleaguered King has tended gradually to overshadow our earlier
sympathy for the Danaids whose incipient violence, rivalling that of
their pursuers, anticipates with prophetic irony still more violent and
polluting deeds to come. For Danaus, by contrast, 'no haven appears,'
as he embarks 'on an unfathomable sea of ruin' (470–1).

The Chorus's supplication of King Pelasgus has succeeded; the
outcome of Danaus' plea (with the King's support) before the Argive
demos has still to be decided. Between these crucial moments of the
action comes the great central ode at vv 524–99. It might be called 'the Io
Song,' for the sufferings and ultimate release of Io form the theme of its
central stanzas (vv 538–89; the second, third, and fourth strophic pairs).
It might equally well be called a Hymn to Zeus, for Zeus dominates
the opening and the closing strophic pairs and it is Zeus' procreation of
Epaphos which delivers Io from her train of woes.[32]

Lord of hosts, most blessed of the blessed, most perfect among perfect
powers, glorious Zeus ... (524–6)

---

32 For an excellent study of the Io theme in this play, and of its significance
   for the Danaids' own situation, see Murray *The Motif of Io in Aeschylus'
   Supplices.*

After this most honorific apostrophe of Zeus,[33] the Chorus pray first for protection against the *hybris* of their suitors and then for their destruction in the purple seas (524–30). In the second stanza, however, the Danaids lay the basis of their appeal: the fact that Zeus is the ἔφαπτορ 'Ιοῦς, 'the one who grasped Io' (535): it is their relationship with Zeus, through Io, which the Chorus are concerned to establish, but it is the image of Zeus as 'the embracer of Io' which lingers in our minds. Io, the song continues, has crossed seas and changed continents in her desperate flight. (So, too, in like desperation, have the Danaids: an implicit comparison which a fuller version of Io's wanderings[34] would have blurred.) At the end of her wanderings, Argive Io reaches Egypt, just as the Egyptian Danaids have now reached Argos. It is the gadfly sent by Hera (541 ff), rather than Zeus as a pursuing suitor, which is blamed for Io's travail (again we may contrast the treatment in *Prometheus Vinctus*). Nevertheless, it was Zeus' amorous approach (cf vv 295, 300–1) which caused Hera's wrath and Io's flight, and it will be the gentle mating with Zeus which will provide her liberation.

In the dramatic context, the Danaids' main intention in this ode is to persuade Zeus, as they have persuaded King Pelasgus, to support their cause. Hence, they set about reminding Zeus of the manner of their relationship with him through the birth of Epaphus, son of Io and himself. But the very circumstances of that connection, Zeus' liberation of another persecuted female, suggests another, less formal, appeal to Zeus:

> Looking down upon this tribe of women, this womanly part of a race sprung from an ancestress dear to you, renew that kindly tale ... (531–4)

'Save us,' sings the Chorus, in effect, 'as once you saved Io!' As one expects in lyric treatments of myths from the past, it is the most wondrous aspect of the myth (here the miraculously gentle, even asexual, impregnation of Io by Zeus) which will receive full treatment:

> – and through the gentle might of Zeus, and through divine on-breathing, Io gained rest ... she took on Zeus' burden in her womb and bore a blameless child. (576–81)

---

33 ἄναξ ἀνάκτων: this typical oriental expression might be applied, as Johansen and Whittle observe, to gods or kings alike: cf δέσποτα δεσποτᾶν at *Persae* 666, as the Chorus invoke the sacred ghost of King Dareios.

34 Contrast Prometheus' account of Io's wanderings at *PV* 561–886 with the Chorus's brief description here.

It is in this transition from the simple facts of 'the Io connection' to its elaboration that the treatment of the myth takes on a new significance. Zeus now appears not only as ancestor of the Danaids and as liberator of a woman in distress but also as providing a model for amorous pursuit and gentle mating ... a model, as it turns out (*mutatis mutandis* again, for Lynceus is only human) for the only suitor of the Danaids destined to survive.

In tune with such a theme (however far from the thoughts of the singers themselves) sound the Chorus's concluding descriptions of Zeus, their hoped-for saviour, in language echoing (by a sort of ring composition) the sonorous Zeus-epithets with which the ode began:

He who rules through time which has no end ... (574)

... Zeus who sends fair breezes [οὔριος Ζεύς] is our total remedy. (594)

Aeschylus tends to reserve passages like this for the most significant and, in first plays, most prophetic moments of his trilogies. In 'the Hymn to Zeus' in *Agamemnon* the Chorus declare their faith in 'Zeus the triple-thrower' (*Ag* 171–2) and their hope that favour, however violently bestowed, will come from the Olympian gods (*Ag* 182–3).[35] If (as we shall argue) that passage signals, for a moment, the resolution of the *Oresteia*, it may not be too fanciful to imagine that the present passage does something of the same kind for the Danaid trilogy.

The third episode (vv 600–24) provides the fulfilment of the 'supplication theme' with Danaus' report of the success of the Danaids' plea. The language of Danaus' report and of the Argive decree which he quotes fairly bristles with contemporary political and legal terminology. The Danaids are to live as residents (μετοικεῖν, 609) of Argos, free, subject to no seizure, inviolable by any man, and no citizen or alien is to carry them off. Any of the land-holders (γαμόρων, 613: cf *Eum* 890) who fails to defend the Danaids from such violence is to lose his civil rights (ἄτιμον εἶναι, 614) and suffer exile by popular decree (φύγῃ δημηλάτῳ 614). The language and tone of this passage has been cited in support

---

35 These passages in the 'Hymn to Zeus' in *Agamemnon* have, to be sure, been given other, rather different interpretations; see my *Aeschylus' Oresteia* pp 11, 83–5 and references there given. For a similar view, expressed in somewhat different terms, of the relation of the Chorus's treatment of the Zeus-Io relation and the probable resolution of their own situation, see Zeitlin 'The Politics of Eros' 226–31, who compares Zeus' gentle liberation of Io with 'the consummated eros [to occur later in the trilogy] that combines both *peitho* ["persuasion"] and *bia* ["violence"].'

of a contemporary political interpretation of the play: namely, that it celebrates in retrospect Argos' provision of sanctuary to Themistocles after his expulsion from Athens in 470–69. The case has been brilliantly argued by its chief proponent,[36] but even if the 'contemporary political' application of the suppliant theme be sound, we need not, I think, regard it as a major raison d'être for the entire work. There are too many other issues, in the play and in the trilogy, for this to be the case.

In the third stasimon (625–709), the Chorus provide their expected song of thanksgiving and prayers for their defenders. Two splendid metaphors introduce these themes: one for Ares, 'reaper of human harvest in alien fields' (637–8) from whose destructive fire they pray protection; the other for Zeus whose 'vengeful eye' (likened to a carrion bird upon the roof-tops, 646–51) the pious Argives have now escaped. Sinister ironies lurk beneath the surface of both these images. In the coming battle and in the coming murder of the cousin-suitors, Ares *will* reap his human harvest in alien fields[37] and, for the shedding of this familial blood, the bird of vengeance will, doubtless, continue to sit upon the roof-tops until the resolution of the trilogy is reached. There follows a series of blessings on the various age-groups of the city: on the youth, that their bloom may not be cut off by Ares (663–6); on the old, that their hearth-fires may keep blazing brightly (667–79); on the future leaders, that 'Artemis-Hecate may preside benignly over their birth' (674–7); on all young people, that Apollo *Lykeios* (Apollo the Wolf-God) may be kindly to them (686–7). Again the ironies appear in connection with the gods invoked or deprecated. Ares is 'Aphrodite's bed-fellow' (664–6), a grim anticipation of the murder of the bridegrooms; Artemis, hailed at the beginning and the end of the

36 See Forrest, 'Themistokles and Argos,' who revives a comparison suggested by Cavaignac 'Eschyle et Themistocle' between the mythical Danaid and the historical Themistoclean situations. Forrest greatly expands the argument by a detailed discussion of Argive politics in the 460s. Forrest remarks of the passage under discussion: 'The praise of democratic Argos in lines 604–24, which is totally irrelevant to any mythological situation and completely relevant in the sixties of the fifth century, shows us more clearly than anything else the gratitude of Aeschylus and other radicals to Argos for her acceptance and support of Themistokles' (p 240). Cf also Diamantopoulos 'The Danaid Trilogy of Aeschylus' and Podlecki *The Political Background of Aeschylean Tragedy* chap 4. Among critics of these political interpretations, see Lloyd-Jones 'The *Supplices* of Aeschylus' pp 357–9, Van Looey 'Mélanges Varia, Tragica I, Aeschyli *Supplices*' pp 489–96, and Burian 'Pelasgus and Politics in Aeschylus' Danaid Trilogy' pp 5–14.
37 Cf *PV* 860–1 where the expression θηλυκτόνῳ Ἀρει is used in the description of that grim wedding night.

play (144 ff, 1030 ff) as the virgin protectress of the Virgin Chorus, is here (676–7) invoked as 'Artemis-Hecate,' to watch over the child-birth of Argive women.[38]

The coming of the Egyptians (vv 710–1017)

Now that 'the suppliant theme' has reached its fulfilment in the decisions of the King and of the Argive people, the more theatrical aspect of the action, the approach and arrival of the Egyptians, takes over. Realistic physical presentation, restricted by the conventions of the early classical theatre, is well supplemented by the vivid descriptions of the approach of the Egyptians, by the growing terror of the Chorus (stemmed at first by Danaus' reassurances, then allowed free rein at his departure), and finally by the entry and harsh, barbaric orders of the Egyptian herald. This theatrical sequence is, of course, much briefer and livelier than 'the supplication sequence.' Nevertheless, the devices for suggesting the rising pitch of emotional excitement, iambic *senarii* (710 ff) leading to an epirrhematic passage (736 ff), followed soon after by an uninterrupted choral song (776 ff), are reminiscent of the technique of the earlier sequence.

First comes Danaus' factual account, vivid but relatively unadorned by figurative language, of the approach of the Egyptians:

> I see a warship ... I see its curtains and its billowing sail. Now the ship's prow looks toward us, threatening, across the watery stretches, and heeds too well the guiding rudder at its stern. Now the black limbs of the sailors show clear against their white and flowing robes. Now the whole panoply of ships has come into view, the leading ship has furled its sails and now the steady beat of oars sounds its approach to shore. (713–23)

---

38 It is tempting to compare, as some commentators have done, this ode of thanksgiving and blessing to the songs of the 'converted' Furies at the end of the *Eumenides*, though some differences should be noted. The Erinyes' blessings come at the end of the trilogy, where hidden ironies are no longer in place; thus there is no sinister aspect to their blessing such as is latent in the present ode. In the *Eumenides*, also, it is only civil war which is deprecated (indeed, martial Athena encourages victories over foreign foes, *Eum* 913–15). See further Solmsen, *Hesiod and Aeschylus* pp 211–14, who points out that 'the song of benediction is one of the old forms of religious poetry which Aeschylus embodies in his tragedy' (p 211), and that in both *Supplices* and *Eumenides* such benedictions are invoked for cities which have shown their worthiness by satisfying 'the demands of Zeus, the guardian of the Right' (p 214).

A series of lyric outbursts, accompanied, no doubt, by frenzied dancing, reflects the Chorus's reaction to this dreadful news, their bestial images for the suitors ('... carrion crows!' 751, 'mad shameless dogs!' 758, 'lewd, sickening beasts!') increasing with their terror. The staid Danaus in his role as comforter serves as a sounding board for these bursts of frantic song and his final prosaic reassurance ('... they'll be a long time anchoring yet!' 765 ff) provides an ironic prelude to the precipitate entry of the Egyptian herald some fifty verses later.

The choral ode which follows Danaus' departure for help completes this sequence of mounting hysteria. Sheer escapism dominates the opening images: the Chorus long to plunge into some black hole, to become smoke drifting to the heavens, or (finally) to vanish utterly into dust and nothingness (776–83). Soon, however, physical revulsion from the violent embrace of the suitors becomes the stronger emotion ('Rather the noose than that a loathed man should seize this flesh!' 787–90) and the images of escape merge into the more violent images of suicide: lonely, snow-clad peaks become, instead of refuges, places whence the fugitives may plunge to their deaths (794 ff). By the end of the second strophic pair, it is thoughts of death and even (in preference to the married state) the state of *being dead* ('the prey of dogs, a feast for native birds ... 800–1) which absorb the Chorus's sick fantasies. As the ode develops, one becomes aware of a new extremism in the Danaids' flight from marriage comparable, in its violence, to the suicidal blackmail of their last appeals to King Pelasgus.

At this point (as at the similar point in the earlier, 'suppliant' action) a certain ambiguity must, I believe, begin to affect the audience's sympathy with the Danaids. (The moment is comparable, perhaps, to that in *Prometheus Vinctus* when [at *PV* 907–27] Prometheus' defiance leads him to predict, falsely, the downfall of Zeus.) If the *Supplices* had ended with the violent 'Egyptian herald scene' which now follows, that ambiguity might well have dissipated in favour of the Danaids. But, as we shall see, the dramatist, with seeming perversity, resists this violent ending in the play's concluding scenes.

The sudden entry of the Egyptian herald brings 'the pursuit action' to its climax. This barbarian treats the Chorus as 'cityless,' and so unprotected, 'honourless' people (853). The Chorus reply with claims of native Argive rights (859–60), but their appeals to Mother Earth and to Zeus, son of Earth (890–3), as they cling despairingly to the altar statues, are ignored by the Herald, who denies respect to the gods of this foreign land (893–4). His physical threats to rend, tear, goad, and even decapitate the Danaids (839 ff; cf 909–10), if they fail to board the

Egyptian ships at once, vindicate their earlier and now repeated horror of Egyptian *hybris*. The Chorus's use of insect and bestial images has increased greatly with the actual arrival of one of their persecutors: the Herald is described successively as a crocodile (878), a spider (887), a serpent (895), and a viper (896). It is interesting, too, to note that 'Earth' is now included (890–2) in the Chorus's prayers for protection.[39]

The intervention of the King comes just in time to save the Danaids. In the ensuing altercation (911 ff), the King's case rests chiefly on the Herald's disregard of the city's gods and of the conduct proper to a stranger ($\xi\acute{\epsilon}\nu os$); here there is a quaint irony in the Herald's appeal (920) to Hermes $\pi\rho\acute{o}\xi\epsilon\nu os$ (protector of strangers), despite his earlier aspersion (893–4, cf 421–3) of Greek gods. What amounts to a formal declaration of war ensues when the King responds to the Herald's threats of warfare (934 ff) by citing the people's unanimous resolve ($\dot{\epsilon}\kappa$ $\pi\acute{o}\lambda\epsilon\omega s$ $\mu\acute{\iota}\alpha$ $\psi\hat{\eta}\phi os$, 942–3) never to yield the Danaids under compulsion. The altercation ends with a fine touch of Argive *hauteur* when the King assures the barbarian Herald that they'll be meeting *men*, not lowly (Egyptian-style) beer-drinkers upon the field of battle (952–3).

If the *Supplices* ended with this violent scene of attempted abduction and its frustration by the King, the interpretation of the play would have been a simpler (though less interesting) task. Conversely, however, attempts to reconstruct the themes of the trilogy as a whole would have been rendered more difficult, for hints concerning the play's trilogic development do appear in the play's closing passages, particularly in the much-debated choral songs at vv 1018–73.

There are, however, two points worth comment in the speeches which King Pelasgus and, after his departure, father Danaus address to the Chorus before these final songs. The first is a minor one but may prove helpful in the attribution of these passages. As the King welcomes the Danaids to their new homes (he offers them a choice of protective accommodations), he uses the expression 'with your dear handmaidens' (if Schutz's emendation of $\phi\acute{\iota}\lambda\alpha\iota s$ $\acute{o}\pi\acute{a}o\sigma\iota\nu$ for MSS $\phi\acute{\iota}\lambda o\iota s$ $\acute{o}\pi\acute{a}o\sigma\iota\nu$ at v 954 is correct, as I believe it to be).[40] This phrase provides the first indication

---

39 Johansen and Whittle compare Aesch *Septem* 69 ff, *Choeph* 722 ff, Eur *Med* 1251 ff, and *Electra* 677–9 for other appeals to Earth for protection. To this we might add (with some trepidation but possibly more appropriateness) Io's cry at *PV* 567. (Cf Sikes and Willson's ingenious defence of the possibility that Mother Earth is referred to here, not on the grounds [etymologically dubious] that $\delta\hat{\alpha} = \gamma\hat{\alpha}$, but on the grounds that $\delta\hat{\alpha}$ might be an abbreviation of the Ionic vocative of Demeter.)

40 Most editors accept Schutz's emendation. Johansen and Whittle, however, find no good reasons for changing the reading of the MSS; to keep it they are forced

of the presence of a group of female attendants of the Danaids. The Chorus (in apparent corroboration of Schutz's emendation) add their own brief instruction to these servants: τάσσεσθε, φίλαι δμωΐδες ('take up your positions, dear [feminine] handmaidens!' 977). These two references to the Danaids' handmaidens prepare us, perhaps, for their role as second Chorus which (at least in the opinion of some critics) they are soon to play.[41]

The second, and perhaps more striking, point of interest concerns Danaus' warning to his daughters (and the Danaids' equally significant reply) concerning their deportment and the protection of their maidenly reputation among the Argives. Here Danaus waxes eloquent on the seductive effect of 'the tender ripeness of youth in bloom' (998), of 'fruit ready for the picking' (1001), and the consequent readiness of beasts and men alike to despoil such youthful beauty. Thus, he urges them strenuously not to suffer what they have all endured such hardships to avoid (1006 ff). This passage may, of course, be taken simply as the rhetoric appropriate to the situation (the expected paternal advice to daughters in a strange land), as those who insist on the conventional, to the exclusion of all other aspects of such set pieces, would undoubtedly assume. It may be, however, that the poet is exploiting such conventional rhetoric for his own dramatic purposes: the passage draws attention, for the first time, to the marriageability (apart from the Egyptians' suit), or at least to the sexual appeal of the Danaids, and perhaps even to their own vulnerability to passion: both points, as we shall see, will be relevant to future moments in their careers. Equally significant for our reading of the Danaids' present attitude and (perhaps) of their future destiny is the Chorus-Leader's firm reply:

> Fear not for my virginity! Unless the gods plan something different, I'll not desert the track of my resolve! (1015–17)[42]

---

to conclude that the attendants in question must be male attendants suddenly bestowed on the Danaids. (Danaus himself, it might be observed, has had to ask the King for *his* attendants and quite a bit is made of *his* need of this favour; see vv 492–504.) Moreover, as Garvie points out (p 195), φίλοις in the sense of 'dear' (on which Johansen and Whittle insist on the somewhat uncertain ground that the meaning 'own' has no parallels in extant Aeschylus) would be an odd modifier for male Argive attendants of the Danaids – much odder than 'dear,' even in the King's mouth, as a qualifier of the *Supplices'* own serving-maids, to which Johansen and Whittle object.

41 This attribution of vv 1034 ff is admittedly very controversial. See below.
42 The foregoing interpretation of this scene between Danaus and his daughters tends to support the tentative view expressed earlier about the motivation of the

This exchange between Danaus and the Chorus has, surprisingly, turned our interest away from the Danaids' particular abhorrence of the Egyptian suitors (which has dominated the play so far) to the broader question of their attitude toward sexual encounters (including, presumably, marriage) in general. It serves as a fitting preparation for the still more surprising choral passage with which the play is now to end.

The final Chorus (1018–73)

It is generally agreed that the lyrical passages (1018–73) which end the *Supplices* are divided between two groups of singers and probably (at 1052–61) between individual singers representing these two groups. As we shall see, differences in tone and content between vv 1018–33 and 1034–51, respectively, indicate the initial division between these two groups, and the shorter exchanges at vv 1052–61 serve to emphasize the contrasting attitudes more sharply. The content of the concluding verses (1062–73) would also seem to indicate that these verses are sung by the singers of 1018–33, that is, by the original Chorus of Danaids, though some editors believe that they are sung by the two groups together. There is no indication in the MSS of such divisions or of any secondary Chorus. There has, inevitably, been considerable disagreement between editors and commentators concerning the nature of this divided lyric and the attribution of the parts just indicated.[43] Some

---

Danaids' flight and of their subsequent attitude to the opposite sex in general. An ingenious and very different interpretation of Danaus' speech in this scene has, however, recently been advanced by W. Rösler in 'Danaos à propos des dangers de l'amour (Eschyle, *Suppliantes*, 991–1013).' Rösler takes as his starting point Sicherl's argument (see above, n 10) that the sole motivation of the Danaids' flight from their Egyptian suitors was the fear induced by the oracle that one of Danaus' prospective sons-in-law would slay him. Rösler goes on to suggest that Danaus' homily to his daughters at vv 991 ff was actually intended by him as a disguised warning to his daughters against marriage with any potential Argive suitors lest the oracle should be fulfilled by an *Argive* son-in-law. But surely the context of the various (non-Aeschylean) passages in which we hear of this oracle indicates that it is only the *sons of Aegyptus* who are to be feared as potentially dangerous sons-in-law of Danaus. Even if, as Sicherl argues, the oracle is indeed relevant to the motivation of the Danaids in this play, its relevance to the present passage seems unlikely. See further, on both Sicherl's and Rösler's arguments, the appendix to this chapter, pp 109 ff.

43 Good summaries of the problem and of some of the positions taken are to be found in Johansen and Whittle's note on *Suppl* 1018–73 (see vol III, pp 306–9 of their edition), and more fully in McCall 'The Secondary Chorus in Aeschylus' *Suppliants*' pp 117–31. In the following notes a sampling only of the defenders of the wide variety of views on this problem will be given.

think that the Chorus of Danaids splits into two somewhat opposed groups of choristers;[44] others that there is a second Chorus composed either of the Egyptian handmaidens of the Danaids[45] *or* of the male Argive guards allegedly allotted to them by the King;[46] finally, one commentator has raised the possibility that the second lyric part may be sung by the Argive king himself.[47]

Certainty among these conflicting views is, in the circumstances, clearly impossible; our choice will depend mainly on the degree of appropriateness we find in one attribution as opposed to another. Thus, supporters of the majority (and in my opinion most acceptable) view, favouring a second Chorus of handmaidens,[48] argue that the opposition

44 This view (despite Johansen and Whittle's advice that it 'be relegated to the oblivion into which it sank nearly a century ago') still has its able defenders, most notably, perhaps, McCall (see preceding note); cf also Carrière *Le choeur secondaire dans le drame grec* pp 50–1 and Ireland 'The Problem of Motivation in the *Suppliants* of Aeschylus' pp 14–29.

45 This attribution is indicated in all the major editions up to (and excluding) that of Friis Johansen (1970). Garvie (pp 194–5) also gives modified support to this view, while admitting some of its difficulties; cf also Sommerstein, 'Notes on Aeschylus' *Supplices*,' who rebuts (pp 76 ff) some of the 'difficulties' advanced against it.

46 Recent editors and commentators have tended to favour this view; see Johansen 'Progymnasmata' pp 61 ff; Johansen and Whittle in their note to vv 1018–73, and Taplin, *Stagecraft* pp 230 ff, who, however, remains relatively open-minded about the various possibilities except with regard to a singing Chorus of handmaidens, which he deprecates. (See also the following note.) West does not commit himself to a choice between this and the alternative just mentioned.

47 See again Taplin ibid p 232, though he favours the preceding suggestion (ie, the Argive attendants).

48 One point which appears to tell against this attribution should, however, be mentioned. In their opening stanza, the Chorus of Danaids urge their hearers, described a moment later as ὀπαδοί (1022) to join in their glorification of the local gods with the words ἴτε ... γανάοντες, and a moment later they add ὑποδέξασθε δ᾽ ὀπαδοὶ/μέλος (1022–3), which probably means 'receive' (just possibly 'take up') our song. Those who think that ὀπαδοί refers to the (alleged) male Argive attendants, rather than to the female Egyptian attendants, can point to the masculine plural of the participle in support of their claim. (Page's argument, in his apparatus, that the masculine is explicable by the inclusion of Danaus in the invitation implied in ἴτε ... γανόοντες strikes one as thin.) It is *possible*, of course, that the masculine participle might be used of a feminine group (cf *Ag* 561–2), and even if this possibility is not accepted, it is still not inevitable that the attendants whom the Chorus address are the ones who actually burst into song at vv 1034 ff. But in the last analysis, it is the content of the verses, both those addressed to 'the attendants' and those which 'answer' and to some degree contradict the first Chorus, which is the most acceptable criterion for guessing their identity. In both cases, the female Egyptian attendants seem to fit the role more appropriately.

expressed at vv 1034 ff to the Danaids' position (which has been clearly re-stated at vv 1030–3) is hardly what we would expect of half of the regular Chorus in this play, and inconsistent with what we know of all the Danaids, except for Hypermestra in the following play. However, similar, though less extreme charges of 'inappropriateness' have been levelled against each of the other candidates for the second lyric part. For the purpose of discussion, I shall adopt the view that the Danaids' handmaidens sing as a second Chorus. Perhaps what matters here is not so much the identity of the second Chorus (if such it be) as the new view of the Danaids' situation which it introduces and which may be thought to have important implications for the trilogic development to come.

The Chorus of Danaids begin (at vv 1018 ff) by repeating their conventional glorification of the gods of the city and their gratitude to their Argive protectors. A new note is introduced, however, in the manner in which they express their change of allegiance from Egypt to Argos, from 'the flowing streams of the Nile,'

> to the rivers which pour their kindly draught over the country, rivers rich in offspring [πολύτεκνοι, 1028] which make glad the soil of this land with their fertilizing streams. (1026–9)

River gods, mentioned already in the Chorus's praise of native Argive deities (1020–1), are of course 'chthonic,' and bestowers of fertility; we are reminded of the Chorus's inclusion of 'Mother Earth' (890) in their earlier appeals for protection. There is also a hint of a paradox (which may be resolved later in the trilogy) in the Danaids' prayer for Argive fertility coupled with their own somewhat frenzied virginity. It is to this latter concern that the Chorus turn at the end of this opening strophic pair:

> May pure Artemis look with pity on this our band, and may marriage never come upon us through the constraints of the Cytherean goddess [Aphrodite]. May *that* prize lead to death. (1030–3)[49]

Though the Danaids' rejection of marriage is here a rejection of that conquest which comes by 'Aphrodite's *constraint*' (ὑπ' ἀνάγκας ...

---

49 I read Στύγιον with Murray and Johansen and Whittle (after Stephanus and Wilamowitz, στύγιον) for MSS reading στύγειον. As Johansen and Whittle point out, this reading (Στύγιον) may be supported as continuing (now, one might add, with a suitably sinister anticipatory irony) 'the river motif' introduced at vv 1021 and 1024–9.

Κυθερείας, 1031–3), we should note that there is still a suggestion of rejection of Aphrodite herself in coupling that abhorrence with her name.[50] It is this hint of blasphemy which the answering Chorus seek to modify:

> But our friendly swarm is not neglectful[51] of Aphrodite.
> For she, together with Hera, is next to Zeus himself. (1034–5)

And in the rest of this stanza, the singers go on to enumerate the honours, attributes, and associations – including, significantly, Persuasion (Πειθώ) and *Harmonia* (1040–1) – which accompany the paths of Love, the whispering preserves of Aphrodite (1034–42).

In their second antistrophe, 'the second Chorus's develop their opposition to the Danaids' attitude to a still more marked degree. This Chorus can see no hope for the fugitive maidens in the coming war on their behalf. The marriage with the Egyptians is 'fated' (μόρσιμον, 1047); it is the will of Zeus (1048–9), as the Egyptians' swift pursuit over the seas has indicated (1045–6). (In their opening prayer to 'Zeus the Saviour,' 29–39, the Chorus of Danaids explicitly asked that the Egyptian suitors should perish in storms at sea, ere they set foot on Argos; this prayer, as the present singers realize, has been rejected by Zeus.) The song ends in acquiescence in this fated scheme of things:

> May this fulfilment [τελευτά] of marriage take place, as with many women before you! (1050–1)[52]

In the ensuing exchange between the Leaders of each Chorus (the rapid alternation of conflicting views suggests such attribution), more

---

50 Cf Johansen and Whittle, *ad loc.*
51 I read οὐκ ἀμελὴς ἑσμὸς (Scaliger's correction of θεσμὸς, M) with Weil, Page, Murray, Johansen and Whittle, but not West. ἑσμός seems to be a favourite word of Aeschylus in this play (it does not occur elsewhere in his extant work); see v 30, where it is used (according to Turnebus's certain correction) of the Egyptian suitors; v 223, where it is used of the fugitive Danaids; and 684, where it is used of the diseases which the Chorus would avert from their benefactors.
52 Again, the text is uncertain and our choice of reading will affect interpretation. If we read προτερᾶν (Bothe) for MSS προτέραν (not an emendation but merely a correction of accentuation), the Chorus-Leader is expressing a wish, as in the translation given; if, on the other hand, we reject the MSS reading and obelize προτέρ (†προτέρ† ἄν), with Johansen and Whittle, following Taube, then the Chorus-Leader is merely expressing what she thinks may happen.

hints of the coming development of the trilogy appear. The more one Leader abjures this Egyptian marriage, the more the other insists that it would be best, and bids the Danaids moderate their words and attitudes to the will of the gods. (If such admonitions [1054, 1059, 1061], like the defences of Aphrodite [1034] before them, sound strange in the mouth of a handmaiden, they would surely sound stranger still in the mouth of an Argive guard, particularly one already dedicated to the defence of the Danaids against their Egyptian suitors.)

In the final song (1062–73), sung by the Danaid Chorus as the sense of the lines must surely indicate,[53] the Chorus pray again for Zeus' protection from 'marriage with hated men,' just as, by the imposition of kindly force (1067), he relieved Io of her woes. Again, a dramatic irony prophetic of the future may be hidden beneath the paradox, for it is in the form of gentle mating that the resolution of the Danaids' turmoil will find its unexpected beginning. If so, such a resolution is lost on the Danaid Chorus, for they declare themselves ready for 'the better part of evil' (meaning, presumably, war and violence as the price of their liberation), provided only that Zeus bestow victory on the women in the end.

53 Not all, however, agree: even among those who accept the Chorus of handmaidens, Smythe (Loeb edition, vol 1) attributes vv 1062–73 to a *combined* Chorus of Danaids and their handmaidens.

APPENDIX

The trilogy

We have already summarized (with references to fuller treatments) some of the mythical material and its sources from which Aeschylus selected for the development of his trilogy in the *Aegyptii* and the *Danaides*, which most scholars believe to be the second and third plays, respectively, of the trilogy.[1] Of the probable death of Pelasgus (since no more is heard of him) during the defeat of the Argives by the Egyptians, we have no details;[2] elsewhere in the tradition Danaus is represented as ruling over the Argives, and so it seems reasonable to assume that, after ordering the murder of the cousin-bridegrooms, he succeeded King Pelasgus as the ruler.[3] Concerning the motive of Hypermestra in sparing her bridegroom Lynceus, there are conflicting views. According to *PV* 865 ff, it appears to have been desire, presumably for her husband, which blunted her murderous intent. Horace (*Odes* III.2.33 ff) immortalized her decision as a 'splendid betrayal' of her father in honour of her marriage vows and a more obscure reference in Ovid has been similarly explained.[4] Which of these motives Aeschylus chose for

---

1 See above pp 78 and n 8. Of the two lost plays of the trilogy, we have (apart from their names, which appear in the catalogue of Aeschylus' plays) no fragments certainly attributable to the *Aegyptii*, and two fragments, one of three verses and one of seven verses, belonging to the *Danaides*.
2 Cunningham 'A Fragment of Aeschylus' *Aigyptioi*?' has argued that *P Oxy* 2251 (reprinted in the Loeb edition of Aeschylus vol II, pp 571–3, as from an unknown Aeschylean play) may be from the *Aigyptioi* and that in this fragment the Chorus (presumably another Chorus of Danaids) is presented as mourning the unjust death of Pelasgus. Cf also 'Second Thoughts on *P Oxy* xx.2251' for Cunningham's (not entirely convincing) defence of her view against criticisms of it by Snell and Lloyd-Jones.
3 Wilamowitz *Aischylos Interpretationen* pp 20 f.
4 Jakel 'The 14th Heroid Letter of Ovid and the Danaid Trilogy of Aeschylus' explains the *timor* and *pietas* which, according to Ovid, kept Hypermestra from husband-murder, as referring to her fear (*timor*) of abandoning the-behaviour-enjoined-by-the-marriage-ritual (= *pietas*). Jakel believes that Ovid has taken Hypermestra's 'motive' from Aeschylus' version in the *Supplices*, but his elaborate argument for this (based on suggested comparison of *timor* and *pietas* with *phobos*

Hypermestra in this trilogy we do not know; if the (perhaps fanciful) idea suggested earlier, that the gentle mating of Zeus and Io celebrated in the *Supplices* provided a symbolic anticipation of Hypermestra's wedding night, then the motive indicated in the *Prometheus* passage would seem to be the more likely one.

If the murder of the cousin-bridegrooms took place between the second and third plays of the trilogy, as seems probable,[5] a suitably dramatic (not to say macabre!) context would be provided for our first (iambic) fragment of the *Danaides*, which appears to be the introduction to the 'awakening song' sung outside the window of bridal couples on their post-nuptial morning:

> And then the bright light of the sun arises while I, in company with youths and maidens, awaken the bridegrooms, gladdening [literally 'softening'] their hearts to gracious disposition with their songs.[6]

If, as some scholars have suggested, these words were uttered by Danaus, rather than by a servant or by the Chorus-Leader, then the grim irony of the words would be intentional, since Danaus would expect that the murder of the bridegrooms would have been consummated. Another, perhaps less probable, view (at any rate, one providing less of a theatrical *frisson*!) is that these verses herald the happy awakening of the Danaids and their *Argive* bridegrooms of a second wedding. According to this view, the fragment would belong near the end of the third play.[7]

The second fragment of the *Danaides* has provided the greatest controversy. The seven iambic verses, spoken by Aphrodite (according to Athenaeus, who quotes them) run as follows:

> Pure Heaven longs to pierce Earth and the passion of Love seizes Earth to attain that union. Rain falling from Heaven in the act of love impregnates

---

['fear'] and *sebas* ['awe, piety'] as Athena uses them in her speech at *Eum* 690–1) seems somewhat far-fetched.

5 If the Egyptians were themselves the Chorus in the play of that name, they could hardly have been murdered during its action. Cf Johansen and Whittle p 50, Winnington-Ingram *Studies* pp 57–8.

6 There are some textual uncertainties in this fragment (fr 24, Loeb, 123 Mette, 43 Nauck); for the emendations involved in the above translation, see the discussion in vol II of the Loeb edition of Aeschylus, p 394).

7 See Garvie pp 228–30 for a discussion of the various views concerning the context of this fragment (Garvie remains uncommitted to any of them).

Earth. And for mortals she brings forth food for cattle and the livelihood of crops. And from that moist marriage the leafy-season-of-the-trees comes to its fulfilment. Of all these things, I, Aphrodite, am the cause.

Even without its dramatic context, one is grateful that this splendid (and seminal)[8] passage has been preserved. Two contexts have been suggested. One is the trial of Hypermestra: in this case Aphrodite would be speaking in defence of Hypermestra for failing to slay her husband.[9] The other is the (second) marriage of the Danaids, to Argive bridegrooms,[10] and so an occasion for celebrating 'fruitfulness.' This is the context for the 'Aphrodite fragment' which has, on the whole, been more favoured by recent scholarship on the trilogy.[11]

What we have been able to gather about Aeschylus' treatment of the Danaid myth so far, particularly in the only extant play of the trilogy, leads us to believe (in company with several of the scholars already quoted) that this second marriage of the Danaids may well have been the climax toward which the whole thematic development has been leading. The Danaids' aversion to marriage with their cousin-suitors (rather than Danaus' fear of Aegyptus and his sons) seems to have dominated the action of the *Supplices*[12] and, as we have seen, this has led, especially in certain passages toward the end of the play, to a sort of generalization of the theme of 'virginity *versus* sexuality and marriage.' In view of these 'expectations,' it would seem improbable that the poet would avoid an extant element in the myth which would allow him to 'convert' the Danaids as a group from the very intransigence to which he had previously drawn attention. And this conversion would

8 Cf, for example, the proemium to Lucretius *De Rerum Natura*.
9 Murray *The Motif of Io* pp 86–7 is one of the most eloquent defenders of this (the traditional) view; he refers to Hypermestra as 'the new Io' who resolves the problem of the trilogy. Cf also Sheppard 'The First Scene in Aeschylus' *Supplices*,' who also speaks of Io as the prototype of Hypermestra.
10 See Pindar *Pythian* IX.114. (This second marriage is not, however, common to all versions of the myth.)
11 See esp von Fritz *Antike und Moderne Drama* pp 188–9 (who argues that the restoration of the Danaids to 'the natural order of things' is the subject of the third play) and Winnington-Ingram (who suggests that Aphrodite's persuasion of the Danaids to reconcile themselves to marriage [with the Argives] is comparable to Athena's persuasion of the Furies at the end of *Eumenides*). Cf also Garvie pp 225 ff and Johansen and Whittle pp 51–2. These views have been instrumental in the general reconstruction of the trilogy's conclusion suggested in this appendix.
12 Cf von Fritz p 181 ff; for the discussion of a contrary view, see below, the postscript to this appendix.

not, of course, be to the acceptance of that forced and violent form of marriage which was at the root of their initial antipathy but rather to the possibility of a joyful form of peaceful married fruitfulness which the new situation at Argos has opened up – and which the imagery not only in the 'Aphrodite fragment' but also in the admonitions of the (second?) Chorus at the end of the *Supplices*. And, indeed, the mention at *Suppl* 1040, by these dissentient choral voices, of 'Persuasion, the softener' (θέλκτορι Πειθοῖ)[13] surely provides the clue (the cue, even) for Aphrodite's appearance in this capacity at the end of the trilogy.

All is, of course, conjecture. The trial (and exoneration) of Hypermestra for disobedience; the trial of Danaus for ordering the murder of the bridegrooms; power struggles (in various forms) between Danaus and Lynceus; the purification of the Danaids by Athena and Hermes, at the command of Zeus; the punishment of the Danaids in Hades by carrying water in leaky jugs; the curious and persistent connection between the Danaids and the water supply at Argos;[14] the legend (reported by Herodotus at II.171) that the Danaids introduced the festival of the Thesmophoria from Egypt to the Pelasgian women in Argos: all of these elements (and others clearly irrelevant to our purposes) occur in one source or another of the complex and varied tradition on the Danaids.

Of these various mythical elements considered as possible candidates for inclusion in Aeschylus' treatment, perhaps the most significant, and most suitable for our view of the trilogy's finale, is the one concerning the introduction of the Thesmophoria, the woman's festival celebrating the institution of marriage. Though Herodotus' reference to this (at II.171) in connection with the Danaids does not mention Aeschylus as the source of the legend, Herodotus' only mention of Aeschylus occurs nearby, at II.156 (where he says that Aeschylus alone of the poets up to that time made use of the account of Egyptian parallels to the Greek gods). It is tempting to conjecture that, if a marriage of the Danaids to Argive bridegrooms provided the climax of the trilogy, it might have

13 The recurrence of the word θέλγω, or its cognates, in this connection in the trilogy is interesting: at *Suppl* 1004–5 (θελκτήριον / τόξευμ' ἔπεμψεν), where Danaus is warning his daughters of the seductive glances of passing Argive youths; at *Suppl* 1040 (above), where soft Persuasion is spoken of as one of Aphrodite's daughters; and at v 3 of fr 24 (Loeb) of *Danaides* (if Heyne's reasonable emendation is accepted). Cf also *PV* 865, where the word is used again, in connection with Hypermestra's decision.

14 Cf Apollod ii.1.4; see also Garvie p 172, Johansen and Whittle, vol 1, 44 and 55, and references there given.

been associated with the Thesmophoria.[15] One is constantly warned not to depend on analogies with our one extant Aeschylean trilogy in theorizing about the poet's 'fragmentary trilogies.' Nevertheless, when a suggestive analogy appears (such as the possible founding of the Areopagus at the end of the *Oresteia*), there seems no good reason for not considering the possibility.[16]

For the plot of the *Amymone*, the satyr-play to the Danaid trilogy,[17] we are dependent on the account given in the myth in pseudo-Apollodorus:

> But the land of Argos being waterless, since Poseidon had dried up even the springs because of his anger at Inachus for testifying that it belonged to Hera, Danaus sent his daughters to draw water. One of them, Amymone, as she was searching for water, threw a dart at a deer and hit a sleeping satyr. He, starting up, desired to force her, but Poseidon appearing on the scene, the satyr fled and Amymone lay with Poseidon, and he revealed to her the springs at Lerna. (Apollodorus ii.1.4, H.W. Smythe's translation in the Loeb edition)

Two associations with the trilogy (apart from the familial connection of Amymone) suggest themselves. There was an ancient tradition connecting Egypt and the Danaids with the bringing of water to dry Argos,[18] and it may be this which gave rise to the passage at *Suppl* 1018–29, where the Chorus sing the praises of the local Argive river-gods and declare their change of allegiance from their native floods of the Nile to the fertile rivers of Argos, 'rich in off-spring.' But a more specific thematic connection between the story of Hypermestra and the story of Amymone has been suggested by Winnington-Ingram:

15 Robertson in 'The End of the Suppliants Trilogy of Aeschylus' is the leading champion of this theory. He is also one of the first to argue against Hermann that the third play did not culminate in the trial and acquittal of Hypermestra.

16 Similar speculation suggests itself in connection with the possible culmination of the Prometheus trilogy with the establishment of the torch festival called the Prometheia; see my *Prometheus Bound* pp 113–14. (Whether the *Prometheus Vinctus* and what we know of its trilogy is completely, or even partially, Aeschylean in authorship has, however, become a matter of some doubt; see below, chap 4, n 58, and references there given.) On the possible similarities between the Danaid trilogy, the *Oresteia* and the Prometheus trilogy, see Herington *Aeschylus* pp 104 ff; cf also Herington 'Aeschylus: The Last Phase.'

17 A mutilated reference in *P Oxy* 2256 (1952), fr 3, indicates that the *Amymone* was the satyr play to the Danaid trilogy; only three fragments, of one verse or less each, are extant.

18 See above, n 14 of this appendix.

In either case a woman who has rejected sexual desire under the mode of *bia*, of force and violence, comes to accept it under the mode of *peithô*, of persuasion and enchantment. She who would not be forced is successfully wooed.[19]

If we allow for a possible exaggeration concerning the role of Persuasion (or at least concerning our knowledge of it) on Poseidon's part, this quotation seems a fair summary of the *Amymone*'s apparent encapsulation of the theme of the Danaid trilogy.

Postscript

As we have noted in the foregoing chapter, at least two recent studies have revived the view that the motivation of the Danaids' flight from their Egyptian suitors in the *Supplices* was the fear induced by the oracle (mentioned in other versions of the Danaid myth) that Danaus would be slain by one of his (prospective) sons-in-law. Since this view, if accepted, may also involve some modification of the view of the thematic development of the trilogy which has been suggested, and some second thoughts on the usually accepted sequence of its plays, it seems right to consider it before concluding this summary of opinions on the matter.

Sicherl places much of his belief in the relevance of this oracle to the *Supplices* (and specifically to the motivation of the Danaids' flight) on a scholiastic comment on *Suppl* 37. This scholion explains the Danaids' words λέκτων ὧν θέμις εἴργει ('marriage which *themis* [= 'all that's right'] forbids') by the phrase διὰ τὸ μὴ θανατωθῆναι τὸν πατέρα ('so that their father might not be killed'). The chief argument against our accepting this scholion as evidence that this was actually the motivation in our trilogy of the Danaids' flight from their cousin-suitors is the complete lack of reference to this motivation in the text of the *Supplices*.[20] Both Sicherl and Rösler (who, as we have seen, support's Sicherl's view) seek to meet this difficulty by suggesting that the Danaids must keep

19 Winnington-Ingram *Studies* p 71.
20 Cf Garvie p 171 and Johansen and Whittle pp 33 and 47. These scholars also take the dominant role of the Danaids themselves (Garvie, for example, speaks of Aeschylus' emphasis on 'the independent nature of the girls' decision) as ground for rejecting any connection in the *Supplices* between the Danaids' flight and the Danaus-Aegyptus feud (including the oracle element). Garvie refers also to *schol PV* 855 which seems to spell out this distinction, at least as far as the latter element is concerned, even more clearly.

this information from the Argives in order for their suppliant claims on the latter to be successful.[21] I find this argument hard to follow, since one would be inclined to think that the threat to their father's life at the hands of one of the suitors would strengthen rather than weaken the Danaids' already strong case for protection against the violent Egyptians.

A further, perhaps niggling, doubt about the accuracy or precision of the scholion on which much of Sicherl's argument depends arises from its form of expression. 'For the sake of [or 'with a view to'] their father not being killed' seems curiously inappropriate phrasing when read in the context of the clause (and *its* context) which it purports to explain. The Danaids are expressing a wish that their suitors may perish at sea, 'before they [the suitors], assuming kin-rights which are not theirs,[22] consummate unwanted [ἀκόντων] unions which *themis* forbids' (*Suppl* 37–9). The run of the clause, in which the Egyptians, not the Danaids, are the subject, rather suggests that any explanation of the marriage which *themis* forbids should, in this context, involve something in the nature of the marriage itself, rather than in the fears which the Danaids might have, for external reasons (such as an oracle about the future activity of the bridegrooms), about its results.

One must, to be sure, allow certain points in favour of the view taken by Sicherl and Rösler. One point is based on the command which we can be reasonably certain that Danaus gave to his daughters to slay their bridegrooms. Sicherl insists that the reason for this command in our trilogy, as elsewhere in the tradition, must have been Danaus' fear induced by the oracle, and, therefore, that the same fear must have been the reason for the original flight of the Danaids from the cousin-marriage.[23] It is true that the murder-command is difficult (though not perhaps impossible) to explain in any other way than that given elsewhere in the tradition, but the Danaids' emphasis in the *Supplices* on their own aversion to kin-marriage and to the violence of their cousin-suitors, together with the complete lack of any mention of the oracle or of the Aegyptus-Danaus quarrel, still make it difficult for us

21 See Sicherl 'Die Tragik der Danaiden' pp 97–8. Rösler (above, n 42 to chap 3) agrees with Sicherl on this point also and, indeed, uses it in his own explanation of why Danaus disguises, in the presence of Argive guards, his (alleged) warnings at *Suppl* 991 ff to his daughters not to marry any Argive swains, who would then (according to Rösler's argument) also become potential murderers of himself!

22 For this translation of v 38, see above, n 16 to chapter 3.

23 See Sicherl 'Die Tragik der Danaiden' p 96.

to accept the oracle-induced fear as the explanation of the flight of the Danaids. (The oracle would have occurred *after* the wedding in the trilogy, as in at least one other version.)[24]

A further strong point (and one which Rösler emphasizes) in Sicherl's argument is that *schol Suppl* 37, which points to the oracle, was presumably composed by someone with knowledge of the whole trilogy. Nevertheless, scholiasts are not always dependable witnesses, and this scholiastic comment could have been made with other versions of the Danaid myth in mind.

The soundness or otherwise of the view of the motivation of the Danaids' flight here being considered has some implications for our view of the trilogy. Rösler argues that if Sicherl's view of this matter is right (as he believes it to be), then one must also conclude that the *Supplices* was not the first play in the trilogy and that the first play was the *Egyptians*, which must have contained the dispute between Danaus and Aegyptus and the further addition to the conflict by the oracle. However, this argument, which is not entirely new, has already been countered, at least to some degree. Garvie, who cites other scholars who have disagreed with this view and who, as we have seen, regards the brothers' strife as irrelevant to Aeschylus' treatment of the myth, claims that the lack of any reference to it in the *Supplices* would be all the more surprising if it had formed the plot of the preceding play.[25]

Sicherl's and Rösler's view of the influence of the dynastic struggle (and, specifically, of 'the oracle') on the action of the *Supplices* does indeed modify, though it does not entirely contradict, the view of the Danaids' attitude to marriage, and so of the future action and larger theme of the trilogy for which we have argued. (That 'future action' could still effect the transformation of an apparently traumatic and 'doomed' nuptial experience into the triumph of love and marriage celebrated by Aphrodite in the final fragment of the *Danaides*.) Nevertheless, neither the motivation of the Danaids in the *Supplices* nor the precise theme of the trilogy can be certainly determined with only one play extant, and the view which we have tended to deprecate in this 'postscript' has a reasonable possibility of being right.

24 See *schol* Eur *Or* 872, referred to by Garvie p 165.
25 Garvie pp 185–6; cf p 171 and his quotation of *schol PV* 855.

PART TWO

CHAPTER FOUR

Imagery

1 Introductory comments

There have been many studies of Aeschylean imagery, both of its
alleged leading characteristics and of its use in individual plays.[1] It may
be useful to cite at the outset a few general observations which occur, in
one form or another, in several of them, and of which this survey will
provide ample exemplification.

1 The following general studies of Aeschylean imagery have been found most useful
(references to studies of imagery in specific plays will be made later) and will be
referred to by author's name alone: Dumortier *Les images dans la poésie d'Eschyle* (the
general approach of Dumortier's work, perhaps the most influential of its kind in the
past generation, will be considered below); Stanford *Aeschylus in His Style* chap 4;
Earp *The Style of Aeschylus* chap 5 (these are two basic introductory studies of the
more traditional kind; they deal extensively with types, subject-matter, location and
provenance of Aeschylean images; Earp provides useful lists along these lines);
Van Nes *Die Maritime Bildersprache des Aischylos* (a careful, scholarly study, which
includes useful categorizations of Aeschylean images); Fowler 'Aeschylus' Imagery'
(particularly good on the imagery in the *Supplices*) and 'The Imagery of *Prometheus
Bound*'; Petrounias *Funktion und Thematik der Bilder bei Aischylos* (perhaps the most
exhaustive and authoritative study of Aeschylean imagery in recent times; the
introduction includes a critical survey of earlier work on the subject); Rosenmeyer
The Art of Aeschylus pp 117 ff (Rosenmeyer is particularly concerned with definitions
and distinctions between kinds of images, but also provides illuminating comments
on certain specific passages); Moreau *Eschyle: La violence et le chaos* chap 1, 'La
métaphore paradoxale' (in this interesting study, Moreau finds the transformation
of peaceful and even idyllic features of everyday life into visions of blood and death
to be a characteristic element of Aeschylean imagery: this apt description of what
Moreau calls Aeschylus' 'métaphores paradoxales' may be found to suit many of
the images which we shall be discussing in this chapter). Finally, reference should

Much has been made, particularly among critics of a generation or so ago, of Aeschylus' alleged tendency to employ in each of his plays a 'dominant image' which typifies, or even symbolizes, the main theme of the play.[2] As we reread the plays, we shall find a good deal of support for this view; there is, for example, much about 'yokes' in the *Persae*, and the flight of doves fleeing before the hawk clearly symbolizes what is happening to the Danaids in the *Supplices*. However, in its extreme form this isolation of dominant images tends to make Aeschylean technique in these matters appear more artificial and contrived than it actually is, and too firm an allegiance to this approach distracts attention from the rich variety and flexibility with which images are deployed in almost all the extant plays.

More illuminating than the 'dominant image' view is the realization recently expressed by Petrounias that in Aeschylus motifs in general are established mainly through images and that, since the poet expresses almost all his dramatic ideas in this form, an appreciative grasp of his imagery is essential to an understanding of his plays.[3] Complementing this view of the fundamental role of the image in Aeschylus is the further recognition, shared by several critics, that 'the metaphorical regularly develops into the literal, until finally the underlying idea is made visible

---

    be made to three more specialized studies, valuable for the specific aspects of our subject indicated in their titles: Smith 'Observations on the Structure of Imagery in Aeschylus'; Silk *Interaction in Poetic Imagery*; Sansone *Aeschylean Metaphors for Intellectual Activity*.

2 This approach is associated particularly with Dumortier, though others have adapted (eg, Stanford) or developed (eg, Petrounias) certain aspects of it. Though valuable, the approach as employed by Dumortier has decided limitations: the critic varies between underlining the obvious and (occasionally) letting his view of the play's theme, rather than the actual prominence or use of the metaphor concerned, determine his choice of the 'dominant image.'

3 See Petrounias pp ix ff and 301 (most of Petrounias's general observations on Aeschylean imagery are well expressed in the introduction and conclusions to his long and excellent study; in between he gives full exemplification of these observations from each of the plays). Cf his concluding remarks:

    Wir haben verfolgt, wie Aischylos durch die Bildsprache die Wirklichkeit interpretiert, d.h. wie seine metaphorische Sprache einen Sinn schafft der durch konkrete Ausdrücke unaussprechbar wäre, und wie ... die Bildsprache den tieferen, unerwarteten Sinn der Welt offenbart. (ibid 301)

    We have traced how Aeschylus interprets reality through images, ie, how his metaphorical expressions create a meaning which would be impossible through realistic speech and how ... figurative speech provides the deeper, unexpected view of the world.

on-stage'[4] – a recognition which brings home to us how easily, because so vividly conceived, the imaginary world can be 'actualized' in the archaic mind.

Turning to more sophisticated matters of technique, other commentators have dwelt on Aeschylus' tendency, more marked perhaps in the later plays which we possess, particularly in the *Oresteia*, to deal in patterns and sequences of images. Valid and valuable as this emphasis has been, the critics involved are sometimes in danger (as we shall see) of stressing the pattern to the detriment of the individual image and even of finding, once the fit is on them, more completely developed patterns than are actually in the text. But further evaluation of the strengths and weaknesses of this approach must await more detailed consideration of the passages and plays concerned.

While admitting the value – and the usefulness for various different aspects of our study – of these various approaches, my own approach will be less conceptual and my purpose considerably more modest. I will be concerned primarily with the dramatic function, in a fairly narrow and restricted sense, of Aeschylean images, adhering to the view that the most important thing to be discussed with regard to any given image is its effect in its immediate context: its power to illuminate that particular moment in the action or, it may be, in the experience of a given character, which it surrounds. That is not to say, of course, that these individual illuminations do not sometimes form part of a meaningful sequence or pattern, as many critics have ably demonstrated, or that, when taken together, the images of any given play may not provide, in the enigmatic form appropriate to poetry, its main thematic statement. But for the audience viewing the play for the first (and presumably the only) time (the audience with whom the poet is directly concerned), the meaning of the images surely lay primarily in their immediate, individual, 'atomized' effects, and only in a truly secondary and, as it were, 'cumulative' sense in the sequential experience. Only through the first of these meanings does the second become possible, and it is with the

---

4 This is A.G. Garvie's neat paraphrase of Petrounias in his review, *CR* 29 (1979) 8. For a similar idea, cf Porter 'The Imagery of Greek Tragedy: Three Characteristics': 'A second characteristic of the imagery of the *Oresteia* is that a number of its recurrent images reflect closely its basic pattern of action.' (One of Porter's best examples is 'the net' in *Agamemnon*, which figures as image in Agamemnon's inflicting of justice on Troy and as 'actuality' in Clytemnestra's infliction of justice on him.) Cf also Porter's references to other critics, especially Lebeck and Knox, on comparable points.

first that we shall be chiefly though not exclusively concerned in this survey.

Two related questions must also be addressed, however briefly, in this foreword. The first concerns what the term 'image' is to be understood as meaning in the present discussion. Except as otherwise noted, the term will be used to refer to any comparison, direct (simile) or implicit (metaphor) which is intended by the author to heighten, render more vivid, or in any way enhance or exaggerate the description of the person, object, state, situation, action, and the like to which the comparison refers (that is, in technical terms, of the *comparandum*). In the case of implicit comparison (metaphor), there must also be some impression of 'otherness,' that is, of something other than 'the actual,' in the new guise given to the *comparandum*. Thus, as used here, 'image' will exclude simple or banal comparisons such as 'black as night' or 'to cry like a baby,' and 'dead metaphors' (that is, expressions in which the comparative or 'literally inappropriate' element has been rendered almost unnoticeable by convention or by use over a long period of time.)[5] More important, it will also exclude all mere descriptions, even though these include 'word pictures,' in which no element of comparison, overt or implicit, is present (that is, the intention is to use the 'image' only in the figurative, 'literary' sense; the distinction, though obvious, needs to be made, if only because it is ignored, for one reason or another, in a few of the studies considered below).

The second, and larger, question concerns what Aeschylus would have regarded as metaphorical in the figurative sense just described. Were some expressions which appear to us to be metaphorical, that is, to imply imaginative comparisons, actually literal descriptions for him? There are admittedly grey areas here, particularly with regard to apparent personifications of abstractions such as Persuasion (*Peithô*), Fate (*Moira*), and Justice (*Dikê*) which are sometimes represented as actual divinities,[6] and with regard to apparent metaphors involving thoughts

---

5 On these matters (ie, on the kind of 'deviation from the terminological norm' involved in metaphor, and on the nature of 'dead metaphor'), see Silk chap 2 'Dead Metaphor and Normal Usage,' esp pp 27 ff.

6 This is admittedly an area of great uncertainty and disagreement. Opinions vary widely, from the view that the archaic Greek mind was incapable of abstract concepts to the view that the 'deification' of such ideas as 'Fate' was itself the end product of a process of poetic personification. Readers will find useful discussions (among many others) of this subject in Dietrich *Death, Fate and the Gods* chap 3, 'Moira and the Moirae,' esp pp 60–6 (note also Dietrich's references to Wilamowitz and Nilsson, both of whom tend to deprecate the 'deification' of Moira until a comparatively

and emotions which some scholars, regarding classical literature as if it were 'a vast physiological treatise,' might call simply expressions of 'anatomical reality.'[7] However, until one knows more than one is ever likely to know about the fifth-century Greek individual's view of 'reality' (and even this view must have varied greatly between that of a poet, a philosopher, and an average member of the Athenian theatre audience), it would seem safer to infer the significance of a given expression from the way in which the poet uses it in its context. As we shall see, there are passages where Justice personified is part of a clearly metaphorical (not mythological) sequence and others where Justice has clearly the trappings of divinity. So also, when we hear of Agamemnon, at the dread moment of decision, 'breathing a changing wind of his mind' (φρενὸς πνέων ... τροπαίαν, Ag 219), and recognize 'changing wind' (τροπαία) as an excellent poetic image for just such a fatal change of mind,[8] we surely need not reject the metaphorical interpretation of such a passage simply because elsewhere φρήν (mind) and θύμος (spirit) are used with 'wind' and other physical elements in what appear to be literal descriptions of thought or emotion.[9] On

---

late date); Lloyd-Jones *The Justice of Zeus*, esp pp 35–6, 44, 50, 86–7, 99–101, on *Dikē* (Justice) as a goddess; Burkert *Greek Religion*, trans John Raffan, chap 3.4, esp pp 184 ff on the personification of abstract concepts. (Burkert [who in turn cites K. Reinhardt 'Personifikation und Allegorie'] perhaps puts this murky problem as clearly as it can be expressed: '... the Archaic Greek personifications come to assume their distinctive character in that they mediate between the individual gods and the spheres of reality; they receive mythical and personal elements from the gods and in turn give the gods part in the conceptual order of things' [p 185].)

7 These expressions occur in Sansone's (mildly satirical?) account of J.B. Onian's view (see n 9, below) of what are to most of us poetic descriptions, of thoughts and emotions, occurring in Aeschylus' time and earlier.

8 τροπαία also appears in other Aeschylean metaphors involving 'change': 'change of fortune' at *Choeph* 775 ('But what if Zeus at some time causes a change [lit. 'sets a changing wind,' τροπαίαν ... θήσει] from troubles?') and 'change of spirit' at *Sept* 706, where τροπαία is used, albeit a shade optimistically, by the Chorus of a possible eventual change of purpose (λήματος ... τροπαίᾳ χρονίᾳ) on the part of the family curse.

9 Onians *Origins of European Thought* (see esp pp 46, 53–4 for the relevant passages here) is the chief proponent of the view that apparently metaphorical passages of the kind mentioned above are really literal descriptions of the processes (in the poet's view) of thought and emotions. Homer *Il* 21.385 f and Aesch *Ag* 1388 f are reasonably cited as literal descriptions, and Empedocles B105 D-K, more than reasonably but not, perhaps, as relevantly in a literary context; from such examples it seems to be assumed that numerous other passages involving 'mind,' breath, and the like (including *Ag* 187 and *Ag* 219) are also intended by the poet as

the other hand, there are, as we shall see, some Aeschylean passages
dealing with the emotions where the physical details enumerated may
well make us hesitate between regarding them as metaphorical or (in
the poet's view of the matter) actual physiological descriptions.

2 Imagery in the *Persae*

Dumortier,[10] with justice, regards 'the yoke' as the dominant image
of the *Persae*. There are five occurrences of ζυγόν (yoke) or cognate
forms used metaphorically for Xerxes' act of bridging the Hellespont
with a bridge of boats,[11] an act which, as we have seen in our discussion of the play, is treated as the deed symbolizing Xerxes' *hybris* in
seeking to extend his rule beyond his *moira*. (In theatrical terms, of
course, Xerxes' bridge of ships is also treated as a hybristic attempt
to subdue to his will the divine element of the sea, 'the stream of
Bosporus, sacred to the god' [745–6, cf 722–3]). Certain words used
with ζυγόν help to emphasize its metaphorical use in these passages:
ἀμφιβάλλω ('cast around'), twice (50, 72); δούλιον ('slavish') once, as a
modifier; αὐχένι ('neck'), once as indirect object, with ζυγόν as direct
object (72). Note also Darius' use later of δοῦλον ὡς δεσμώμασιν ('en-
slaved as if by chains,' 745) to describe how Xerxes foolishly hoped
to restrain the 'sacred Hellespont.' This symbolism ('the yoking of the
sea' to suggest the imperial overreaching of Xerxes) is particularly
well illustrated at v 736, where Atossa tells the ghost of Darius about
Xerxes' return, after his defeat, to the bridge 'yoking the two continents' (γέφυραν, ἐν δυοῖν ζευκτήριον, 736). Other uses of 'yoke words,'

---

literal descriptions. Cf also Van Nes, 15–16, who clearly takes *Ag* 187 and *Ag* 219
metaphorically, while still referring respectfully in a later context (cf p 54) to
Onians's approach.

10 Dumortier chap 2. On imagery in the *Persae* see also the good discussion in Smethurst
Artistry pp 240 ff. Smethurst describes perhaps more subtly than Dumortier
Aeschylus' treatment of the yoking of the Hellespont: 'The moral (involved in this
image) is expressed in terms of the sea and the land in the contrast which Aeschylus
sets up in the lyric parodos' – which contrast Smethurst then proceeds to elucidate
in her analysis of the first three strophes of that parodos. Another excellent feature
of Smethurst's treatment is her observation, with good illustrations, of Aeschylus'
practice in the *Persae* of interweaving, and sometimes fusing, 'tenor' and 'vehicle'
(Smethurst's terms for the literal and the figurative in the poet's descriptions) in his
account of the Persian force and the disaster which it suffered at Salamis.

11 *Persae* 50, 72, 130, 722, 736.

in a context other than Xerxes' bridging of the Hellespont on his way to enslave European lands, complement this metaphorical usage. In Atossa's dream, Xerxes 'yokes' (ζεύγνυσι) to his chariots the two women representing Persia and Greece, and sets yokes (λέπαδνα) about their necks (191). (The yoking here is only marginally metaphorical since of the dream itself it is a literal description.)[12] And a particularly poignant metaphor, again involving the same image, is used for the sweeter yoke of (all-too-recent) marriage with absent warrior husbands which lonely brides now long for (... ἀνδρῶν ... ποθέουσαι ... ἀρτιζυγίαν, 541–2).[13]

While the 'yoke images' may be the dominant ones in the *Persae*, perhaps the most vivid and sinister ones belong to the sea and its inmates, for this is in keeping with the nature of Xerxes' catastrophe. Sea and its floods are used in general images of disaster ('a great sea [πέλαγος ... μέγα] of ills [433], 'a flood [κλύδων] of troubles' [599] – in both cases of the Persians' woes) and the expression 'a mighty stream [μεγάλῳ ῥεύματι] of men' (88) is used, with false confidence, by the Chorus of the doomed Persian host. Hideously vivid are the 'sea and fish images' used in connection with the luckless occupants, sailors and soldiers, of the ships destroyed by the Athenian navy:

Like tunnies, or any mess of fish they whacked and boned us with bits of wreckage and the shaft of oars. (424–6)

Gnawed by the swirling sea, mangled by the voiceless children of the deep ... (577–8)
[πρὸς ἀναύδων ... παίδων τᾶς ἀμιάντου: a marvellously Aeschylean phrase for fish!]

12 Rosenmeyer, 122–3, gives this passage as one of his examples of 'asyntactic' comparison operating without explicit 'as' and 'so' connections. '... the yoking of the two women to the chariot implies the unspoken comparison: "as one would yoke two horses, so he yoked the two women."' Be that as it may, one might also suggest a metaphorical element in the 'dream symbolism' implied, in which the two women yoked by Xerxes represent Persia and Greece.

13 On the voluptuous description of the marriage beds in the same passage (*Persae* 541 ff), see Moreau 22–3, who finds in it a possible ironic anticipation of *Persae* 624, where *thalamoi*, often used for 'nuptial chambers,' refer to 'abodes of the dead.' (Moreau finds a similar paradoxical replacement at *Sept* 333–5 and 363–8, where the expectation of wedding rites for marriageable Theban maidens is replaced by fears of rape by the besieging soldiers.)

Finally, and perhaps most ghoulishly, there appears the terse image for the drowned body of the hero Tenagon, truest born of Bactrian sons, who 'now noses [πολεῖ, lit. 'frequents' or 'comes and goes from' like a fish at a rock or a bit of submerged timber] Ajax's sea-smitten isle' (306–7).

There are more metaphors involving earth and its produce than one might expect in a tragedy whose central catastrophe is a seabattle. Sadly these involve, for the most part, the young men doomed to die in that battle, the 'flower' (ἄνθος) or 'blossoming fruit' of the Persian land as they are repeatedly called (59–60, 252, 925). Here, too, the land itself is presented as mourning for the fruit of its own nurture, in two passages which express rather beautifully the productive as much as the national or political aspects of the mother country. In the first of these

> … for them the whole land [χθών] of Asia, which nourished [θρέψασα] them cries out [στένεται] with great longing (61–2)

the verb στένεται (which usually has a connotation of lamentation) anticipates the actual fate of the Persian youth, while now (at this early point in the play) simply bemoaning their absence.

In the second passage the implicit contrast between land and nation becomes more poignant, as the land mourns what it has produced only to have it consigned to Hades by its ruler:

> And the land mourns the youth-of-the-land [γᾶ δ' αἰάζει τὰν ἐγγαίαν / ἥβαν], in the power of Xerxes, the Hades filler. For many men now dwellers-in-Hades[14] the flower of the land, archers, a countless throng of heroes, have now perished utterly. (922–7)

But perhaps the most beautiful of these metaphors celebrating the fruits of the earth even as they are returned to 'earth-the-receiver,' occurs in Atossa's speech describing the offerings which she pours out as 'appeasements of the dead' (νεκροῖσι μειλικτήρια, 610) while summoning the ghost of Darius:

> … this glory of an ancient vine, a pure draft from a wild mother, and further sustenance, the fruit always found amid the foliage of the lovely-scented

---

14 Ἀιδοβάται, 'Hades-walkers' or 'Hades-dwellers,' is Hermann's emendation for the unintelligible ἀγδαβάται of the MSS; however, the emendation itself implies an Aeschylean coinage.

yellow olive trees, children, too, of all-bearing mother earth [παμφόρου γαίας τέκνα]. (614–19)

Consistent with this use of fair images blended with sad thoughts and catastrophic moments in this play (fruits offered to the dead and blossoms doomed to die) are two striking passages depicting brilliant sunshine (once at dawn, once at high noon) which are to spell disaster at different moments in the Persian débâcle. The first of these describes the dawn of that day at Salamis which Xerxes expected would herald the Greek disaster:

When white-steeded day filled the whole land with it radiance (386–7)

The second passage describes that fatal high noon, as the Persian host crossed the all-too-lightly frozen Strymon, on their bitter journey home:

But when the sun's bright orb, with its flaring rays, reached the middle of its journey, blazing like a torch-fire ... (504–5)

Like the images of wealth and glory, and of flowers and fruitfulness in this play, these images of radiant sunshine presage not hope or joy but yet another disaster for Xerxes' expedition.

Just as the images already discussed are all used, in this 'single-minded play,' to heighten the expectation of Persian disaster, so too most of the personifications are used with similar intention and effect. Several of these are, to be sure, of a fairly conventional kind readily found elsewhere in Aeschylus. Thus the cities, and the land of Persia, are apostrophized by the Messenger (249–50) after the Persian defeat, just as, in the *Agamemnon* (503 ff), the Herald, this time with joy, hails his native Argos after the victory at Troy. So, too, in the *Persae*, emotions, feelings, and thoughts, here again all concerned with gloomy foreboding, are also personified in the usual manner.[15] However, it is the more unusual personifications, such as occur in Atossa's expression of fear about wealth, which provide the more striking images:

15 Eg, 'my prophetic spirit' (κακόμαντις ... θυμός, 10–11); 'anxiety tears at my heart' (με καρδίαν ἀμύσσει φροντίς, 161); 'my black-robed heart is torn with fear' (μελαγχίτων / φρὴν ἀμύσσεται φόβῳ, 115–16).

... fearful am I lest great wealth, in its hurry over the threshold, should trip up the true prosperity which Darius amassed, not without the help of some god. (162–4)

Personifications of *hybris* and *atê*, elements so essential to Xerxes' fatal career, become so familiar in Aeschylus that one wonders whether these conceptions (abstract as they may seem to us) may not, in the poet's mind, be actually endowed with a sort of baleful spiritual reality. Be that as it may, two such passages lead to particularly vivid sequences, involving favourite Aeschylean metaphors, which may be said to sum up the beginning, middle, and end of Xerxes' tragedy. The first comes in the Chorus's gloomy premonitions of Persian doom:

For Delusion ["Aτη], all fawning and friendly at first, beguiles a man into her nets [ἄρκυας] whence no man can escape uninjured (97 ff = 111 ff in Müller's transposition)[16]

The second comes in Darius' account of its fulfilment:

Hybris, blossoming, has produced a sheaf of *Atê* [now in the sense of Destruction] whence it now reaps its crop of utter disaster. (821–2)

3 Imagery in the *Septem*

The imagery in the *Septem* is, in some ways, among the 'strongest' in the plays of Aeschylus, in that the most repeated images are most closely related to the main theme and are, perhaps for the same reason, the least complex and subtle. As has been noted by several commentators, the most frequently recurring subjects for imagery are those connected with ships and their handling; those connected with storms, wind, and weather (often, though not always, in relation to ships at sea); and those connected with the earth and vegetation in general.[17]

---

16 The text and sequence of these lines have been much debated (see Broadhead's notes to 93–6, 111–13, 114, Müller's numbering), but the general sense is clear.

17 Among the many commentators on the imagery of the *Septem*, several have noted one or more of these 'dominant images.' See Dumortier chap 3; Stanford chap 4; Dawson *The Seven against Thebes* intro. pp 18–22; Cameron *Studies in the Seven against Thebes of Aeschylus* chaps 4 and 5; Thalmann *Dramatic Art in Aeschylus' Seven against Thebes* chap 2; and especially Van Nes, passim. (See Van Nes's table of contents for

Just as the theme of the play varies between emphasis on the safety of the city and on the fate of individual heroes, especially the two brothers, so 'ship and storm imagery' is used to highlight and illustrate dangers now to the first and now to the second of these, and eventually to both together.[18] As Cameron has observed, 'the *Septem* provides the most extended metaphor of the ship of state in ancient literature.'[19] The image of the ship and its captain, for the city and its commander, begins at the very beginning of the play, with Eteocles' opening words:

> Citizens of Cadmus, it is necessary that anyone who is in charge of defence, guiding the rudder on the ship of state [ἐν πρύμνῃ πόλεως / οἴακα νωμῶν], should speak what's fitting, not letting his eyes blink with sleep. (1–3)

Fragments of nautical images, whether for ships, or their accessories, or for seamen and their activities, are slipped in, unobtrusively, throughout the dramatization of the defence preparations. Thus, among Eteocles' instructions to the citizens we hear the expression 'man the bulwarks!' (κἀπὶ σέλμασιν / πύργων στάθητε, 32–3), where the word for 'bulwarks' is the same as for 'decks' or 'rowing benches,' even as he rebukes the frightened Chorus with an extended nautical image:

> What! Does a sailor seek safety, when his ship wallows in the waves, by dashing from stern to bow? (208–10)

So, too, the Scout's various exhortations to his Commander keep taking a nautical turn: 'Guard the city like a skilled pilot [οἰακοστρόφος]!' (62–4) and, somewhat later, 'Send wise and good defenders against [ἀντηρέτας, lit. 'rowers against'] *this* attacker!' (595–6). The Chorus, in its terrified imaginings, describe the coming attack on the city as 'a wave of lofty-crested warriors aroused by Ares' blasts' (114–15). The Scout's

---

references to various aspects of 'ship and sea imagery' in Aeschylus; see his index for specific references to the *Septem* in this connection.)

18 Thalmann, *Dramatic Art* p 79, extends this view to cover *all* the imagery in the *Septem* and presses the contrast rather further than is suggested here. A table synopsizing the author's findings on these matters is provided on pp 80–1.

19 Cameron *Studies* p 58. *Septem* 2–3, 760–1 provide the most explicit examples of this image. Van Nes, pp 71 ff, regards the 'ship of state image' as not only the most prevalent but also the richest of Aeschylus' 'ship and sea images,' especially in its use in a 'storm-tossed' context, to depict the city-state as a bulwark against a hostile environment. He reminds us how often the fate of Athens depended on its fleet and how once the Athenians abandoned their city, in flight from the Persians, for their ships.

final admonition to Eteocles, after he has given the dread news of the attacker at the seventh gate, is once again expressed in nautical terms:

> Blame not the bearer of these tidings: think, rather, how *you* must captain [ναυκληρεῖν] now our ship of state! (651–2)

Storm and wind imagery take over again as the climax of the play approaches. Eteocles, sure now that he is doomed to meet his brother in fratricidal combat, describes that doom as 'the wind-driven fate of Cocytus' which bears his family to its fate (690–1), while the Chorus, still seeking to restrain him, suggest that the Curse (here, δαίμων) 'blowing with a changing-wind of purpose at last [τροπαία χρονία], might still come with gentler breath' (705–8).[20] However, when Eteocles refuses to listen to their warnings and rushes off to battle, their worst fears are expressed (during the great ode on the family curse) in a fine storm image for the disasters which they now see threatening the city and its leaders:

> Mind-destroying madness [παράνοια] brought the bridal pair [Oedipus and Jocasta] together. Like the sea, that primal folly sends waves of evil, each wave seeking the next, then rising, triple-crested,[21] around the timbers of the ship of state. (756–61)

This passage is followed a little later in the same ode by another image involving an imperilled ship, but now the context has changed, the avoidance of shipwreck by jettisoning cargo being used as a minatory image to suggest the dangers of too great prosperity. The primal curse is still maintained as the root cause of the danger (to individuals as to the state), as we see from the transitional passage (766–8) between the two images, but it must be admitted that the second image suits the theme of the dangers of prosperity (and the avoidance of those dangers) much better. The apparent inconsistency (which is hardly ruinous, given the frequently loose thought sequences of even Aeschylean choral lyrics)

20 Van Nes, 12–13, quotes this passage in connection with his statement: 'Als brausender Wind erscheint in der Tragödie manchmal das Schiksal' ('Fate often appears as a storm-wind in tragedy'). Hutchinson, Van Nes, and others compare the use of τροπαία at *Ag* 219 (πνέων τροπαίαν), though *there*, of course, it is used of a human change of purpose: it is Agamemnon who 'blows the changing wind of his mind.' Cf above, nn 8 and 9.
21 For further examples of 'water imagery,' see below, n 27.

may be seen if we quote both the transitional passage (between the contextually different images) as well as the second image:

For grievous resolutions[22] of curses uttered long ago are now coming to fulfilment. Disaster passes by poor men.[23] But prosperity of profit-seeking men when grown too great requires cargo-jettisoning [ἐκβολὰν] over the ship's stern. (766–71)

In this passage, then, both the ship-and-storm image and its application have undergone considerable change. The beleaguered ship is still implied, though no longer as clearly present to the mind's eye, by the mention of cargo-jettisoning, and the dangers being metaphorically presented are no longer those due to some ancestral or parental 'folly' (cf παράνοια, κ.τ.λ., 756 f) but those due to the too-great wealth of greedy men. Further difficulties are provided by the strophic pair of stanzas immediately following. These stanzas deal with the fall of Oedipus (in no way occasioned by too-great wealth, jettisoned or not) from great honour to the misery which led to the self-blinding and the cursing of his sons, and it is with this end result and the Chorus's fear lest the swift-footed Erinus may now be fulfilled that the ode, with dramatic appropriateness, now ends.

What, then, is the explanation for the insertion of that curious little passage (769–71) in which the image clearly illustrates the dangers of, and the remedies for, too greedily accumulated wealth?[24] Other critics and editors have, of course, seen the similarities between this passage and *Ag* 1005–13 (where it is said that unswerving prosperity, when it strikes a hidden reef, can still be saved by jettisoning cargo, when the house is too wealthy, and then 'the ship sinks not'). The Chorus in the

22 καταλλαγαί, lit., 'reconciliations,' which here has a grimly ironic meaning, for the curses will be resolved, or fulfilled, by the only kind of 'reconciliation' (mutual slaughter) possibly between the brothers.

23 The text is quite uncertain here. Bücheler's emendation, πενομένους, at least seems to fit the sense of the following sentence (pace Hutchinson, who takes this and the following sentence quite differently: see below, n 24).

24 I find it impossible to accept Hutchinson's view of these verses. In order to make their sense jibe with the passage on Oedipus which follows at 772 ff, he takes ὄλβος to mean simply 'good fortune' ('The fortunes of the house – and especially the house of Oedipus – have flourished too highly ...'), which, of course, it often does in other contexts; ἀνδρῶν ἀλφεστᾶν to mean not 'rich men' (or, presumably, 'profit seeking men') but 'mortals' (see his refs. to Hesiod, *ad loc*); and (most difficult of all) the cargo which must be jettisoned, the whole prosperity of the house. He rejects the comparison with the meaning of *Ag* 1008–14.

Agamemnon go on to say (1017 ff) that, unlike the dangers of wealth and surfeit which can be averted, blood once shed upon the ground can never be recalled. Possibly the poet is thinking of a similar contrast here: unlike the curable excess figured in 'the jettisoning image' at *Sept* 769–71, the familial dooms stemming from the deeds of Laius and Oedipus cannot be turned aside. Admittedly the contrast, if intended, is not carefully spelled out. It may be that the image of the storm-beleaguered ship introduced at vv 758 ff has called to the poet's mind the more traditional 'moral metaphor' of the-overladen-ship-saved-by-jettisoning-cargo, and so he introduces the latter idea briefly and elliptically in the image at 769–71. But it is tempting to think that some such contrast based on traditional gnomic wisdom[25] (and anticipating the contrast of a slightly different kind described at *Ag* 1005–21) may be being suggested here.

The sequence of 'ship and storm images,' particularly as involving the 'ship of state,' is finally brought to a peaceful conclusion with the arrival of the Messenger and his initial announcement concerning the safety of the city:

> The city is in calm water once again. Even amid the worst blows of the storm it did not founder. (795–6)

Contrary to the usual beleaguered ship images, while the ship is saved, it is the captain who has perished. The poet does not, however, provide us with this final image. Once the ship of state is saved and the battle over, we are no longer invited (by the Messenger or by the poet) to think of Eteocles, the captain of that ship, alone:

> The city is saved. But of the two royal brothers, the land has drunk their blood, when they fell by one another's hand. (812–13 = 820–1, codd.)

While thoughts of the embattled city call up, as we have seen, many images of a storm-lashed ship at sea, Thebes is a land-locked city and one whose citizens, descendants of earth-born parents, would think first of their native soil in any deeds of self-defence. Thus, we find in the

---

25 Cf *Ag* 750 ff, where the Chorus refer to the ancient saying (παλαίφατος ... λόγος) that prosperity of itself begets misery. It is true that the Chorus here reject this view, but it is clear from subsequent passages (eg, 772 ff, 1005–13, cited above) that the Chorus, and perhaps the poet, held enough of the traditional view to regard excessive wealth as at least dangerous and, perhaps, usually associated (as Solon would associate it) with greed and ill-gotten gains.

Septem numerous passages referring to nurture and growth, whether of Thebes' citizens or of the fruit its land produces.[26] Not all of the passages involving 'land' or 'growth' employ figurative expressions (though the ones which do provide some of the play's most striking metaphors), but all of them may, one feels, be treated as belonging to the same thematic complex, as their sharing of similar ideas and, sometimes, language, would seem to indicate.

In his opening speech, Eteocles calls on all citizens in turn, *by the stages of their growth*, to defend their native land:

> Now 'tis fitting that each of you, he who still lacks his full maturity and he who has passed it, and likewise he who nourishes to the full his body's growth, that each should now defend the city ... (10–14)

and as Eteocles continues he makes it clear that this defence is to include not only the city and its children but also ...

> Mother Earth, our dearest nurse, welcoming all the toils of child-rearing, the young ones crawling on her kindly bosom, nourishes her inhabitants to be her faithful defenders in her hour of need. (17–20)

The Chorus too, as they sing their fears of what may happen, continue this emphasis on danger to the nurturing land:

> Fruit fallen to the ground gives pain: bitter sight for the householder, when earth's produce is carried off in useless floods.[27] (357–62)

Ironically, and yet perhaps fittingly, the one 'good' member among the enemy chieftains is allowed a share in the language and imagery of the earth. Amphiaraus, after rebuking Polyneices for seeking to sack his paternal city and obliterate his maternal source (μητρός τε πηγὴν, 584),[28] confidently prophesies that he 'will enrich this land when he, a prophet, lies buried under enemy soil' (587–8). The Messenger,

26 Cf Dawson *The Seven* pp 19–22.
27 Cameron, *Studies* p 66, notes several other 'rushing water' images for the invaders: 80, 85–6, 360–2 and (less aptly) 797 and 556–7. See further (pp 66–8) his rather complex overall interpretation of all the water images (of floods *and* stormy seas) in the play.
28 For an ingenious explanation of the Scout's mildly paradoxical quotation of Amphiaraus concerning Polyneices' 'paternal city' (πόλιν πατρώιαν, 582) and 'maternal source' (μητρός ... πηγήν, 584), see Dawson *The Seven* pp 20–1.

apparently accepting this 'tribute' from an honourable enemy, respectfully describes Amphiaraus as

> reaping the rich furrows of his mind from which grow worthy prophecies.
> (593–4)[29]

Eteocles, in turn, complements his Scout's tribute (and further continues
the 'earthy' metaphor) with the explanation of the undeserved fate of this
'just man' as the sad fruit (καρπὸς οὐ κομιστέος, 600) of evil association.
The 'earth images' are given a more sinister aspect as the Chorus sings
of the sources of the primal curse, in the offence of Laius and the birth
of Oedipus:

> father-slaying Oedipus, who sowing the sacred field of his own mother,
> whence he was sprung, a bloody root [ie, a source of bloodshed, especially
> of the two brothers, Eteocles and Polyneices] ... (751–6)

Earth, however, is not only the producer of life but also the receiver
of the dead, and the recipient of shed blood (as Aeschylus frequently
reminds us) when life is spent. The poet saves the most striking of the
metaphors involving earth and its fruits for the Chorus's fear of the fratricidal deed, that 'bitter-manslaughterous-fruit of blood forbidden,'[30] if
they should fail to restrain Eteocles from the seventh gate. The Messenger is soon to fulfil their fear with the news that, though the city is
saved, the brothers have slain one another and 'earth has drunk their
blood.'[31]

One would expect a fair number of 'animal images' in an early
Greek play involving siege and battle descriptions (and the *Septem* is,

---

29 For a similar metaphor and a similar (though not identical) idea, cf vv 617–18: 'but
    he [Amphiaraus] knows that he must die in battle, if there is to be fruit [εἰ καρπὸς
    ἔσται] in the prophecies of Loxias.' See also Sansone's interesting comments, pp 34 ff,
    in this connection. Sansone lists *Sept* 618 with *Ag* 620–1, *Eum* 714 and fr 284a.5–6 as
    examples of truth *being reaped* (or not reaped) from prophecies which come true (or
    don't come true). He argues that a prophecy or a λόγος can grow truth, ie, become
    true, like a seed becoming a tree, or a tree producing olives, in time, when it does
    not have them earlier in the year.
30 πικρόκαρπον ἀνδροκτασίαν ... αἵματος οὐ θεμιστοῦ, 693–4: the tightly compacted meaning
    of the first two words of the Greek here is almost untranslatable.
31 See vv 820–1; these verses have, however, been variously placed and misplaced by
    various editors; see Hutchinson's note to v 804, though I do not agree with him that
    the verses should be suppressed altogether.

in this respect, the most 'epic' of Aeschylean tragedies), but such are not particularly prominent. In their preparations for battle, the Argive attackers are reported (by the Scout) to be sacrificing bulls and dipping hands in their blood, but they are not actually compared with bulls. They *are* compared, in a very conventional simile, to 'lions gazing furious warfare' (53). Snakes, another favourite in the more sinister kind of bestial comparisons, appear in two images: once (in another quite conventional simile) when the Chorus fears the enemy at the walls as some timorous dove fears a snake in the nest (290–4); and once (more strikingly) when Tydeus' battle screams are compared to 'the serpent's noon-day hiss' (381). But attempts to find a 'dominant animal image' in the play are not impressive. One critic finds the attacking Argives particularly associated with equine imagery,[32] but of the few actual horse images occurring, the more vivid ones are used by the female Chorus of themselves: once when they fear being grabbed like horses by the fetlock (328) and once when they speak of their domicile as 'the fillies' quarters' ($\pi\omega\lambda\iota\kappa\hat{\omega}\nu$ ... $\dot{\epsilon}\delta\omega\lambda\dot{\iota}\omega\nu$, 454–5)[33] whence they fear being dragged away.

Other figurative expressions in the *Septem* (such as 'yoke of slavery,' at vv 75, 471, and 'balance-scale,' v 21, for the vicissitudes of war) tend to be of a fairly conventional kind. The same is true of the usual personifications of abstract ideas such as Justice ($\Delta\dot{\iota}\kappa\eta$, at v 662), Curse ($\dot{}A\rho\dot{\alpha}$, at v 70), and familial destiny ($\delta\alpha\dot{\iota}\mu\omega\nu$, at v 705).

There are, however, striking personifications, particularly in the third stasimon, referring to the Curse which is at the heart of the play, to its manner of fulfilment, and to its feared effects. Thus, the primal offence of Laius is described as 'born of old' ($\pi\alpha\lambda\alpha\iota\gamma\epsilon\nu\hat{\eta}$) yet now 'swift of vengeance' ($\dot{\omega}\kappa\dot{\upsilon}\pi\sigma\iota\nu\sigma\nu$) as it abides even unto the third generation (742 ff), and the generation sequence of the Curse's 'frenzied madness' is pictured again as a 'triple-crested wave crashing about the ship of state' (758–61). The fratricide itself is also the occasion of various vivid personifications. First there is the Chorus's fear of the 'never ageing pollution' ($\mu\dot{\iota}\alpha\sigma\mu\alpha$, 682) which would result from it.[34] Then the actual means by which the brothers are to divide their inheritance appears in another veiled, yet vivid, personification:

32 See Cameron *Studies* chap 5, pp 74–80.
33 This is, of course, only a conventional (and possibly male chauvinistic) metaphor (cf Hutchinson's note) of no particular dramatic significance.
34 On this aspect of the pollution from the shedding of familial and other blood, see Hutchinson's note *ad loc*, and the references (including his reference to Parker *Miasma* 104 ff) there given.

> The Chalybian stranger, visitor from the Scythians, divides the inheritance, harsh arbiter of possessions, savage steel ... (727–30)[35]

The same personified expression occurs again in the Chorus's subsequent lament for the brothers, when their fate has been fulfilled:

> Bitter was the resolver of the strife, sharp steel, the fire-forged *stranger* from across the sea ... (941–3)[36]

Here we should note, also, that what is actually a metaphor for the fatal sword as 'a Chalybian stranger,' 'an arbiter from across the sea,' may well have contributed to an original ambiguity, confusing to the brothers, in their father Oedipus' curse upon them. Once again we see (as Petrounias has reminded us), how intimately major themes in Aeschylean drama are related to their imagery.[37]

4 Imagery in the *Supplices*

As with other Aeschylean plays, the close relationship between the imagery of the *Supplices* and its main dramatic theme has been frequently observed. Nevertheless, excessive emphasis on, for example, dominant images reflecting 'the fugitive maidens' theme,[38] perhaps

35 Literally translated, the word (σίδαρος) is 'iron,' though in similar passages cited below the reference is to 'wrought-iron' or 'steel.' The Chalybes, sometimes referred to as a Scythian race, were said to have discovered iron-working.
36 There is also a metaphor (perhaps only a 'dead' one), of a different kind from those being discussed here, in the expression ἐκ πυρὸς, lit., 'sprung from fire.'
37 Cf Petrounias pp ix ff, and his conclusions at pp 310 ff. The *Septem* provides Petrounias with particularly rich examples of the major theme of his own book. Note also Thalmann's comment on the play's use of 'the allotment image': 'In *The Seven*, Aeschylus uses the process of allotment as an image for the duel between Eteocles and Polyneices, in accordance with the terms of their father's curse. He thus distorts the procedure whereby an inheritance would customarily be shared in peace into an expression of the brothers' enmity and doom ... The lot suggests an arbiter – in this case the iron of Ares. One of the technical terms for this mediator implies division, but the division which results is not one of property, as would be expected, but of the brothers' bodies' (Thalmann *Dramatic Art* p 77). On the practice of arbitration in the case of disputed inheritance, see also Hutchinson's note to vv 727–33 and his reference to Thalmann *Hermes* 110 (1982) 385 ff.
38 See, eg, Dumortier chap 1 pp 7 ff, and passim; Stanford chap 4; both these critics choose 'doves pursued by hawks' (cf *Suppl* 223 ff) as the dominant image of the play.

fails to do justice to the particularly rich and imaginative use of figurative language throughout this play. Every aspect of the theme is
illustrated by appropriate images; every fresh development of the
plot, particularly at its most exciting moments, is highlighted by a
flurry of highly visual metaphors and similes. It is true that this
figurative, pictorial style is so characteristic of Aeschylus that there
may be some uncertainty as to how 'conscious' the metaphorical usage actually is, to what degree the poet himself would distinguish
it from his literal descriptions. Such uncertainty would, however, be
justified in only a small number of cases, at the most. The poet's
occasional ironic use of metaphor (to indicate, as we shall see, contrasting aspects of the same situation) and, more specifically, his
choices of appropriate metaphors to emphasize his own mythical adaptations, surely indicate a fairly sophisticated level of technique in this
matter.

   An example of this latter feature may, perhaps, be noted early in
the play. Aeschylus' original use of the Io theme[39] as the basis of the
Danaids' supplication of the Argives seems to explain the unusual
metaphor in the Chorus's initial prayer to the gods of the land and to
'Zeus-of-the-suppliants' that they be received 'with reverent breath of
the land' (αἰδοίῳ πνεύματι χώρας, 28–9). Only a few verses earlier they
have explained their choice of Argos for their refuge as

   the land where our own race had its origin from the gadfly-driven cow [Io],
   impregnated by the touch and the breath [ἐπιπνοίας] of Zeus. (15–18)

And indeed the 'breath image' of vv 28–9 is ringed by this reminder of
the Danaids' claim on Argos when they claim as their champion

   the off-spring of our ancestress, the blossom-browsing *breath-impregnated*
   cow, [Epaphos], the touch-born son of Zeus. (41–5)

   The early references to Zeus as Saviour and ancestor, and the early
images used in connection with him, are benign and gentle (1, 26,
14–17, 41–5). But such descriptions of Zeus soon give way to images
expressing the power and (more troubling) the impenetrability of Zeus'
dark resolve:

---

39 See above, chap 3, on the *Supplices*. Cf also Fowler 'Aeschylean Imagery' pp 16–17,
   for her comments on various relations between the use of 'the Io theme' in this play
   and its imagery.

Not easy to track down is the transcendant will [ἵμερος]⁴⁰ of Zeus. Its ways are murky and obscure and hard for men to understand. Safe and not upon its back it falls, whatever in the mind of Zeus has been determined for fulfilment. In darkness all around it flares forth, boding dark misfortune for mortal men. (87–95)

The Danaids no doubt intend this splendid passage as an expression of confidence that Zeus' will will be exerted against their violent suitors, and indeed a passage following shortly after this one ('Let him [Zeus] look on mortal violence [ὕβριν],' 104 ff) so assures us. But it may be that the poet's intent in having the Chorus use metaphors emphasizing the obscurity as well as the power of Zeus' will is somewhat different from that of the singers. If 'the ways' of Zeus' will are really so 'murky,' it may be that the Chorus themselves do not fully comprehend them and that Zeus' will, which 'falls not upon its back,' portends a future for the Danaids and their suitors different from what the Chorus have in mind.

A similar though perhaps more striking ambiguity may be noted in the use of 'bird imagery,' which also occurs first in the initial statement of the suppliant theme. The Danaids' plaintif comparison (57 ff) of the sound of their lament to the voice of Tereus' wife, the hawk-chased nightingale, leads (as we have seen) to the brilliant little picture of Mêtis, the bird-victim transformed, in time, into a bird of prey destroying her own kin in her destructive fury.⁴¹ Thus, we are prepared, when we come to the Danaids' further comparison of themselves and their pursuers to 'a swarm of doves in fear of hawks, feathered like them, kin-enemies polluting their own race' (223–6), to suspect that these timid victims might also, in time, turn into bloody avengers. What we know of the myth, and of its development in this trilogy, indicates that this indeed turned out to be the case, but the loss of the *Aegyptioi* prevents our knowing whether this sequence was depicted (as it is at *Prometheus Vinctus* 856 ff) through a recurrence of the dove-hawk simile of the present play. Later in the play we are to see a continuation of this bird imagery in connection first with the defenders of the suppliant Danaids and subsequently with their assailants.⁴² (There are also other

---

40 Johansen and Whittle are probably right in rejecting (in their note *ad loc*) any reference to Zeus' desire for Io in this passage; see their references indicating that 'no sexual or affectionate connotations are necessarily inherent in ἵμερος and ἱμείρειν.
41 See above, chap 3, p 83.
42 See below, p 137 on vv 646 ff and 751–2, respectively.

images which are used sometimes in a benign, sometimes in a sinister, context. 'Swarm' (ἑσμός) is used, as one would expect, in a pejorative sense, once of 'the violent swarm of Egyptians' (30), and once of 'the sad swarm of diseases' (683–4), but the term is also used, somewhat surprisingly, of the Danaids themselves at v 223. 'Blossom,' 'fruit,' and 'harvest' images also undergo, as we shall see, a striking change in significance in response to the dramatic context in which they are used.)

As we have noted earlier,[43] the Danaids' initial supplication of the Argive king Pelasgus is not completely successful. Two interesting images appear as the Chorus-Leader begins to apply the screws of persuasion to the King. The first involves a return to 'the ship-of-state' image (originally used in the *Septem*), as the Chorus-Leader points toward the suppliant boughs upon the altar:

Respect the city's stern thus garlanded! (345)[44]

The second, in contrast to this brusque warning, is an unusually extended image, a simile of almost Homeric proportions, which provides a good example of the Danaids' skill at switching from the minatory to the pathetic mode in their appeals:

Behold me, the fleeing suppliant, racing like the wolf-chased heifer amid steep mountain rocks where, trusting in this defence, it lows its woeful message to the herdsman. (350–4)

As the tension surrounding the King's looked-for decision increases, so do the images, both in number and complexity. The King defers his judgment to that of the people's decision (365–9; 397–401), and the Chorus (now singing), sensing that the crucial moment is being reached, intervene with a well-known image for just decision:

Zeus, being kin to both parties, looks down upon these matters, weighing both sides, rightly separating the unjust matters into the scale of the wicked,

---

43 See above, chap 3, pp 90 ff.

44 See Johansen and Whittle's note to *Suppl* 345 for references to the other Aeschylean occurrences of this 'ship of state' image (*Sept* 2–3, 760–1; *Eum* 16, 765). Note also their interesting comments on the, as it were, double metonymy involved at *Suppl* 345, where 'the garlanded stern of the city' stands for the city's garlanded altar but also becomes involved in an implicit 'ship of state' image.

just matters into the scale of the lawful. Since these matters are thus weighed out with due proportion, [why does it pain you?][45] to do justice? (402–6)

The three images through which the King expresses his dread dilemma, his sense of being on the edge of an abyss, are among the most striking in the play. He begins with the simile of the diver:

Now is there need of deep and salutary thought, as the eye, like a diver, peers down into the depths below. (407–9)

This is followed by two depictions of the fixed Necessity in which any decision must plunge the city, first by the image of a ship held inexorably in the launching ways by the windlasses,[46] second by the poignant contrast between 'the arrow which the tongue shoots' (which may be softened) and kindred bloodshed (446 ff).[47]

The climax of this supplication scene is reached with the Danaids' threat (expressed initially by the grim metaphor 'to decorate these altars with tablets of a new kind,' 463) to hang themselves from the altars. It is this that brings about the King's decision (not, of course, to grant sanctuary of his own accord but to seek to persuade the city to do so), which he reaches after expressing his horror in another series of varied metaphors. The Danaids' threat he describes as 'a whiplash of the heart' (466), which has plunged him into 'a deep sea of disaster' (470), and promises 'pollution unsurpassable' (lit. 'which cannot be shot beyond,' ὑπερτοξεύσιμον, 473), though here, perhaps, the conscious metaphorical force of the expression may no longer be present.[48]

The Danaids' great 'thanksgiving ode' (after they have won sanctuary with the Argives) provides further examples (and dramatically more significant ones) of the ironically ambiguous use of imagery which we have noted earlier in this play. All three of the images involved, despite their benevolent context, carry a prophetically sinister significance. In the strangest of these, a return in more sinister form to the earlier bird

---

45 Text is uncertain as to the main verb; cf Johansen and Whittle's text and note.
46 This seems to be the most probable meaning of the admittedly obscure expression at vv 440–1.
47 The comparison is actually left unspoken, as if too awful to mention; instead, the King goes on to indicate how kin bloodshed may be *avoided*, eg, by many sacrifices to the gods.
48 Johansen and Whittle take *ὑπερτοξεύειν, the verb one must supply as the basis of this adjective, as 'simply a poetic variant of ὑπερβάλλειν.'

imagery,[49] Zeus' scout is figured as a vengeful 'watcher-on-the-roof' whose polluting the Argives have avoided by their piety toward the suppliants (vv 646 ff). Yet the pollution will return nearly fifty-fold with the kin-murder of the fifty cousin-bridegrooms. The 'bird of Zeus' image is surrounded on each side by two striking 'harvest images' (632 ff and 663 ff) used in deprecation of Ares, the grim reaper. Both are ironically apposite to the future situation in ways which the singers cannot realize. In the first, Ares is called 'a wanton harvester of bodies in fields tilled by others' (636): a strange conceit whose sexual and murderous overtones suit the conjugal and murderous sequel soon to come; in the second, the Chorus pray further that 'man-slaying Ares,' now called 'Aphrodite's bed-fellow,' may not cull the bloom of Argive youth (663-6). Again, in the sequel, the lustful suitors (Aphrodite's bed-fellows in intent) will indeed spill the blood of the Argives, now sworn to defend the grateful Danaids.

The crisis of the Egyptians' arrival provokes a fresh series of excited images from Danaus and his daughters. The approaching ship acquires a sinister life of its own as it 'gazes ahead with (painted) eye along the forward course and heeds too well the rudder at the stern' (716–18). The ship's occupants, by contrast, are described, by a sort of reverse personification as 'raving dog-bold [κυνοθρασεῖς] creatures' (758) and compared, for their impious minds, with 'crows, which [more 'bird pollution'!] care nothing for the altars of the gods' (751–2). Danaus, however, seeks to reassure the terrified maidens with reminders that ships' captains ('herdsmen of ships') have no confidence in landings after dark. The scene ends with a gynaecological metaphor – 'for the wise pilot, night is wont to produce sore travail' (ὠδῖνα τίκτειν, 769–70), which may again look forward to the travail ensuing from the Danaids' bridal night – for the bridegrooms rather than the brides.

The terrified ode which follows the departure of Danaus (in search of help) provides the most splendid 'escape image' of the play:

> Would that I might become black smoke up among the clouds of Zeus, so that I might perish as I flutter aloft unseen entirely, like wingless dust. (779–83)

As the ode develops, the escapist images ('Where might I find a seat high in the air, where the watery clouds turn to snow?' 792–3) become more literally related to thoughts of suicide ('or a steep crag, lonely,

---

49 Cf above, p 134.

vulture-haunted, unobserved, to witness my mortal fall?' 794–7). But
still the Chorus find consolation in prayers to Zeus-of-the-suppliants
(814–16) and the ode ends with a recurrence of the image, once so
confidently used (402–6), invoking the scales of Zeus' justice (822–4).

Toward the end of the *Supplices*, various images for fruitfulness
make a sudden and somewhat surprising reappearance. Previously
such images have occurred in a negative context, as in the descriptions
(637–8, 665–6) of Ares the grain harvester. Now the images are applied
to the Danaids themselves, as Danaus, directing his daughters to the
shelters provided by the Argives, warns them to behave prudently
among strangers, 'for tender fruit [τερειν' ὀπώρα] is never easy to
protect' (998). The maidens repeat the same image in their reassurance
to their father:

> Fear not, father, about my fruitfulness [ὀπώρας]. For, unless something new
> is being planned by the gods, I'll not turn aside from the earlier track of my
> intention. (1015–17)

Thus, though the context of fruitfulness, as it is now applied to the
Danaids, is still in a sense negative, the last quotation provides a hint,
however unconscious on the Chorus's part, that it may not always be
so. Indeed, these two images prepare us, perhaps, for other, surprising
passages in the final lyrics of the play which emphasize 'fruitfulness'
in less inhibited contexts,[50] first in the Chorus's homage to the rivers
of Argos, 'rich in offspring' (πολύτεκνοι, 1028), 'gladdening the soil
with their fertilizing streams,' and later in the Chorus of handmaidens'
reminders[51] to the Danaids of the charms of Aphrodite and her seductive
acolytes:

> Not unregarding of Cypris is this well-disposed swarm of ours ... For she
> along with Hera is closest to Zeus ... And Desire and Persuasion, to whom
> nothing is denied, follow their dear mother as her acolytes. And to Harmony
> also has been given a whispering share of Aphrodite and the well-worn
> paths of making love [τρίβοι τ' Ἐρώτων] (1034–42)

This song of propitiation to Aphrodite (in which figurative and
literal senses seem insolubly blended) anticipates, as we have seen,

---

50 Cf Fowler 'Aeschylean Imagery' pp 17–20, on the significance of various images
   involving 'blossoms' and 'fruitfulness' in this play.
51 See above, chap 3, p 102.

the revolt of Hypermestra (in the second play of the trilogy) against the aggressively virginal will of her sister Danaids. The modulations which we have just observed throughout the *Supplices* in the images of fruitfulness and their contexts provide us with a striking example of the poet's use of metaphorical language not only to express the themes of his plays but also signal their major dramatic movements.

Apart from their primary function, already stressed, in their immediate context, can we detect in the uses of imagery in these earlier plays any significant features or, possibly, signs of 'development' in these uses?

In the *Persae*, the yoking image (called by some 'the dominant image') does provide a sequence of a limited kind. Thus, the Chorus's early description of Xerxes' intended 'yoking of Greece' is answered, after the catastrophe, by Darius' shocked reaction to what he describes as his son's 'yoking of the Hellespont.' Other recurrent images which we have noted in this play include various images for land (as nourishing, mourning, and burying its youth) and for the sea and its inhabitants (in the descriptions of the disaster suffered by the Persian fleet). None of these recurrences, however, can be called 'sequences' in quite the sense we shall see the term used in descriptions of imagery in the *Oresteia*.

So it is with imagery in the *Septem*. Here again, 'ship and storm images' do provide a kind of sequence, but the images concerned adhere throughout to the same two elements (the city and the warring brothers) of a joint destiny, the one achieving the peace of 'calm waters' only with the destruction of the other.

Something new and exciting seems to happen in the use of imagery in the *Supplices*. Here each new moment in the action, each aspect of the theme as it appears, is expressed, as we have seen, with a fresh flood of images, each uniquely suited to its function. Here, too, we noted the occurrence (for perhaps the first time in extant Aeschylus) of the dramatically ironic use of certain images, where a sinister prophetic sense lurks beneath the ostensible meaning. In the case of 'the bird images' discussed, this double significance resides in images occurring early and late in the play, the sinister meaning becoming stronger in the later occurrence and so leading the audience to speculate on possible future disasters, in the trilogy's development. Such a use does, indeed, involve a 'sequence' but, as with the 'yoke images' of the *Septem*, it involves images situated at the beginning and end of the play, joined, in this case, by the sinister meaning underlying each.

Finally, we may note, in these earlier plays, Aeschylus' love of vivid and imaginative personifications, so characteristic of all his extant work and here applied to such phenomena as the emotions of fear and anxiety and to traditional ethical concerns such as family curses, *hybris, atê*, and the dangers of excessive wealth. Again (though this may be merely an accident of its theme), the *Supplices*, with its descriptions of the mysterious plans of Zeus and of the worried thoughts of the Argive king, seems to show a level of imagination not in evidence before.

5 Imagery in the *Oresteia*

Even a brief indication of some of the dramatic uses of imagery in the *Oresteia* may serve to suggest certain developments of features already observed, as well as some striking innovations, at least as far as we can tell from the small number of earlier plays extant. Here we shall be concerned mainly with the new ways in which images are made to serve the plot and theme of their plays, with new subjects chosen for metaphorical description, and with apparent changes in the manner and even the significance of the comparisons involved.

With regard to the first of these concerns, recent studies of the *Oresteia* have stressed particularly the dramatic deployment of patterns or sequences of images to a much greater degree than we have observed in the earlier plays. These are repeated (so critics have claimed) in such a way as to reflect the changing moods of the three plays and, in some cases, the changing fortunes (both within individual plays and in the trilogy as a whole) of the house of Atreus.

William Scott has provided an excellent example of this approach.[52] He sees all the passages, whether metaphorical or merely descriptive, involving 'wind' or 'breath' as a sort of dynamic sequence, which he describes, towards the end of his discussion, as follows: 'The wind is not merely an image: it is inextricably involved with the dramatic events. It follows each person in reaching the point at which he commits his unfortunate act; and once he has committed it, it turns to accompany and even aid the avenger of this act.' Individual readers of the *Oresteia* will, no doubt, have their individual quibbles with this account.[53]

---

52 See Scott 'Wind Imagery in the *Oresteia.*' For a very different kind of discussion of 'wind images' in the trilogy (and elsewhere in Aeschylus) see Van Nes pp 7–29.

53 Thus, exception might be taken to Scott's treatment (at pp 463 ff) of *Ag* 187, where he includes the description of Agamemnon's 'breathing with the sudden blasts of [mis]fortune' (my translation) as one of several examples where the wind 'follows each person in reaching the point at which he commits his unfortunate act.' But it is clear from the context (both the lines immediately preceding and those immediately

On the whole, however, Scott succeeds in demonstrating this poetic cooperation of image and 'reality,' from (to provide a few examples) the adverse winds of Strymon (*Ag* 219 ff) and Agamemnon's 'breathing from out his mind the unholy ... change of wind' (*Ag* 219–20); through the Chorus's song, prospering Orestes' vengeance 'by blowing on it with favouring wind' (*Choeph* 819 ff [?]); to the converted Erinyes' final prayer for beneficent breezes over Athens (*Eum* 938), when all has been resolved.

J.J. Peradotto's rather more ambitious study of several kinds of 'nature imagery' in the *Oresteia*[54] also stresses the close relation between this imagery and the action of the trilogy. Like Scott, Peradotto also combines both metaphorical and actual descriptions of nature in his treatment. In this connection, Peradotto speaks of archaic literature as showing 'explicit awareness that the benevolence or hostility of nature *depends upon* the moral decisions of men, especially the rulers,' and of Aeschylus as seeming 'to be most archaic in his use of nature imagery.' 'Nature in the *Oresteia*,' he continues, 'both actual and as metaphors of internal states, appears in a pattern consonant with and asserting the movement of the entire trilogy.' Peradotto proceeds with a brilliant demonstration of three types of 'nature imagery' (at least as he has defined it), 'Vegetation,' 'Weather,' 'Light and Darkness,' which show initially sinister, then gradually improving or redeemed, and ultimately (by the end of the *Eumenides*) beneficent aspects of nature *pari passu*, as it were, with the progression of the tragic plot and theme.

Both Scott's and Peradotto's studies seem to indicate that, in the matter of patterns or sequences of imagery, the *Oresteia* does show a marked advance in a technique which we have noted as gradually developing in the earlier plays. Still, both studies tend to err, perhaps, in casting their nets too widely, or else in forcing *some* images too

---

following v 187) that the 'winds,' or the '[mis]fortunes,' which Agamemnon is here represented as 'breathing with,' or accepting, are the adverse winds of Aulis, not some other, metaphorical winds of fortune which the critic imagines as bringing Agamemnon *to* Aulis. Cf also Van Nes p 15, who also understands that it is Agamemnon's reaction to the adverse winds encountered at Aulis which is being referred to here.

54 Peradotto 'Some Patterns of Nature Imagery in the *Oresteia*'; see p 378 for the following two quotations. (In addition to the articles by Scott and Peradotto, I have found the following studies particularly useful for discussion of imagery in the *Oresteia*: Porter 'The Imagery of Greek Tragedy,' Lebeck *The Oresteia*, and the works of Moreau and of Petrounias cited in n 1 to this chapter.)

rigorously into the suggested patterns. In many cases, Aeschylus' use of a given image can best be described in terms of the poetic need of the moment, of the poetic response to a particular situation or kind of situation. (In this respect, the dramatic uses of imagery are similar to those noted in the earlier plays, especially the *Supplices*, except, perhaps, that the *Oresteia* provides more striking examples of Aeschylus' mastery of this technique.) 'Storm and shipwreck images,' for instance, are often used in paradigms for crucial moments of disaster in a man's career; in some cases there is little to be gained, critically speaking, in seeing them as part of a pattern specifically related to the larger theme of the play. Thus, at *Eum* 553–65, the Erinyes, as part of their warning that they should not be set aside, depict the lot of the transgressor calling, when disaster strikes, upon the gods, as one struggling in a shipwreck; however, the emphasis of the image here lies in its development, on the laughter of the god as he looks down upon the helpless wretch, once so arrogant and boastful. This splendid image belongs to its context alone. It loses its point if it is forced into an alien sequence (that is, as part of an image-pattern of storm-tossed vessels representing the house of Atreus).

In contrast to the 'patterns' or 'sequences' which we have been considering in the *Oresteia*, we may note the use of the same or similar images to provide quite different effects in several different contexts. A good example (among several) of this is the use of the archery image in the *Agamemnon* to convey the accuracy of Zeus' aim against Paris (at *Ag* 363 ff); to express the Chorus's pondering of the right meed of praise for their returning King ('... neither overshooting nor falling short of the right amount' (*Ag* 786–7); and finally to phrase Cassandra's ironically triumphant question ('Have I erred? or like some bowman have I hit the mark?' (*Ag* 1194), after she has recounted for the Chorus the primal curse upon the house of Atreus. (With these occurrences we may contrast the still further contrasting uses of 'bow imagery' at *Choeph* 380–1 and 1033 and at *Eum* 676.)

The varied uses of 'the chariot-racing image' illustrate a virtuosity of a still more striking kind. This image appears first in Clytemnestra's ironic warning to the victorious Argives at Troy that 'they must still bend back along the other stretch of the double course, before arriving home in safety' (*Ag* 343–4). But the image is used to far greater dramatic (and poignant) effect to express the crucial balance between reason and madness in Orestes' desperate experiences of matricide and its aftermath. Before the matricide, Orestes has been likened by the Chorus to a young colt yoked to a chariot of woe (*Choeph* 794 ff). But it is *after* the matricide, as Orestes desperately seeks to justify his deed before madness seizes him, that the charioteer image finds its most vivid fulfilment:

> ... like one carried off-course as he drives his chariot-horses, my crazed wits over-master me and carry me away! (*Choeph* 1022–4)

(This last use of imagery which we have noted has, perhaps, been anticipated to some degree, in the *Supplices*, where we have noted the contrasting effects which the poet has achieved, in contrasting circumstances, with his bird images, and his images for harvests and fruitfulness.)

Personifications, which have always been a rich source of metaphor in Aeschylus, run riot in the *Oresteia*. Abstract ideas, including weal and woe and what we would call virtues and vices, striking events such as murder and bloodshed, emotions and various psychic states, are all given, at one time or another at least a fleeting animation and perform exciting actions within the brief compass of their figurative life. One of the most celebrated examples occurs in the great ethical coda to the second stasimon of the *Agamemnon*. Anticipations of the imaginative conceit here involved have, to be sure, occurred in the earlier extant plays, most notably in the *Persae*, at vv 93 ff [= 111 ff, West] and at 821 ff. Nevertheless, there is a certain exuberance in the great sequence at *Ag* 750 ff not seen before in such personifications. Here, the Chorus illuminate their argument that not excessive prosperity but evil deeds of violence cause familial disaster by clothing both the rejected and the new belief in one long, slendid metaphor. *Hybris* and 'the impious deed,' rather than wealth and prosperity, are endowed with the power of creating offspring like themselves, but the fate of just houses is seen to be blessed with fair and noble progeny. Other abstractions, such as Justice (*Dikê*), which is described as 'looking askance' (*Ag* 777) at homes with ill-gotten gains, also receive particularly vivid personalities in the *Oresteia*'s imagery.

While several of the personifications of social and ethical concepts (wealth, *hybris*, *atê*, and the like) have already appeared, though in perhaps less vivid form, in the earlier extant plays, there are a few others appearing in the *Oresteia* which seem to break new ground, at least as far as, with our limited knowledge, we can tell. These include the vivid picture of 'the last old age' (*Ag* 79 ff) and the poetic series of metaphors involving time' (*chronos*), which is pictured as 'growing old' at *Eum* 286 and, at *Ag* 894, as 'sleeping with' Clytemnestra during her allegedly lonely nights of Agamemnon's absence. A still more unusual conceit occurs at *Choeph* 965–8, where time is made to represent all the pollution which has occurred during its passage and so to be expelled, along with the slain usurpers, from Agamemnon's palace![55]

These few examples, then, must suffice to suggest the ways in which the personifications found in the *Oresteia* strike one as more imaginatively conceived than in the earlier extant plays.

In the introduction to this chapter, I have noted the recognition by several critics of the tendency of some Aeschylean images to be transformed, as the action of the play or the trilogy progresses from the metaphorical to the actual; a prime example of this tendency (as has also been noted) is the development of 'the net image' in the *Oresteia*.[56] Here the image also undergoes a tragic declension from the triumphant to the catastrophic,[57] as it is transformed from 'the net of slavery' cast over Troy (*Ag* 360–1), through Clytemnestra's gruesome imaginings about her husband's battle-wounded body ('more riddled than a fishing-net,' 868), to its literal fulfilment in the confining meshes of the murder-robe ('the net of Hades,' as Cassandra calls it, *Ag* 1115) in which the Queen ensnares her victim.

A related feature of this 'actualization sequence' (though not an inevitable concomitant of it) is that, as the image moves closer to reality, metaphors may be replaced by the more direct comparisons of similes. Once again, the prime example is to be found in the *Oresteia*. The hunting and tracking images which appear in metaphorical contexts in the *Agamemnon* (368, 1184–5) are succeeded in the next play by the similes of Orestes' escaping 'like a fawn' (*Eum* 111) and of the sleeping Furies whimpering like a dog (*Eum* 131–2), till finally image and reality almost blend when the Furies keep sniffing along Orestes' bloody trail (*Eum* 244–7).

The terms 'development' and 'innovation' which have been used in the foregoing summary of Aeschylus' uses of imagery must always be accepted with two major reservations, if, indeed, they are acceptable at all. One is the obvious one (which has been alluded to several times in the course of our discussion) that we have an insufficient number of

---

55 'Time which fulfils all things will soon pass through the doors of the palace, when from the hearth the whole defilement is driven away by cleansings which expel disaster.' (*Choeph.* 965–8)

56 See above, p 117 of this chapter; Porter in particular illustrates this feature by reference to 'the net image' in the *Oresteia*.

57 Cf Lebeck p 63.

Aeschylean plays for us to be sure of what is an 'innovation' in any given play, or to recognize with any certainty a clear line of development of any given technique. The second is, of course, the equally obvious fact that the particular dramatic needs of individual plays or trilogies must dictate, to a considerable degree, the kinds and uses of images chosen for each of them. Nevertheless, I think it has been possible, within these limitations, to observe certain similarities and differences in the uses of imagery in the plays which we have considered, and to suggest certain trends and developments observable, in this matter, between the earlier extant plays and the *Oresteia*.

6 Imagery in the *Prometheus Vinctus*

(As has been observed in the Preface, uncertainties about all or parts of the *Prometheus Vinctus* [and, I might add, particularly the un-Aeschylean features which have been noted of its choral odes, where the richest use of imagery might be expected] must qualify expectations of significant similarities or developments in the use of imagery in this play, when compared with other plays of the Aeschylean corpus.)[58]

After the glories of the *Oresteia*, readers of the *Prometheus Vinctus* (if they happen to read them in that order!) may regard its use of imagery as something of an anticlimax.[59] Ever Dumortier's praise for the skilful deployment of the play's alleged principal metaphor, 'the harness of

58 On the question of the authenticity of the *Prometheus Vinctus*, see Griffith, *The Authenticity of the Prometheus Bound*; on his treatment of the Chorus of the *PV* in this connection, see esp pp 123 ff. Cf also my *Aeschylus: Prometheus Bound*, appendix 1, for a summary of Griffiths's and other views of 'the authenticity question.' (I am, however, no longer impressed by my own suggestions, ibid pp 147–8, of possible explanations of the apparently 'un-Aeschylean' features of the choral odes of the *PV*.)

59 Several commentators on Aeschylean imagery take a much more positive view of this aspect of the *Prometheus Vinctus* than that suggested in this section. Dumortier, chap 4, pp 56 ff, thinks that the play anticipates some of the metaphorical effects of the *Oresteia*, though he should not perhaps be criticized for the probable error in dating, as it would now appear, involved in this judgment. Earp, p 121, counts no fewer than one hundred and ten metaphors in the play, forty-seven of which he lists as 'striking'; here we must simply agree to differ from this critic's criteria and, perhaps, from his method of approaching the subject (cf chap 5 of his study). Fowler, 'The Imagery of *Prometheus Bound*' pp 173 ff, introduces an excellent discussion (to which we shall return) of medical metaphors in the *Prometheus Vinctus* with the somewhat extravagant statement that the drama 'exists ... in the play's imagery.' Even Petrounias, as we shall see (below, n 62) shares some of the enthusiasms of Dumortier and Fowler, cited above.

Prometheus,' and its development by related expressions, turns out to be rather misleading. Obviously, the theme and plot of the play require numerous references to binding and associated expressions; however, by no means all of the terms which Dumortier insists on in this connection are used metaphorically, and of those which *are* so used, not all are used of Prometheus.[60] Indeed, it is not until Hermes' vivid description of Prometheus near the end of the play as 'a newly-yoked colt biting the bit and fighting the reins' (1009–10), a passage which Dumortier describes as presenting 'la métaphore principale dans toute sa netteté,'[61] that 'the harnessed horse image' for Prometheus is fully expressed at all.

It is easy to mistake the images which a reading of the *Prometheus Vinctus* conjures up in one's mind – and which are, indeed, conveyed by vivid descriptive language – for imagery in the stricter, figurative sense involving comparisons (for the most part implied), with which we are at present concerned. Imagery of this kind is not particularly prominent or striking in the *Prometheus Vinctus*. There is not, *pace* Dumortier and Petrounias,[62] really a dominant metaphor in the play, or even a marked sequential pattern of metaphors such as we find in the 'ship and storm images' of the *Septem*, or the 'fugitive images' of the *Supplices*, or the 'light and darkness images' of the *Oresteia*. Medical imagery certainly comes closest, in the *Prometheus Vinctus*, to comparable status, and the two last-named critics tend to rank it as the play's dominant motif. As Fowler has noted, 'sickness' ($\nu\acute{o}\sigma os$ and $\nu\acute{o}\sigma\eta\mu a$) is used both of

---

60 See Dumortier pp 59 and 64–7 for his list of words which he regards as contributing to the play's leading metaphor, 'the harness of Prometheus.' Of these, $\psi\acute{a}\lambda\iota o\nu$, 'curb-chain,' occurs once (at v 54) and $\pi\acute{e}\delta a\iota$ ('fetters') twice (at vv 6 and 76), both of Prometheus but in a *literal* sense; $\chi a\lambda\iota\nu\acute{o}s$, 'curb' or 'bridle,' is used in a metaphorical sense (at 672), but of Zeus' threat to Io's father; $\sigma\tau\acute{o}\mu\iota o\nu$, 'bit,' is used in a completely literal sense by Ocean, at 286–7; it is finally used metaphorically of Prometheus at v 1009; $\acute{\eta}\nu\acute{\iota}as$, 'reins,' used in connection with Prometheus at v 1010, is perhaps faintly metaphorical. Cf also Moreau p 65 and nn 4 and 6, who quotes Dumortier with approval on this metaphorical emphasis in the *Prometheus Vinctus*. Even so, the expressions which Moreau selects (in n 4) to illustrate the 'shackled horse' metaphor, as he calls it, all occur in the first 176 verses of the play, and many of the 'bondage descriptions,' metaphorical and other, referred to in nn 4 and 6 show no specifically equine connection.

61 Dumortier p 95.

62 For Dumortier, see the preceding notes; for Petrounias's views on this matter, see Petrounias pp 98 ff and 108 ff, where he describes *der kranze Arzt* ('the sick doctor') and *das neuangeschirrte Fohlen* ('the newly yoked colt') as the two leitmotifs of this play.

the indignation of Prometheus at Zeus (977–8) and for what ails Zeus himself, in that Prometheus declares that 'the disease of tyrants is to forget their friends' (224–5).[63] Certainly the most interesting medical passage occurs in the brief dialogue ending the scene between Ocean and Prometheus, when Ocean describes words as 'the healers of a distempered spirit' (ὀργῆς νοσούσης, 378), and Prometheus reminds him that they must be administered at the right time; that 'one must not seek to reduce a swollen spirit by force' (καὶ μὴ σφριγῶντα θυμὸν ἰσχναίνῃ βίᾳ, 380).[64] However, the various medical metaphors, striking as they are, are restricted to a few passages: 224–5; 377–85; 472–5; 977–8. It *may* be that illness is hinted of Prometheus in order to qualify the audience's admiration for the Titan's heroic revolt against Zeus; and of Prometheus *and* Zeus, in order to suggest that some change of attitude on the part of both will be needed before reconciliation can take place. Nevertheless, one feels that the 'medical metaphors' in the *Prometheus Vinctus* represent the new 'scientific,' or perhaps merely sophistic, way of looking at things at the time the play was composed,[65] rather than that they present a significant symbolic image or leitmotif for the meaning of the play as a whole.

Attempts to discuss other images in *Prometheus Vinctus* by their subject-matter reveal that there is really no significant sequence or thematic relation between members of the same group, though several subjects familiar from other plays recur. The sea provides six unrelated images. Of the two most effective of these, one provides Io with a frenzied ending to her scene ('My wild words beat at random against the waves of fell destruction!' 885–6), the other announces the approaching cataclysm ('What a storm and triple wave of ills will come upon you!' 1015–16) which is to sweep Prometheus himself away at the end of the play. So, too, a 'ship image' provides the Chorus with one of the most significant questions ('Who then is the helmsman of Necessity?' 515) which they are to ask in the play. Of 'vegetation metaphors' (another favourite Aeschylean type) we find three such uses of ἄνθος, 'blossom,' at vv 7, 23, and 420, none of them a particularly brilliant image. Animals

---

63 See Fowler 'The Imagery of *Prometheus Bound*' pp 174–8. She makes the wise reservation, however, that νόσος as 'hatred of the gods' is not necessarily metaphorical (p 174).

64 See ibid for comments on the significance of these and similar terms in contemporary medical thought.

65 Whether by Aeschylus or not, *Prometheus Vinctus* was almost certainly not composed before the mid-450s and was quite possibly composed later than this. See above, n 58, and references there given.

(also favourites elsewhere in the Aeschylean corpus) supply a wide variety of images from the vivid though mixed metaphor describing Typho's volcanic eruptions ('rivers of fire devouring the smooth plains of Sicily with savage jaws!' 368–9) to the banal description of primitive man living 'like little ants' (452–3) in caves. In between these extremes we find two rather colourless 'dog metaphors' (at 803–4 and 1022), the fine image (1009–10, already quoted) for the rebellious Prometheus, and the sinister 'aural metaphor' for thunder (again of the final cataclysm) as a particularly formidable kind of cattle lowing (βροντῆς μύκημ' ἀτέραμνον, 1062).

We do not find in the *Prometheus*, as we have in certain other plays at which we have looked (most notably perhaps the *Supplices* and the *Septem*), that there is an outbreak of brilliant metaphors at particularly dramatic or descriptive passages in the play. Despite the imaginative range of Io's wanderings and the vivid accounts of Prometheus' sufferings, there are in these passages only a few metaphorical images which linger in the mind's eye. One of these occurs in Prometheus' *captatio* of the Chorus's sympathy, as he bids them alight and listen to his woes:

> ... for trouble, in its wandering, tends to settle [πλανωμένη ... πημονὴ προσιζάνει] now on one of us, now on another. (275–6)

Another describes the eagle, the 'winged bird of Zeus,' which Hermes describes as 'a daily uninvited guest' which will soon be gnawing at the great rag of Prometheus' body (1021–4).

Personifications are also of a somewhat different kind in the *Prometheus* from those of other Aeschylean plays. Though comparatively few, there are some excellent ones involving the sights, sounds, and other effects of natural forces, for instance, 'the tireless stream' of Ocean (139–40), 'swift-winged breezes,' and the lovely, if almost untranslatable, expression ποντίων τε κυμάτων ἀνήριθμον γέλασμα ('the numberless smiles of the rippling sea-waves,' 89–90). Another personification worth noting is 'harsh stepmother of ships' (727), a tersely effective description of 'the harsh sea-jaw of Salmydessus' (726). But one misses the brilliant animations of abstractions-made-concrete (in, for example, the depictions of *Hybris* and *Atê* at *Persae* 821–2, 96 f, respectively, and at *Agamemnon* 763–71); of the emotions, such as that of Fear, which is both 'dream-prophetic' (*Choeph* 33) and 'making the hair-to-stand-on-end' (*Choeph* 32); and of other human weaknesses, such as 'sleep and weariness, dread conspirators' (at *Eum* 127). Time, it is true, 'grows old and teaches all things' even in the *Prometheus* (981), but this favourite subject of Aeschylean personification is given much richer treatment elsewhere by the poet (see, for example, the elaborate conceits at *Ag* 893–4, 984–7 and at *Choeph* 965–8).

For the rest, the great majority of images in *Prometheus Vinctus* are of a fairly conventional kind, as when, for example, Zeus is described as 'warmed by the shaft of love' (649–50), or when the Chorus speak of Io's woes as 'chilling their souls' (692–3). Many of the play's metaphors are limited to single words, usually adjectives (such as 'iron-minded Zeus,' or Prometheus' 'whetted words') or verbal expressions (such as when Prometheus is said to have been 'chastened' or 'controlled' [ἐρρύθμισμαι, lit. 'measured out,' 241] or not to have been 'melted' [τέγγῃ] or 'softened' [μαλθάσσῃ] by Hermes' prayers, 1008.) (Some of these usages – and there are numerous examples of this kind in the *Prometheus* – had perhaps become sufficiently commonplace for them to be ranked as 'dead metaphors'.)[66] Thus, while the language of the *Prometheus* is still highly figurative, in the 'elevated' style of Aeschylean tragedy, it tends to lack, apart from certain splendid exceptions already noted, the consistent metaphorical excitements which so often illuminate the dramatic high points of Aeschylean plays.

66 On 'dead metaphors,' see Silk *Interaction in Poetic Imagery* pp 27 ff.

CHAPTER FIVE

The Chorus

1

Of the various characteristics of Greek tragedy, none reflects the ritualistic elements in its origins as clearly as the songs and dances of the
Chorus. As Walther Kranz has shown (at least with regard to the use of
the Chorus), Aeschylus' dramatic art stands at the boundary between
ritual and drama, and Kranz has illustrated this point by several observations of ways in which Aeschylus has exploited, in secular contexts,
various originally ritualistic or 'cultist' elements.[1] It is true that in some,
though by no means all, of these observations, Kranz, like other earlier
commentators on Aeschylus' use of the Chorus, was misled by the belief
that the *Supplices* was the earliest, and so the closest to pre-dramatic
ritual, of the extant tragedies. Since the correction of this early dating
of the *Supplices*, and of consequent misconceptions based on it about
the *dramatic* importance of the Chorus in the earliest Greek tragedies, it
is generally agreed that the conventional and perhaps the original use
of the Chorus was to provide comment and lamentation on the tragic
action.[2]

1 Kranz *Stasimon* pp 127 ff. Elements which Kranz particularly singles out for comment
   in this regard are the use of parallel or repeated expressions (such as were originally
   used, perhaps, in magical formulae) for emphasis or decoration; various examples
   of triplicity in the deployment and structure of choral odes and thematic passages;
   the thematic harmony or parallelism between the anapaestic introduction and the
   lyrics of the *parodoi*; the hymn-like subject matter, and sometimes even 'naming' (as
   in ὕμνος ... δέσμιος φρενῶν, *Eum* 331–2; cf 306) of certain odes, eg, threnodies, and
   songs of praise and thanksgiving.
2 See above, chap 3 (on the *Supplices*), p 76 and references, esp to Garvie, *ad loc.*

Thus, laments such as we find at *Septem* 875–960, *Persae* 908–1077, and in 'the great kommos' of the *Choephori*, 306–478, and also, perhaps, hymns of praise and thanksgiving (as at *Suppl* 625–709 and *Eum* 916 ff), probably reflect the most traditional forms of choral activity in Greek tragedy. Signs of the traditional nature of the laments appear in their antiphonal or (in the case of the *Choephori* passage) kommatic form and, again in the latter case, in the actual terms θρῆνοι ἐπιτυμβίδιοι (*Choeph* 342) and τίμημα τύμβου (*Choeph* 511).[3] Consequently, one would not expect these passages to represent Aeschylus' more original uses of the Chorus. Nevertheless, in the case of the kommos of the *Choephori*, the poet certainly adapted the threnody so that it became a dynamic element in the development of the vengeance action. There the Chorus uses this medium to lead Orestes from his matricidal decision to the deed itself: 'Mourning becomes revenge,' as one critic has put it.[4] And in the case of the choral benisons at *Suppl* 625 ff, the poet invests the prayers for Argive good fortune with sinister overtones anticipating hidden catastrophes to come.[5] In both cases, then, the poet enriches choral passages of conventional mourning and thanksgiving, respectively, with meanings more specifically relevant to the dramatic action of the play or the trilogy.

Another effective dramatic deployment of the Chorus by Aeschylus is its use, early in the tragedy, to instil in the audience a sense of foreboding, of impending doom. This the Chorus may do by direct expressions of concern (as in the worries of the Persian elders, in the *Persae*, at the long absence of the army); or, more effectively (again in the *Persae*), by the dramatically ironic use of Aeschylean 'danger words' (such as ἰσόθεος, 'equal to god,' πολύχρυσος, 'rich in gold'), even in passages where the Chorus is seeking to buoy up confidence in the one to whom they are applied; or (finally) in the slow but inexorable

---

3 In connection with these two points, cf also Kranz *Stasimon* pp 12 and 135, respectively. For the view that 'the song of benediction is one of the old forms of religious poetry which Aeschylus embodied in his tragedy,' see F. Solmsen *Hesiod and Aeschylus* p 211, and above, chap 3, on the *Supplices* n 38.

4 For this feature of the kommos of the *Choephori*, and for the phrase 'mourning becomes revenge (*Klage wird zu Rache*),' quoted from Reinhardt, see my *Aeschylus' Oresteia* chap 2 (on the *Choephori*), section 3.

5 See chap 3 (on the *Supplices*), pp 94–5. On the comparison of the above-mentioned passages from the *Supplices* and the *Eumenides* as examples of 'the song of benediction ... one of the old forms of religious poetry which Aeschylus embodies in his tragedy,' see the reference to Solmsen in n 38 of this chapter on the *Supplices*.

movement of an ode from an opening full of confidence to a gloomy or even despairing close. Striking examples of this last, more extensive, device occur in the parodos of the *Persae* (as we have seen) and in the early odes of the *Agamemnon*.[6]

Similar to this 'foreboding' device is what might be called, for want of a better expression, the 'atmospheric' use of the Chorus, that is, its use to convey to the audience a sense of *immediacy*, usually fraught with awe or terror, with regard to the particular dramatic situation, the dramatic moment, even, in which the Chorus find themselves. Perhaps the most vivid example of this use is to be found in the parodos (78–180) of the *Septem*, of which the primary effect must surely be to transport us within the walls of the besieged city of Thebes, there to share the near hysteria of the Chorus of Theban women as they shrink before the threatening advance of the attackers.

A similar sense of disaster about to strike is achieved, in a very different context, at the beginning of the third stasimon of the *Agamemnon*, as the Chorus watch the King treading the purple tapestries into the palace:

> Why this persistent fear, hovering and fluttering before my mantic heart? Unbidden and unpaid, my song sings a song of prophecy, and confidence sits not at my heart's throne to spurn these fears away like murky dreams. (*Ag* 975–83)

> With my own eyes I've seen him safely home, yet still my spirit, self-taught, within me hymns its lyreless Fury-chant. (*Ag* 988–94)

'Premonitions of disaster' are also achieved by the Chorus's evocations of dangerously significant moments in the past of the doomed figure in the play.

> When he put on the yoke of necessity, breathing the impious, impure, unholy changing-wind of his mind, from that moment he changed direction to ponder the most outrageous deed. (*Ag* 218–21)

> Then [raised aloft], with her saffron robe trailing the ground, she smote each of her sacrificers with the piteous weapon of her eye, appearing, as in a painting, as if she longed to speak ... (*Ag* 239–43)

6 Cf above chap 1 (on the *Persae*) and chap 1 of my *Aeschylus' Oresteia* (on the *Agamemnon*). Cf also Rosenmeyer *The Art of Aeschylus* p 151.

It is by such immediate word-pictures as these that the terrible moments in Agamemnon's past are injected into the bloodstream of the tragedy.[7] Indeed, evocations of the past, whether of individual heroes or of past generations, are a particularly recurrent feature of Aeschylus' use of the Chorus. Such passages are rarely provided simply for the case of giving 'background information' to the audience; rather, time and again, the past is shown to be, as it were, a present element in the dramatic action and in the tragic meaning of the play. As Aeschylus well recognized, it is only through his choral lyrics that such connections can be so powerfully and 'immediately' effected.

Rather different from this use of the Chorus to evoke the past is its use, in several plays, to introduce 'mythical analogies' to the dramatic situation. Sometimes, as when (at *Choeph* 603 ff) the Chorus rehearses the deeds of legendary 'wicked Women' along with Clytemnestra's, the dramatic application of these mythical elaborations is pointed and intentional. Sometimes, as in the Danaids' self-comparison with Mêtis, the 'hawk-chased [but ultimately vengeful] nightingale' (at *Suppl* 58–67) or in their songs of Io's wanderings and liberation (at *Suppl* 524–99), the analogies to the singers' own careers will, ironically, prove closer than they realize. Sometimes, again, as in the Argive elders' celebration (at *Ag* 355–402) of the justice of Zeus overtaking Paris and the Trojans, the full significance of their song for the present action is left for the audience to infer.[8] What seems important to realize, in the case of these and similar passages, is that 'extra-dramatic myths' are seldom mere decorations in Aeschylean choral songs and usually have a significant relation to events and persons in their tragedies.

Aeschylean choral odes have also been traditionally celebrated for passages of religious fervour (such as the praises of Zeus sung at *Suppl* 590 ff and *Ag* 160 ff) and for passages of ethical grandeur or social and political admonition, such as we find at *Ag* 750 ff and *Eum* 526–37, respectively). Such passages should not, however, be regarded as hymns or sermons, separable from their context. Whether or not the poet agrees with them, they are usually very much the Chorus's own reflections, suited to the particular moment at which they are sung in the play,

7 Kitto (*Greek Tragedy* pp 72–3) was one of the first critics to express clearly the function of the Chorus in the *Agamemnon* in making the audience 'feel that the Past is an active factor in the Present.'

8 For more detailed discussions of the passages mentioned see (on *Choeph* 603 ff) my *Oresteia* chap 2, pp 115 ff; (on *Suppl* 57–67 and *Suppl* 524–99) above chap 3 p 83 and pp 91 ff; and (on *Ag* 355–402) my *Oresteia* chap 1, pp 17 ff.

and for this reason, they are more easily discussed in their dramatic context.[9]

There is, however, one curious exception to these generalizations about the 'moralizing' passages in Aeschylean choral odes: there are several passages concerning the dangers of wealth which do not seem as closely relevant in their dramatic context as do the passages just mentioned. This is not, of course, true of the play exhibiting the most obvious examples of excess and its attendant dangers. In the Chorus's descriptions (replete with unconscious irony) of Xerxes and his expedition in the early songs of the *Persae*, the poet exploits the traditional Greek attitudes to wealth and ostentation as a major way of building tragic expectation in his audience. In the *Agamemnon*, however, and even more so in the *Septem*, there are choral reflections about wealth which seem to fit their respective dramatic themes less well.

In the *Agamemnon*'s best-known passage about wealth, the Chorus make a sharp distinction between *their* view and the traditional one: it is not 'wealth grown great' which begets insatiate misery but rather 'the impious deed' (τὸ δυσσεβὲς ... ἔργον), the hybristic act, which produces more violence and, ultimately, disaster (see *Ag* 750–71). Here the Chorus's observations do indeed express the tragic theme: it is not the wealth of Agamemnon (or his family) but his impious deed (and that of his father) which begets his ruin (compare the Chorus's earlier description of Agamemnon's intent at Aulis, φρενὸς πνέων δυσσεβῆ τροπαίαν, 'breathing the impious changing-wind of his mind,' *Ag* 219). Nevertheless, the topic of morally dangerous wealth creeps back, in one guise or another, in the same play and even in the same ode. 'Justice shines in smoky hovels,' sing the Chorus at 776–7, 'leaving with averted eyes houses gold-encrusted with ill-gotten gains' (σὺν πίνῳ χερῶν). However, in *this* disparagement of wealth, 'the ethical element' is still preserved.

Other passages in the *Agamemnon* suggest, without qualification, that wealth is dangerous. There is, as we have seen, a passing reference to wealth in the first stasimon (at 374 ff) when the Chorus associate excessive wealth with excessively warlike activity, a critical attitude to wealth which they continue in the next stanza with the reminder that wealth provides no defence against divine punishment for injustice. Finally, in the third stasimon, in one of the nautical metaphors favoured by Aeschylus, the Chorus sing of the possibility of avoiding the dangers

---

9 See below, section 2 of this chapter; cf also above, in the chapters on the plays concerned.

of too much property by jettisoning some of the cargo, whereas no such remedy is to be found in the case of 'blood once shed' (*Ag* 1008–21).

Thus, despite the disavowals in the 'ethical coda' to the second stasimon, the theme of 'dangerous wealth' does seem to keep recurring in the play. Yet, unlike the case of Xerxes in the *Persae*, the downfall of Agamemnon (who enters just after the deprecation of unjust wealth at *Ag* 776 ff) is not significantly related to his wealth. And even Paris, whose punishment along with that of the Trojans is the occasion of at least the first of the references to the dangers of excessive wealth (at *Ag* 373–7) suffers primarily for his offence against 'Zeus of the guests' (see vv 362 ff and 369–72). Could it be that, in having his Chorus regularly include 'excessive wealth,' whether fully relevant or not, in their ethical deliberations, Aeschylus is following, consciously or unconsciously, conventional thought patterns of his age?[10]

Another choral comment on wealth, this time from the *Septem*, tends to support this rather bold hypothesis. The Chorus sing thus, in the second stasimon, of the fate of Oedipus:

> For the fulfilments of the curses spoken long ago involve bitter reconcili-
> ations. But disaster bypasses the poor [reading πενομένους].[11] The wealth
> [ὄλβος] of gain-seeking men, when grown too great, requires casting over
> the stern. For what man have the gods or fellow citizens or the thronging
> crowds of his age honoured as greatly as they honoured Oedipus ...?
> (*Septem* 766–75)

Now wealth or prosperity, in the form of material goods which could be jettisoned, can hardly be called a causative factor in the downfall of Oedipus. Again one is tempted to wonder whether the Chorus's

---

10 Cf my *Aeschylus' Oresteia* chap 1 (*Agamemnon*), pp 28–9 and nn 56, 57, 59 and
   references there given. (Denniston and Page's note [in their edition of the *Agamemnon*]
   on *Ag* 757–62 is particularly useful for references to sixth- and fifth-century Greek
   authors on the subject of wealth, in various contexts, in relation to the downfall of its
   possessor.)
11 Hutchinson rejects Bucheler's emendation πενομένους (at *Septem* 768) on the grounds
   that it 'produces a very strained connection between this clause and the clause
   before, and ... spoils the connection of the following stanza with this ....' But the
   allegedly intrusive element provided by πενομένους (ie, concerning the greater safety
   of the poor over the rich) is in any case introduced in the next sentence. Moreover,
   some such statement as that provided by reading Bucheler's πενομένους is needed to
   give point to the following sentence, as the translation of this passage as given above
   will indicate.

opinion here does not simply reflect a conventional association of excessive wealth with any disaster which befalls the great.

In general, then, Aeschylus' treatment of religious and ethical themes, like his treatment of the myths antecedent or comparable to the dramatic situation, shows a close relation to theme or the action of his plays. Only occasionally, as in the case of a few passages just discussed, does the poet allow his ethical generalizations to acquire conventional or traditional overtones at the expense of dramatic relevance.

Having considered, however superficially, a number of specific dramatic uses to which Aeschylus put his Chorus, we may turn now to one or two larger questions which must always vex modern readers, unfamiliar as we are with the theatrical conventions which an ancient audience would unthinkingly accept.

To what degree (we ask ourselves) does the Chorus in an Aeschylean tragedy have a more or less consistent dramatic personality, or at least a specific dramatic function, tailored to the theme and structure of its particular play? To what degree, on the other hand, does the poet use the Chorus in a similar way (with allowances for special cases like the *Supplices*) in his plays generally, making only the simplest adaptations (such as 'male,' 'female,' 'citizens,' 'sympathetic visitors,' and the like) to suit the dramatic situation?

Among recent commentators, Rosenmeyer has addressed these questions, particularly the initial ones mentioned above, most seriously. Several times throughout his chapter on the Chorus in Aeschylus he repeats, in different forms, his conviction that there is something which may be called a 'choral voice' common, in some sense, to all Aeschylus' plays (or at least to all the plays which we know).[12] This common choral voice Rosenmeyer relates on the one hand to the function of the Chorus as a sort of middle-man, with whom the audience could to some degree identify, between the play and the audience;[13] and on the other hand to their role as commentator on the action of the play, a function including the giving of information, the direction of the audience's sympathy, and the like.

Rosenmeyer does not, of course, deny some element of individual 'choral personality' attaching to individual choruses in different plays,

---

12 See Rosenmeyer chap 6, passim, esp pp 145–6, 164–9, 171–5, for the major point in his discussion to be considered here.

13 Ibid pp 145–6: 'The audience recognizes in the Chorus an institutionalized part of itself, a delegate ... of the community, connecting the two worlds without removing the barrier necessary to maintain psychic distance.'

but he believes that Aeschylus is quite ready to let the Chorus abandon such dramatic personalities (even, as at *Eum* 490 ff, in the case of such marked ones as that of the Furies in the *Eumenides*) when he wishes to make use of the Chorus's 'community voice' (which seems often to be what he considers the Aeschylean 'choral voice' to amount to). This view tends to lead (at least in some contexts) to the identification of the 'community voice' with 'the voice of the poet,' but Rosenmeyer is rightly cautious on this point. He rejects Wilamowitz's view, for example, that in the parodos of the *Agamemnon* the poet states the religious and ethical views which are to be our guide in appreciating the drama. Nevertheless, he suggests (reasonably, it seems to me) that both at *Eum.* 919 ff and at *Eum* 490–565 the Chorus express thoughts and sentiments with which the community would be in hearty agreement. Another passage where Rosenmeyer believes that the Chorus's 'community voice' replaces that of their dramatic personality occurs at *Suppl* 1034 ff, where in contrast to the strongly virginal line which they have previously followed, the Chorus revert to 'the typical choral insistence on the wrongness of excess.'[14]

For the most part, however, the Aeschylean chorus, in Rosenmeyer's view, functions successfully enough as 'the voice of the community' *within* its dramatic personality. In the case of the *Agamemnon*, he argues reasonably that the Chorus's inconsistencies (that is, with regard to their criticism and subsequent praise of the King) are not out of keeping with the sort of inconsistencies which citizen bodies, even conservative ones, often manifest. In the case of the Chorus in the *Choephori*, he stresses that their counsels of vengeance really express the proper 'community view.'

Rosenmeyer's views have been summarized at some length here because, though we may not agree with them in all their applications, he raises several important problems of perspective which the modern reader faces when confronted by Aeschylean choruses. His view of a common choral personality as a sort of 'voice of the community' is shared by several critics, especially with regard to Aeschylus' earlier plays.[15] It contrasts, however, with Aristotle's view of the Chorus:

14 Ibid p 174–5. (We will return to the question of the identity of the singers at *Suppl* 1034 ff later in this chapter; see below pp 175–6.)
15 See, for example, Kranz *Stasimon* pp 162 ff, who describes the Chorus of the *Persae* as 'not individuals but the voice of the people.' Cf also Dale 'The Chorus in the Action of Greek Tragedy' pp 17–27, most of whose points about the Chorus (though admittedly she is not speaking specifically of the Aeschylean chorus) emphasize its dramatic limitations.

The Chorus ought to be regarded as one of the actors and be a part of the whole and take part in [συναγωνίζεσθαι] the action, not as in Euripides but as in Sophocles. (*Poetics* 1456a25–7)

Whatever qualifications one may feel inclined to make about Aristotle's rather general prescriptions here,[16] they do, I think, point us in the right direction, that is, toward viewing the Chorus as very much a part of the dramatic situation, and the dramatic structure, of its play, and not as simply, or even primarily, reflecting the conventional reactions of the community to that situation. Thus, in the case of Aeschylus, the poet provides his Chorus with the kind of group personality which the theme and action of the play require, and just so much or so little 'characterization' as is needed to complement the properly 'dramatic' roles played by the actors.[17] So, too, the needs of the dramatic action and of the audience's understanding of the theme will take priority over our nice modern concerns regarding inconsistency on the part of the Chorus, though the poet will usually attempt to mitigate or to justify, in one way or another, any major contradictions in attitude or sentiment which the Chorus may be required to express at different moments in the dramatic development.[18]

2

Some illustrations from various plays may now help to clarify the foregoing generalizations. Since it is the dramatic requirements which tend to dictate the way in which the Chorus is used, the comparative date of the plays concerned will not be a major consideration in determining the sequence of these illustrations.

The *Septem* provides an excellent example of Aeschylus' skill at suiting (or limiting) the group characterization of the Chorus to the needs of the action. It is this group characterization of the Chorus of terrified women which occasions, in the early odes, the vivid cameos

16 The context of this passage (which concerns 'plot' and the exclusion of material irrelevant to it) would appear to indicate that Aristotle is concerned here more with the integration of the Chorus with the tragic action than with any precise equation between the Chorus and 'one of the actors.'

17 This aspect of the Chorus's subordination to the formally dramatic element is, of course, in keeping with the primacy of the dramatic action on which Aristotle so rightly insists (*Poetics* 1450a19–24).

18 We might find this to be the case at, for example, *Suppl* 1034 ff, *Ag* 799 ff, and *PV* 1036–9, 1063 ff.

of 'the city besieged' and (in their fevered imaginings) of 'the city captured' which we have seen to play a major part in highlighting the significance of Eteocles' later decision to defend the city at all costs. This characterization of the Chorus is also essential to the characterization (still of a fairly elementary kind) of Eteocles, for it is the Chorus's hysteria which provokes the expressions of stern discipline and resolute confidence so typical of the commander-in-chief. Once the Chorus have fulfilled these dramatic functions and have failed (at their most dramatically active moment) to restrain Eteocles from confronting his brother in battle, they are free to play a more conventional choral role in the latter portions of the play. Abandoning the wilder, dochmiac measures of the earlier odes for quieter, mostly iambic, metres of the second stasimon,[19] the Chorus now dwell on the family curse (which they review while its last fulfilment is taking place offstage) and, when the fatal news arrives, sing lamentations for the fratricidal pair. This change in function on the part of the Chorus requires, in this instance, only a minor change in the way in which they are presented, but it is indicative of the kind of change in their dramatic personality which the Chorus may undergo to suit the changing requirements of the dramatic action.

Of equal importance is the contribution of the Chorus to the structural design of the *Septem*. The fate of the *polis* and the fate of the doomed brothers are the two poles in the themes of this play, and the Chorus plays an essential part in their demarcation. Its contribution here has been well expressed by Oliver Taplin's comment on the two songs (the first and second stasimon) on either side of the so-called *Redepaare*, the long and crucial exchanges between Eteocles and the Scout: '... the shift in choral emphasis reflects the thematic shift of the whole play. The fear in the earlier song ... was for the city and the women themselves; in the later song ... the fear is for the brothers and the race of Laius.'[20] As Taplin has also observed, this significant choral framing is further

19 The first strophic pair of this ode (720–33) on the mythical background of the play is in ionic verse, but the remaining four strophic pairs are mainly in various iambic metres. The choral lamentations after the death of the brothers are also mainly iambic. Readers wishing fuller metrical discussions of these and other Aeschylean choral odes should consult Dale 'Metrical Analyses of Tragic Choruses' and, for a brief summary of Dale's analyses, Webster *The Greek Tragic Chorus* pp 112 ff. See also the excellent studies of Scott, Rash, and Chiasson to which references will be made later in these notes, in connection with various aspects of Aeschylus' uses of lyric metres in relation to the themes of his odes.

20 Taplin *The Stagecraft of Aeschylus* p 166 and, for the following point, p 167.

emphasized by additional structural features, each ode being preceded by epirrhematic, then stichomythic, passages followed (in the second instance after a brief speech) by the exit of Eteocles.

The *Persae* is the most formal and, as it were, impersonal play which we have from Aeschylus: its action seems to proceed at more than one remove – as is to be expected in view of its *muthos* – from the audience in the theatre. Partly for this reason, its Chorus is the least individualized of all the choruses in the extant plays (including the *Prometheus Vinctus*, of dubious estate). Here, indeed, the Chorus do express 'the voice of the community,' in this case, of the Persian elders left at home when Xerxes and the army go to war, and there will be no occasion, within the relatively simple structure of the *Persae*, for any major departures from that voice. Nor are the Chorus of the *Persae*, concerned citizens though they be, as closely involved in the action of the play as are the Chorus in the *Septem*, for what the dramatist requires of them is something very different from the 'atmospherics' and hysteria provided there.

The Chorus do, however, play an essential part in the formal structure of the *Persae*, marking (sometimes alone, sometimes in subordinate cooperation with one of the characters) the successive phases – anticipation, fulfilment, retrospection. and, finally, exhibition – in the presentation of the Persians' tragedy. Thus, in the parodos the Chorus provide, as we have seen, a nice blend of confidence in Persian magnificence and sombre premonitions of the disaster which that magnificence is to bring; in the kommos shared with the Messenger of that disaster, and in the lament which follows the Messenger Speeches, the Chorus reflect the community's reception of the catastrophic news; in the two odes surrounding 'the Darius episode,' the Chorus first prepare us, in the second stasimon, for the arrival of that ghostly figure and then, in the third stasimon (sung in stately dactyls), look back regretfully on the prosperous empire of the former King; finally, in their kommos with Xerxes 'the Hades-filler' (923–4), the Chorus, completing a sort of vast ring-composition, rehearse the fates of the various glorious leaders whom they had celebrated so heroically in their opening anapaests.

It is interesting that in a play which presents the tragic theme of *koros-hybris-atê* more starkly than any other Greek tragedy, the Chorus themselves indulge in no overt moralizing. The hint of danger in the emphasis, in the parodos, on Persian gold and luxury, is a dramatically ironic one, not consciously imparted by the Chorus. In the first stasimon, when the Chorus ask, rhetorically, why Darius, in contrast to Xerxes, remained scatheless, they do not provide an answer, moralistic or of any other kind. (Indeed, the only explicit suggestion of 'the voice of the poet' occurs, in a different context, when [at 584–97] the Chorus celebrate, in terms more suited to Athenian democrats than to loyal Persian elders, the destruction of the royal power and the freedom of the people from its yoke.)[21] So also, in the final kommos with Xerxes, the Chorus bewail the glance of heaven-sent *Atê* (1005–7) but do not relate it to Xerxes' *hybris*. Instead, we hear from the Chorus's relentless questioning of Xerxes about the fate of various individual heroes, a regular roll-call of the dead, to balance the general picture of their heroic magnificence in the parodos. This, and the appearance of Xerxes, once called ἰσόθεος (80), makes the point for the Athenian audience, in dramatic and spectacular terms rather than by choral moralizing.

Nevertheless, despite the dignified formalism which we have accorded to the chorus of the *Persae* as it supports the perfect structural balance of its play, we should not forget that it also provides some of the most quietly moving passages to be found in Aeschylus' lyrics. Two of these, among several, may perhaps be quoted again to remind us of this: one from the Chorus's description of the lonely wives as they await news of their absent husbands:

> Marriage-beds are drenched with tears of longing for absent husbands, and Persian wives, each softly grieving for the eager spearman she sent to war, are left in single loneliness. (*Persae* 133–9)

and one from the choral lament after the disaster has been announced:

> And Persian wives, weeping softly with longing to see their bridegrooms, abandon the delicately woven sheets of their marriage beds wherein they took their youthful joy, and mourn with grief insatiable. (*Persae* 541–5)

The Chorus of *Prometheus Vinctus* has often been assailed for its 'un-Aeschylean features,' most notably, perhaps, for the brevity, and the lack of poetic inventions and thematic development, of its choral odes. In the context of this discussion (which is not, in any case, primarily concerned with the authorship of the play), let us leave aside

---

21 Other critics have, of course, made this or similar points about this curiously 'out of character' passage from the Chorus at *Persae* 584–97. Cf Broadhead's note *ad loc* and references there given, especially to Kranz (p 88), who regards this passage as the invention of the poet and contrasts it with Atossa's words at vv 213–14. On the possible significance of this contrast, see Schenker, 'The Queen and the Chorus in Aeschylus' *Persae.*'

these aspects of the *Prometheus*'s Chorus and concentrate on the nature and consistency of its dramatic personality and on the part which it plays in the structure and thematic development of the tragedy.

The 'group personality' of the *Prometheus*'s Chorus is of a simple but on the whole consistent kind; they are the gentle, very feminine Oceanids, who come, full of sympathy and some curiosity, to visit Prometheus, suffering on his lonely crag. This role they sustain, with some interesting variations and perhaps one surprise, to the end of the play. Indeed, whatever this Chorus may lack in other respects, they fill their dramatic role admirably. Moreover, they depart less from their dramatic 'group personality' than any other Aeschylean chorus: what inconsistencies they may be thought to show are the fluctuations, and changes in attitudes, which a dramatic character might be expected to exhibit at different stages in the action.

The chief dramatic function of this Chorus, and the one which is most helpful in aiding its limited, yet powerful, dramatic development, is that of helping, as a sort of midwife of the emotions, in the self-revelation of Prometheus, and of the meaning of his struggle with Zeus. Prometheus is silent before his persecutors in the Prologue, and even in his opening soliloquoy, telling us he can neither be silent, nor not be silent, about his fortunes (106–7), he reveals only the bare bones of his offence against Zeus. It is only through the gentle prompting of the Chorus ('this company which approaches you in friendly wise,' 128–30) that Prometheus is gradually prevailed upon to make the great series of avowals (his services to gods and men and the particularities of his offence against Zeus) which inform the first half of the play. While it is through the sympathy which the Chorus express in song that they succeed in reaching Prometheus, we should not neglect the role played by the Chorus-Leader. It is she, in default of any other character available to do so (Oceanus arrives to fulfil a very different function), who makes the first specific request for information ('Reveal everything ... tell us!' 193–6); more strikingly, it is the Chorus-Leader again, who presses Prometheus, in two highly charged passages of dialogue (246 ff and 515 ff), to be more explicit on two essential matters. The first of these concerns Prometheus' particular gifts ('blind hopes' and 'fire') to mortals; the second, which Prometheus is not yet prepared to divulge in full, the possible limitations of Zeus' power. This function of the Chorus and the Chorus-Leader as catalysts for revelations which are themselves an essential part of the dramatic action, is, I think, unique in Greek tragedy, but it arises quite simply and naturally from the needs of the dramatic situation.

When these revelations relating to the past of Prometheus have been completed, the Chorus hand over to Io their role of principal catalyst in the action, but not before they have repeated the advice, previously but more tentatively advanced at the end of the parodos (at 178 ff), to bow before the superior power of Zeus. This they do in the first stasimon (526–60), an ode sung, for two stanzas, in the solemn dactylo-epitrite metre,[22] expressing more fully than elsewhere in the play the Chorus's own pious submission to the ruler of the universe. In the final stanza the Chorus (somewhat abruptly) sing of happier days when their song was in celebration of Prometheus' wedding to Hesione. This rather strange adversion to a marriage theme serves to introduce the sudden arrival of fugitive Io, fated to be the bride of Zeus: a thematic frame which the Chorus are to complete in the brief third stasimon, after Io rushes madly from the scene.

In the central part of the play, it is Io who becomes Prometheus' chief interlocutor but even here it is partly through the Chorus's interjections (see vv 631–4 and 782–5) that the subtle interweaving of Io's and Prometheus' fates, and of the past, present and future times involved, are so skilfully effected.

The other main function of the Chorus in the *Prometheus Vinctus* is that of urging moderation in their advice to their rebellious friend. In these passages, to be sure, the Chorus do seem to be speaking with the conventional wisdom and piety of 'the voice of the community,' the 'common choral voice' described by Rosenmeyer. Nevertheless, even here the poet has a dramatic surprise in store for us. True, the Chorus keep up their 'voice of moderation' even in the face of Hermes' threats to Prometheus, but then, at the last minute, when Hermes warns them to stand clear or suffer with Prometheus the icy avalanche of Zeus, they throw in their lot with their friend:

Sing me some other song which will persuade me ... With *him* I wish to suffer what must be. For I have learned to hate false friends the most, and betrayal more than any other bane. (1063–70, in part)

22 Webster (*The Greek Chorus* p 131) comments: 'the stately metre is probably chosen to contrast with the wild monody of Io which follows it.' However, the fact that this metre (the dactylo-epitrite) occurs in no other extant play of Aeschylus has, of course, provided one of the arguments (though not, perhaps, one of the stronger ones) against the authenticity of this play. See Griffith *Authenticity* chap 3, pp 40–7, where the problematical metrical analysis of the second strophic pair, 545–60, is also considered.

Though some have found a startling inconsistency in these two reactions,[23] they actually represent the two functions which the Chorus have maintained throughout the play: the reasonable 'community voice' familiar from other Choruses and the more 'personal' voice of sympathy which we have seen to be so necessary in breaking through the silence of the suffering god. And in the end, perhaps, they provide as well a signal, if one is needed, to the audience that, however much Prometheus may have willed his own catastrophe, we too are to stick with him in the end. Thus, whatever the choral odes of the *Prometheus* may lack (for one reason or another) in thematic grandeur and poetic effectiveness, the actual contribution of the Chorus should not be underestimated. Indeed it is difficult to see how the play, whose 'second actor' is repeatedly used for visitors with their own specific functions, could have achieved a successful dramatic structure without the Chorus's role.

The three plays of the *Oresteia* provide an excellent opportunity to view within a single related whole several of the different ways in which Aeschylus can use his chorus, in each play, both as a dramatic instrument helping in the advancement of the plot or in the deployment of his characters-in-action and as a medium for expressing themes fundamental to the play or to the trilogy.

It has been observed that the female Choruses of the second two plays (the *Choephori* and the *Eumenides*) play an increasingly aggressive role in their plays, in contrast to that of the Chorus of elderly males in the *Agamemnon*; however, this is not, I think (as has also been argued), in order to aid the alleged contrast between the 'powerful, resolute, intelligent, violent' females of the trilogy and the 'hesitant, ineffectual' males.[24] It is hard to see how such a contrast would aid the poet in his expression of the ultimate victory and vindication of the male avenger. The poet merely uses his Chorus in each case simply in response to the dramatic needs of the play: it is in these terms, rather than in terms of significant gender contrasts, that we should seek to explain the radical

---

23 Cf Taplin, *Stagecraft* p 271, who regards the two passages, 1036 ff and 1063 ff, as a particularly blatant example of inconsistency on the part of the Chorus. Cf also his references to Dawe *HSCP* 76 (1972) p 91 f on the same point. See also Griffith, *Authenticity* p 135, who regards the alleged inconsistency of the Chorus at this point as destroying 'the continuity and credibility of the Chorus as characters,' and as one more argument against the Aeschylean authorship of the play. Cf also his comment in his *Prometheus Bound*, note on vv 1063–70.

24 See McCall 'The Chorus of Aeschylus' *Choephori*' pp 17–30; for the second point cited above, see p 27.

differences in the group personalities of the three Choruses of this trilogy.

The main theme of the choral odes of the *Agamemnon* is retribution, the sins of the past catching up with the present, and the main dramatic effect of this theme is to switch the mood of the Chorus (and of the audience) from a sense of optimism and triumph to that of the inevitability of coming catastrophe. In the parodos, for example, this motif is first set up by the treatment of the sacrifice of Iphigenia and its mysterious motivation. Typically of the choral technique of this play, the ode opens with rousing description, in heroic dactyls, of the marshalling of the expedition against Troy and an account of the apparently auspicious 'omen of the eagles' at Aulis, heralding the eventual sack of Troy. Then, suddenly, all is clouded by the prophet's warning of Artemis' anger, and now the Chorus, quoting Calchas, ranges murkily from hints of the coming sacrifice of Iphigenia back to the other child-murders, by Atreus, and forward, again only by veiled expression, to the vengeance of Clytemnestra:

> ... [Artemis] speeding on another sacrifice, some lawless and unsavoury one, a fashioner of strife growing as the race grows and fearing not the husband. For the fearful, late-arising, treacherous house-keeper abides, the ever-watchful, child-avenging wrath. (*Ag* 149–55)

Switching sharply from the splendid dactyls of the opening stanzas, the Chorus now sing, in a series of (trochaic) *lecythia*, the so-called Hymn to Zeus (160–83) in which (at least as I interpret this passage) the singers find consolation, for the dreadful events foreshadowed, in Zeus' harsh prescription that it is by suffering that man reaches understanding. From here on, the ode acquires an increasingly gloomy and despondent tone. Even before the second pair of trochaic stanzas is over, we are back again at Aulis and (as the metre changes once more, this time to lyric iambics)[25] the Chorus sing the whole bitter story of Agamemnon's dilemma and the sacrifice of Iphigenia, to end with the

---

25 The metrical shifts in this ode (mainly from dactylic to trochaic *lecythia* to lyric iambics) seem particularly significant in relation to the themes introduced; indeed, particularly in the case of the last two metres, they are thought to be indicative of Aeschylus' use of dominant metres in the trilogy as a whole. Scott *Musical Design in Aeschylean Theater* p 38 claims that in this ode: 'the two thematic meters of the trilogy have been clearly defined and established, each within a context: lecythion for humanity's progression under the kingship of Zeus, and iambic for the infatuation that leads men to sin and punishment.' Certainly the two

repeated solemn reminder that justice brings knowledge to those who have suffered.

Similarly, in the first stasimon, the Chorus (after it has learned of Agamemnon's victory) moves by a series of transitions from triumphant celebration of the justice of Zeus on Paris and the Trojans to sing of the people's curse and the wrath of the gods against Agamemnon. In the second stasimon, Helen as Zeus' seductive instrument of destruction against the Trojans prefigures Clytemnestra's temptation of Agamemnon, in the following scene, to tread the purple tapestries to his doom. Finally, in the third stasimon, as Agamemnon enters the palace, the Chorus, after abandoning all confidence (in the first strophic pair) hints darkly at the inevitable consequences of 'blood once shed.'

Overt dramatic action by the Chorus is, of course, far more limited in the *Agamemnon* than it is in the following two plays of the trilogy: it is not what the Chorus is needed for in this play. Even so, the Chorus do have a group personality and certain problems do arise in blending the Chorus's thematic role (with its lofty strains on the justice of Zeus, preparing us for Agamemnon's doom) and their more immediate dramatic role as the loyal subjects of the King. In their latter capacity, they seek, somewhat tentatively (at 788–98), to warn the King of dangers at home, and here the Chorus make a gesture at smoothing over the inconsistency of their present loyalty with their earlier criticism of the war and of the sacrifice of Iphigenia:

> When you first raised the military expedition for Helen's sake, you were regarded, for I'll not hide it from you, in no friendly way by me, as not directing the rudder of your mind aright when by certain sacrifices you gave heart to starving men. But now I feel a deep and abiding good-will for those who have successfully accomplished their undertaking.[26] (*Ag* 799–806)

From this point on (during the scene with Cassandra, during the off-stage murder of Agamemnon, during the epirrhematic and

---

metres to which Scott attaches particular significance (*lecythion* and iambic) are indeed used, though not perhaps as exclusively as he suggests, for the themes which he assigns to them. Inevitably, however, qualifications will be suggested to such broad claims as these. Chiasson, for example, in 'Lecythia and the Justice of Zeus,' though agreeing with much of Scott's approach, tends to regard 'the justice of Zeus' and 'sin and punishment' as one theme, and to associate it with *lecythia*.

26 I have followed Page's text here; see Denniston and Page's notes on the uncertainties of vv 803–4 and 806.

kommatic scene with Clytemnestra after the murder, and during the final scene with Aegisthus) the Chorus are entirely consistent as the King's loyal supporters. During the off-stage murder, the problem of consistency does, to be sure, arise again, in a somewhat different form: intervention seems required by the elders' stated loyalty to the King: non-intervention by choral convention. Once again, the poet seeks to preserve a semblance of dramatic probability, this time by means of a delaying action: the twelve *choreutae* each advance a different view of what should be done until the Queen with her murdered victim appears on the *ekkuklêma* and it is too late for *anything* to be done.

In the long epirrhematic passage with Clytemnestra (1407–1576) which follows the Queen's vaunt over the bodies of her victims, the Chorus again perform a useful dramatic role, moving Clytemnestra, by their outrage and by their threats of citizen fury against her, from bold declarations of sole responsibility to defensive claims that she is merely the instrument of the family curse.[27]

In the final scene with Aegisthus, the Chorus-Leader provides, at least to the degree allowed by convention and by the Chorus's age, sufficient motions of loyal resistance against the usurpers to allow the Queen to intervene and bring the action of the play to a close amid rebellious mutters presaging the action of the coming play.

In the *Agamemnon*, then, the most important contributions of the Chorus, especially in the earlier part of the play (where the dramatic shape of a tragedy is usually decided), operate above and around the action itself: great odes highlighting significant moments in the past of Agamemnon, and hymning the inevitability of Zeus' justice and of retribution for blood once shed. Only in the latter parts of the play do the Chorus, sometimes through the Chorus-Leader, begin to play some part, as loyal champions of the King, in the dramatic action of the play; even here, as we have seen, the poet takes some pains to keep this role consistent both with the conventions limiting choral intervention and with the more generalized choral voice of the earlier odes.

This relation of the Chorus to the theme and action of the play is almost reversed in the *Choephori*. Here the Chorus play a very active role, at times almost dominating the youthful avengers in the earlier scenes but later turning to more conventional choral functions (possibly

---

27 Contrast Clytemnestra's speech immediately after the murder, esp vv 1379–87, with 1497 ff. Cf my *Aeschylus' Oresteia* chap 1 (on the *Agamemnon*), pp 48 ff, and my paper 'Interaction between Chorus and Character in the *Oresteia*' pp 324–30.

better suited to their group personality in this play) during and after the execution of the murders.

The device of having the action of the play begin with the Chorus carrying libations from Clytemnestra to appease the spirit of the King is a brilliant dramatic idea, for we have seen that in this play songs of mourning shared between the Chorus, Electra, and Orestes around the King's tomb are to be converted into vengeance. The identity of the Chorus is also well suited to these functions: it is natural that household slaves with access to the Queen's bed-chamber should attend Clytemnestra when she is startled from her sleep by the ominous dream. Thus, it falls naturally to this Chorus (along with Electra) to bear the propitiatory libations to Agamemnon's tomb and later to be the ones to inform Orestes about the content of Clytemnestra's dream. The leading role which the Chorus play during the actual conversion of mourning to vengeance in the great kommos is also to be explained in terms of the dramatic requirements: their relative aggressiveness here helps in preserving a suggestion of innocence, or at least reluctance, on the part of the matricidal avenger. (Here it is important to think of the *Choephori* as part of a trilogy as well as a tragedy in its own right, for Orestes is to be acquitted in the final play.)[28]

The parodos provides appropriate preparation for this role which the Chorus are soon to play: here lamentation for the King encircles the Chorus's songs of Clytemnestra's dream and the sure vengeance which must follow 'blood once swallowed by the nurturing earth' (66). In the first episode, the Chorus-Leader herself initiates that vengeance with her brisk instructions to Electra to pray (as she pours the libations) 'for one who will kill, in requital, those who have killed' (121–3). But it is the great kommos (306–475), shared between the Chorus, Electra, and Orestes, which of all Aeschylean passages must be regarded as the one which best represents 'choral action.' Here it is the Chorus which, at every turn (in the initial anapaests and in the lyric triads), keep directing the initially hesitant Electra and Orestes to vengeance and to goading their father's ghost to help in that

---

28 These explanations concerning what some have felt to be the unusually active role to be assigned (here and later in the play) to a Chorus of slave-women seem more natural and 'dramatic' than that suggested by McCall (see above, p 164 and n 24). (I agree with McCall, however, on one point concerning the identity of these 'household slaves' of the Chorus: that they are not, in all probability, Trojan captive women, or, at any rate, that there is nothing to indicate that they are.)

vengeance.[29] And even when the great kommos is over, the Chorus still continue their active role in telling Orestes the content of his mother's dream (and so providing him with the final fillip to the matricidal deed) and in directing the Nurse, Cilissa (contrary to the orders of Clytemnestra), to bid Aegisthus to hurry home alone, without his guard (766–73).[30]

In addition to this unusually active participation, the Chorus of the *Choephori* also fulfil a more conventional function in their various songs showing sympathy and support for the central figure. Here, too, however, it will be noted, the Chorus are more consistently partisan than elsewhere in extant Aeschylus, anticipating the actions and in places even the language of Orestes and celebrating his final victory. Thus, the first stasimon (as we have seen) provides us with a splendid example of the use of the Chorus to enlarge the dramatic situation by the use of mythological paradigms, painting a vivid series of pictures of female monsters 'whose loveless passion ... defeats the paired unions of men and beasts alike' (599 ff).[31] But the main dramatic purpose of this ode is surely to mitigate, for the audience, something of the horror of Orestes' deed by placing its victim firmly in the midst of this mythological rogues' gallery. So, too, the combined appeal to Justice and to violence in the final strophic pair ('For the sake of Justice trampled underfoot the sharp sword strikes,' 639 ff) insists still more emphatically on the 'justification' of Orestes, even as the final stanza of this ode introduces (albeit a shade ambiguously) the avenger himself, who is now about to make his entry:

The famed Erinys, deep-plotting, now ushers the son into the house, to avenge the pollution of ancient blood-shed. (648 ff)

The second stasimon is concerned mainly with prayers to the gods for the success of the deeds of vengeance now about to be attempted. Again

29 See my *Aeschylus' Oresteia* chap 2 (on the *Choephori*), pp 108 ff, and references there given, for more detailed interpretations of the great kommos.
30 Garvie comments (in his note to *Choeph* 730–82): 'The Chorus is obeying Orestes' orders (cf 581–2 n) but its interference in the plot is still a surprising and unusually bold use of the Chorus as an actor in the drama.' A comparable intervention of the Chorus may be found at Euripides' *Ion* 756–62, 780 ff, where the Chorus-Leader reveals to Creusa that the Oracle has bestowed Ion on Xuthos as his son, and so triggers the (ultimately forestalled) murder plot against Ion.
31 For fuller discussion of this ode, see my *Aeschylus' Oresteia* chap 2, pp 115 ff (on the *Choephori*).

the Chorus's close identification with 'the young master' is, perhaps, suggested by their choice of imagery in their prayer to Zeus (789 ff) to set 'a saving rhythm' to the pace of the 'orphaned colt [Orestes] now yoked to a chariot of woes,'[32] for the image anticipates Orestes' own image for his incipient madness, after the matricide, when he likens himself to a charioteer driving his team of horses far off course (1022–3). Mingled with these prayers are images of 'the light of freedom' (809 ff) and of fair sailing with favouring wind (821) with which the Chorus hopefully anticipate a victorious outcome. But at the end of the ode, the Chorus return again, at least for a moment, to their hortatory role (827–30), anticipating Pylades' advice to Orestes (900 ff) to ignore maternal pleas, when the dread moment of action finally arrives.

The final ode (the third stasimon, 935–71) is a victory ode, pure and simple. As we have seen, themes and images from earlier in the play and the trilogy now reappear in triumphant form, and Justice (*Dikê*) and Apollo (rather than *Erinys* and the darker powers from Hades) are celebrated as the coadjutors of Orestes' vengeance. Images of light and liberation dominate the Chorus's final refrain:

> Now is the light plain to be seen, for the great curb has been lifted from the halls and the house looks up again! (961–3)

It is in the *Eumenides* that Aeschylus displays his most striking and original *dramatic* use of the Chorus in the trilogy and possibly in all his extant plays. Here, as in the *Supplices* (and in no other extant Aeschylean play) the Chorus's dramatic personality and treatment is central to the tragic action of the play. Orestes, his trial and acquittal, are, in one sense, the focus of that action and of the resolution of the larger action of the trilogy as a whole. But just as the theme of the trilogy transcends the fates of the individuals concerned (of Iphigenia, Agamemnon, Clytemnestra, Orestes), so too the resolution of the larger theme, the evolution of a new order of justice, centres more on the poet's treatment of the Chorus of Erinyes than on dramatization of Orestes' acquittal.

This treatment has already been fully discussed in the various studies of the *Eumenides*. In this context, it will suffice to recall its major features to illustrate the poet's skill in combining, for the most part successfully, a strong dramatic characterization of his Chorus with its use to express,

---

32 Garvie, however, rejects this 'usual interpretation' (as he calls it) of this sentence; see his note *ad loc.*

with the directness possible only in the lyrical part of the drama, ideas essential to its theme.

In the *Eumenides*, then, the Chorus's dramatic personality emerges first as a vampire-like version of the Furies, single-minded in their pursuit of Clytemnestra's murderer; develops gradually into a collective force defending social order of every kind; returns, during the trial scene, to its more specific function as avengers of the Queen; and is finally transformed, after Athena's persuasions, into benevolent (though still potentially punitive) guardians of society.

The great central ode, the second stasimon, marks an essential transition point in this development, though there have been anticipations of the more 'institutionalized' Erinyes in the preceding ode.[33] It is in the second stasimon also that the poet succeeds in introducing, as part of the Chorus's 'in character' warnings against the acquittal of Orestes, certain social principles championed by them which are to remain operative (even after the acquittal of Orestes and the subsequent placation of the Furies) under the new dispensation of justice instituted by Athena:

> There is a place where dread [τὸ δεινόν] should abide as guardian of men's minds. It is fitting that by constraint man should learn the ways of wisdom [σωφρονεῖν ὑπὸ στένει]. (*Eum* 517–21)

These expressions of the Chorus's own sentiments at this dramatic moment of the play anticipate, as well, words of Athena in her address to her new court during 'the Trial Scene': 'awe and its kindred fear on the part of the citizens shall restrain them from unjust deeds' (690–2).

It should be admitted, however, that some of the political and ethical generalizations in this ode do strike one as 'out of character' utterances for the Chorus, particularly at this juncture in the play. When they sing, 'Praise neither the anarchic nor the despot-ridden life' (526–8), and 'violence [ὕβρις] is the off-spring of impiety but from moral health of mind comes prosperity much loved by all' (533–7), we do feel that the sentiments involved belong with the general ethical admonitions found elsewhere in Aeschylus[34] rather than with the more characteristic utterances of this particular Chorus. It is for this reason Rosenmeyer believes that in this ode the poet simply suspends the

---

33 See, for example, vv 391–3, where the Erinyes claim an office (θεσμός) sanctioned by fate and by the gods; cf also v 312, where they claim to be εὐθυδίκαιοι, 'of right judgment.'

34 *Ag* 758–71 provides a typical parallel example.

dramatic personality of the Chorus and lets it revert to what he regards as the more usual choral voice: 'they [the Chorus in this ode] barely refer to themselves ... The ode is simply an encomium of the middle way, with plain justice and the principle of fear providing the guidance. The emphasis is on law and order, and on the dangers posed by permissive courts.'[35] Nevertheless, before we agree completely with Rosenmeyer's view, we should note how skilfully the poet, initially at least, dovetails these two 'voices' of his Chorus. At the beginning of the ode, the Chorus have been threatening, in their 'dramatic' role, what will happen to society if Orestes is acquitted: they, the Furies, will withdraw (see especially vv 494–516) and kin-murder, executed with impunity, will become rife. It is from this threat that the Chorus develop, quite in character and in context, their little homily (517–25) on the place of fear in society. From this point on, however, the Chorus go on to consider the well-being, and otherwise, of the body politic at large and of individuals in it, in a wider context than that crime of kin-murder, with which the Furies in this play are particularly concerned. Thus, initially at any rate, Aeschylus has his Chorus universalize, or express in general terms, what 'Clytemnestra's Furies' express through their attempts to avenge her murder; once embarked on their moralizing, however, the Chorus is allowed to develop their song 'withersoever (as Socrates might have put it) the *logos* leads it.' But it is *dramatically* essential, for the sake of 'the trial scene,' that the Chorus should revert, after this central ode, to something like their earlier, personally vindictive role.

I have dealt with the second stasimon of the *Eumenides* at some length because it seems to me to present not only the clearest example of a place where the individual 'dramatic voice' and the conventional 'choral voice' meet, but also because it exemplifies one of the poet's most earnest attempts to have the general ethical themes of the play expressed through a Chorus which still maintains, to a considerable degree, a marked dramatic personality.

Of necessity, the Chorus-Leader plays a prominent part in the Trial Scene of the *Eumenides*: indeed, the Chorus's role as plaintiff or prosecutor here is almost equivalent to one normally played by an actor, except that, as A.M. Dale has observed, of the Chorus generally, 'it never makes a speech, never marshals arguments.'[36]

---

35 Rosenmeyer p 174; cf pp 167–8.
36 Dale 'The Chorus in the Action of Greek Tragedy' p 18; see p 20 for her application of this observation to this passage in the *Eumenides*.

After their defeat in the Trial Scene, the Chorus, true to the near perfect blending of choral and dramatic elements in this play, continue their furious resistance to Athena's blandishments for two strophic pairs of repeated stanzas (778 ff, 808 ff, and 837 ff and 870 ff, respectively). Thus, they supply Athena with full opportunity for a splendid demonstration of Persuasion (Peithô, whom the goddess herself invokes at v 885) to balance the sinister uses to which this power has been put earlier in the myth and the trilogy.[37] And, formally at least, the gradual effects of Peithô may be observed in the slight changes of emphasis (from threats to self-pity) and of metre (which changes from intermittently to exclusively dochmiac) between the first and second strophic pairs of the Chorus's sung answers to Athena's offers, till finally (as Athena's language becomes increasingly convincing in a fifth-century context!) the Chorus's capitulation is completed in a brief passage of stichomythia between the Chorus-Leader and Athena.

Even with the conversion of the Erinyes, the dramatic functions of the Chorus in this play are not completed. The most striking feature of the final epirrhematic passage (916–1020) is the counterpoint set up between the Chorus's songs of blessings and Athena's sombre chants reminding the citizens of the Erinyes' more sinister powers.[38] Even as the Chorus now become exclusively benign, Athena becomes more severe in her warnings, with constant reminders that these new guardians are hard to please (δυσαρέστους, 928), avengers of crimes bred from ancient crimes (934 ff), and kindly only to those who honour them (note the significant reciprocity indicated by '... εὔφρονας εὔφρονες ...,' 992). Thus, the Erinyes are still to provide that element of dread which Athena has warned her new Court (690–2) is necessary for the just state. The Chorus, then, even more than Orestes, the technical protagonist, is really at the dramatic heart of this tragedy. Any doubt that the conversion of the Erinyes, and the new order of justice which their continued presence ensures, do not provide the thematic finale of the trilogy must surely be dispelled by these two epirrhematic passages, between the two orders of the gods, with which it ends.

In the case of the Supplices, where the fate of the Danaids is itself the dramatic and thematic centre of the play, our previous questions concerning the successful integration of the Chorus with the action must

37 Peithô has been involved in the 'temptation' of Paris (Ag 385 ff) and in Clytemnestra's inducements to Agamemnon to tread the purple tapestries (Ag 931 ff).
38 Cf my Aeschylus' Oresteia chap 3, pp 172 f; and now cf also Aeschylus, Eumenides ed Sommerstein, pp 260–2, in his head-note to Eum 916–20.

take a rather different form. How does the poet deploy his Chorus here in order to compensate for the lack of an individual, dramatic character whose fate is the dramatist's main concern? And how does he do this without sacrificing the effects, pictorial as well as 'universalizing,' which we tend to associate with the Aeschylean Chorus?

As far as the 'dramatic personality' of the Chorus of Danaids is concerned, their dominant characteristic of aggressive virginity is established in their initial declaration of 'self-chosen avoidance of men' (8), is sustained by many of their statements and images throughout the play, and is confirmed by their vehement assurances to their watchful father (at 1015 ff) with regard to the lascivious glances of local Argive males.

This Chorus's effect on the dramatic *action* is also strongly marked. Indeed, the 'Supplication Scene' (291–467), in which the Danaids 'persuade' King Pelasgus to plead their case before the Argive assembly, provides a splendid example of how choral action, skilfully handled, can replace individual dramatic action when the situation requires. The scene begins quietly with a stichomythic exchange between the Chorus and the King; increases in emotional tension in an epirrhematic sequence, with the whole Chorus singing in agitated dochmiacs and the King answering in iambic senarii; reaches a still higher pitch in a sustained lyric by the Chorus; and then ends, surprisingly and very dramatically, with a brief and grim passage of stichomythia in which the Chorus-Leader finally forces the King's agonized capitulation by threats of mass suicide upon the Argive's altar.

Aeschylus sustains this strong choral characterization and activity in the *Supplices* without sacrificing the pictorial delights, the mythological enhancements, and even the hymnic elements which we associate with his choral odes. This he does by relating each of the elements to the central focus of the tragedy, which is, of course, the Danaids themselves and their lot. Thus, the songs of Io's wanderings and deliverance, and the magnificent celebration of Zeus' power and benevolence, become a part of the Danaids' supplication (of Zeus as well as of the Argives) on their own behalf.[39] So, too, throughout the play, the Chorus use

---

39 Detailed studies of metre in relation to theme in the choral odes of the *Supplices* have been attempted by J.N. Rash in *Meter and Language in the Lyrics of The Suppliants of Aeschylus*. Particularly interesting arguments for such relations will be found in Rash's comments (pp 106 ff and 137 ff) on metrical devices allegedly used for marking different stages in the Danaid-Io theme, and also on the use of the dochmiac metre (with variations, possibly for sinister effect) to suggest an apprehensive note

their most vivid imagery to highlight their own nature and plight, as 'wearing away soft, Nile-warmed cheeks, ... they feed on flowers of lamentation' (70–3, in part). Similarly self-referrent are the vivid images near the end of the play for the Danaids' terrified despair at the approach of the Egyptian suitors:

> May I become like a cloud of black smoke reaching the clouds of Zeus, or like a puff of dust soaring aloft, invisible, in wingless flight. (779–83)

and

> O, that I might find some lofty seat amid the storm-clouds' flurries, some barren crag, lonely and steep, to witness my leap into the depths, rather than suffer perforce a marriage which would scald my heart! (792–9)

Any discussion of the Chorus as 'group protagonist' in the dramatic action of the *Supplices* must take account of the 'problem passage' at vv 1034 ff where, as we have seen, the Chorus (or half the Chorus, or possibly a second Chorus)[40] suddenly abandon the previous stance of the Danaids to celebrate the power of Aphrodite and her delights. Soon these singers even suggest that the will of Zeus (which is παραβατός [1048], 'not to be transgressed') may actually be marriage for the Danaids, as for many women before them. After a brief stichomythic exchange which follows between the leaders of the two factions of the Chorus (or possibly the leaders of the two Choruses), the voice of moderation is finally silenced and the (whole?) Chorus of Danaids ends with a prayer to Zeus for protection and 'victory for the women.'

Rosenmeyer seizes on the passage at *Suppl* 1034 ff as one where the conventional choral voice manages to reassert itself. He argues as follows:

> Whether the lines are sung by some members of the Chorus who thus stand in opposition to the rest, or whether the whole Chorus ... relaxes its former rigidity, what matters is that the lines give us the typical choral insistence on

---

in the Danaids' later thankful prayers for the Argives. Sometimes one wonders, however, whether the audience would connect the various detailed metrical effects which Rash observes to the thematic shifts and developments to which he relates them.

40 For the controversy over the attribution of these verses, see above, chap 3 (on the *Supplices*) pp 99–101 and nn 43–8.

the wrongness of excess ... The warnings are similar to others pronounced by choruses ... in many Greek plays ... that moderation and compromise are to be preferred to one-sided worship, or neglect, of specific divinities. The self-criticism of the women ... rights the balance and restores the choral norm, after the experimental use of the chorus in this unusual play had for a while effaced the distinction between chorus and principal.[41]

Rosenmeyer is, of course, quite justified in asserting that the Chorus at vv 1034 ff do indeed advise moderation and compromise in the manner of the more conventional Aeschylean choral utterances. Nevertheless, if, as seems quite possible, these verses are sung by *half* the Chorus of Danaids, they become quite dramatic, rather than merely a reflection of conventional wisdom; in that case the Chorus, as a group, is indulging in self-debate (which becomes more vivid in the stichomythic passage), and those hinting at submission to Aphrodite and the suitors are, in effect, dramatically anticipating the choice to be made by Hypermestra in the lost second play of the trilogy. And if, as some scholars have argued, this 'counsel of moderation' is voiced by a second Chorus of handmaidens, then this shared ode and dialogue play a still more dramatic role in the tragedy.

Whatever choristers utter the controversial verses at 1034 ff, we may surely conclude that the overall presentation of the Chorus in this play represents a tour de force of successful characterization as 'group protagonist' of the tragedy, while still preserving the essential elements traditionally associated with Aeschylean choral songs. For this reason, consideration of the Chorus of Danaids provides a fitting conclusion to this discussion of Aeschylus' virtuosity (evident even from the small number of plays available to us) in his dramatic uses of the Chorus in such a wide variety of ways.

41 Rosenmeyer *The Art of Aeschylus* p 174; for the whole of his discussion of this passage, see pp 173–4.

Bibliography

This bibliography is restricted to works referred to in the book and to a few additional works also found valuable in its preparation.

Editions, translations, commentaries

Bacon, Helen, and Hecht, Anthony *Seven against Thebes, translation with introduction and notes* New York and London 1973

Belloni, Luigi, ed *Eschilo I, Persiani* Milan 1988

Broadhead, H.D., ed *The Persae of Aeschylus* Cambridge 1960

Dawson, Christopher *The Seven against Thebes, a translation with commentary* Englewood Cliffs 1970

Denniston, J.D., and Page, Denys, eds *Aeschyli septem quae supersunt tragoediae* Oxford 1972

Grene, David, and Lattimore, Richmond, eds *The Complete Greek Tragedies* vol I *Aeschylus* Chicago 1959

Griffith, Mark, ed *Aeschylus, Prometheus Bound* Cambridge 1983

Hecht, Anthony. See Bacon and Hecht

Hermann, Gottfried, ed *Aeschyli Tragoediae* Leipzig 1852

Hutchinson, G.O., ed *Septem contra Thebas* Oxford 1985

Italie, G. *Index Aeschyleus* second edition ed S.L. Radt, Leiden 1964

Johansen, H. Friis, and Smith, Ole, eds *Aeschylus The Suppliants: Text, Introduction and Translation* (Johansen); *The Scholia* (Smith) Copenhagen 1970

Johansen, H. Friis, and Whittle, Edward W., eds *Aeschylus: The Suppliants* 2 vols Copenhagen 1980

Lattimore, Richmond. See Grene and Lattimore

Linwood, W. *Lexicon to Aeschylus* London 1897

Lloyd-Jones, Hugh. See Smyth, H.W.

Mazon, Paul, ed *Eschyle* 2 vols, third edition (Budé series) Paris 1966 and 1968

Mette, H.J. *Die Fragmente der Tragoedien des Aischylos* Berlin 1959

Munro, D.B., ed *Homer, Iliad* books I–XII, fifth edition, Oxford 1953

Murray, Gilbert, ed *Aeschyli septem quae supersunt tragoediae* Oxford Classical Texts, Oxford 1938; second edition, 1955

Nauck, A. *Tragicorum Graecorum Fragmenta Supplementum*, ed Snell, Bruno, Hildesheim 1964

Page, Denys. See Denniston and Page

Paley, F.A., ed *The Tragedies of Aeschylus, re-edited, with an English commentary* fourth edition. Oxford 1924

Perrin, B., ed and trans *Plutarch's Lives* vol I, Loeb Classical Library, London 1914

Rose, H.J. *A Commentary on the Surviving Plays of Aeschylus* Amsterdam 1957–8

Roussel, L., ed *Eschyle, Les Perses, texte, traduction et commentaire* Montpelier 1960

Sidgwick, A., ed *Persae* Oxford 1903

– ed *Tragoediae* Oxford 1900

Smith, Ole. See Johansen and Smith

Smyth, H.W., ed *Aeschylus, with an English translation* 2 vols, Loeb Classical Library, Cambridge and London 1956–7 (appendix to vol II, Hugh Lloyd-Jones)

Tucker, T.G., ed *The Seven against Thebes* Cambridge 1908

Vürtheim, J., ed *Aischylos' Schutzflehende* Amsterdam 1928 and 1967

Weil, H., ed *Aeschylus. Quae supersunt tragoediae* Giessen 1958–67

West, Martin *Aeschyli Tragoediae cum incerti poetae Prometheo* Stuttgart 1990

Whittle, Edward W. See Johansen and Whittle

Wilamowitz-Moellendorf, U. von, ed *Aeschyli Tragoediae* Berlin 1914

Books

Arnott, Peter *Greek Scenic Conventions* Oxford 1962

Bloom, Harold, ed *Modern Critical Interpretations* New York 1988

Bolton, J.D.P. *Aristeas of Proconnesus* Oxford 1962

Bremer, J. *Hamartia* Amsterdam 1969

Burkert, W. *Greek Religion* trans John Raffan Oxford 1985

Cameron, H.D. *Studies in the Seven against Thebes of Aeschylus* The Hague 1971

Carrière, Jean *Le choeur secondaire dans le drame grec* Paris 1977

Conacher, D.J. *Aeschylus' Oresteia: A Literary Commentary* Toronto 1987

– *Aeschylus' Prometheus Bound: A Literary Commentary* Toronto 1980

Croiset, M. *Eschyle* Paris 1928

Dale, A.M. *Collected Papers* Cambridge 1969

– *The Lyric Metres of Greek Drama* Cambridge 1968

Deichgräber, Karl *Die Persentetralogie des Aischylos* Wiesbaden 1974

Dietrich, B.C. *Death, Fate and the Gods* London 1965

Dodds, E. R. *The Ancient Concept of Progress and Other Essays on Greek Literature and Belief* Oxford 1973

– *The Greeks and the Irrational* Berkeley and Los Angeles 1951

Dumortier, J. *Les images dans la poésie d'Eschyle* Paris 1935

Earp, F.R. *The Style of Aeschylus* Cambridge 1948

Else, Gerald F. *The Origin and Early Form of Greek Tragedy* Cambridge, Mass 1965

Finley, J.H., Jr *Pindar and Aeschylus* Cambridge, Mass 1955

Fischer, Ulrich *Die Telosgedanke in den Dramen des Aischylos* Hildesheim 1965

Frankfort, H.A., trans *Greek Tragedy* by Albin Lesky, second edition, London and New York 1967

Gagarin, Michael *Aeschylean Drama* Berkeley and Los Angeles 1976

Garvie, A.F. *Aeschylus' Supplices: Play and Trilogy* Cambridge 1969

Goldhill, Simon *Reading Greek Tragedy* Cambridge 1986

– *Language, Sexuality, Narrative: The Oresteia* Cambridge 1984

Gomme, A.W. *Greek Attitudes to Poetry and History* Berkeley 1954

Griffith, Mark *The Authenticity of the Prometheus Bound* Cambridge 1977

– and Mastronarde, D., eds *The Cabinet of the Muses* Chico, Calif 1990

Hall, Edith *Inventing the Barbarian* Oxford 1989

Heller, John L., ed *Serta Turyniana* Urbana, Ill 1974

Herington, C.J. *Aeschylus* New Haven and London 1986

Hexter, Ralph, and Selden, Daniel, eds *Innovations of Antiquity* New York and London 1992

Highet, Gilbert. See Jaeger, Werner

Ireland, S. *Aeschylus, Greece and Rome*, New Surveys in the Classics no 18, Oxford 1986

Jaeger, Werner *Paideia*, vol I, second edition, trans Gilbert Highet, New York 1945

Jones, John *On Aristotle and Greek Tragedy* London 1962

Kaimio, M. *The Chorus in Greek Tragedy within the Light of the Person and Number Used* Helsinki 1970

Kitto, H.D.F. *Poiesis: Structure and Thought* Berkeley and Los Angeles 1966

– *Form and Meaning in Drama* London 1956

– *Greek Tragedy* second edition. London 1950

Knox, Bernard *Word and Action, Essays on the Ancient Theatre* Baltimore and London 1979

Kranz, W. *Stasimon* Berlin 1933

Lamphere, L., and Rosaldo, M., eds *Women, Culture and Society* Stanford 1974

Lattimore, Richmond *The Poetry of Greek Tragedy* New York 1958

Lebeck, Anne *The Oresteia, A Study in Language and Structure* Cambridge, Mass 1971

Lesky, Albin *Greek Tragedy* second edition, trans H.A. Frankfort, London 1967

Lloyd-Jones, Hugh *The Justice of Zeus* Berkeley and Los Angeles 1971

Lupas, L., and Petre, Z. *Commentaires aux Sept contre Thèbes* Bucharest and Paris 1981

Mastronarde, D.J. *Contact and Discontinuity, Some Conventions of Speech and Action on the Greek Tragic Stage* Berkeley and Los Angeles 1979

Mastronarde, D. See Griffith and Mastronarde

Méautis, G. *Eschyle et la trilogie* Paris 1936

Michelini, Ann N. *Tradition and Dramatic Form in the Persians of Aeschylus* Leiden 1982

Moreau, Alain *La violence et le chaos* Paris 1985

Murray, Gilbert *Aeschylus, the Creator of Tragedy* Oxford 1940

Murray, R.D. *The Motif of Io in Aeschylus' Supplices* Princeton 1958

Mylonas, G., and Richmond, Doris, eds *Studies Presented to David Robinson* St Louis 1953

Onians, J.B. *Origins of European Thought* Cambridge 1954

Owen, E.T. *The Harmony of Aeschylus* Toronto 1952

Patin, M. *Études sur les tragiques grecques* Paris 1965

Parker, R. *Miasma* Oxford 1983

Petre, Z. See Lupas and Petre

Petrounias, Evangelos *Funktion und Thematik der Bilder bei Aischylos* Göttingen 1976

Pickard-Cambridge, A.W. *The Dramatic Festivals of Athens* Oxford 1968

– *The Theatre of Dionysus in Athens* Oxford 1946

Podlecki, A.J. *The Political Background of Aeschylean Tragedy* Ann Arbor 1966

Pohlenz, M. *Die griechische Tragödie* second edition, Göttingen 1954

Raffan, John *Greek Religion* trans W. Burkert, Oxford 1985

Rash, J.N. *Meter and Language in the Lyrics of The Suppliants of Aeschylus* New York 1981

Reinhardt, Karl *Aischylos als Regisseur und Theolog* Berne 1949

Richmond, Doris. See Mylonas and Richmond

Rosaldo, M. See Lamphere and Rosaldo

Rosenmeyer, Thomas G. *The Art of Aeschylus* Berkeley and Los Angeles 1982

– *The Masks of Tragedy* Austin 1963

Sansone, David *Aeschylean Metaphors for Intellectual Activity. Hermes Einzelschriften* 35. Wiesbaden 1975

Schmid, Wilhelm *Geschichte der griechischen Literatur* I.3, Munich 1940

Scott, William C. *Musical Design in the Aeschylean Theater* Hanover and Dublin 1984

Selden, Daniel. See Hexter and Selden

Silk, M.S. *Interaction in Poetic Imagery, with Special Reference to Early Greek Poetry* Cambridge 1974

Smethurst, Mae *The Artistry of Aeschylus and Zeami* Princeton 1989

Smyth, H.W. *Aeschylean Tragedy* Berkeley and Los Angeles 1924

Snell, Bruno *Aischylos und das Handeln im Drama* Leipzig 1928

Solmsen, Friedrich *Hesiod and Aeschylus* Ithaca 1949

Stanford, W.B. *Aeschylus in His Style* Dublin 1942

Stoessl, Franz *Die Trilogie des Aischylos* Baden bei Wien 1937

Taplin, Oliver *Greek Tragedy in Action* Berkeley and Los Angeles 1978

– *The Stagecraft of Aeschylus* Oxford 1977

Thalmann, William *Dramatic Art in Aeschylus, Seven against Thebes* New Haven 1978

Thomson, George *Aeschylus and Athens* third edition, London 1966 [1941]

– *Studies in Ancient Greek Society* London 1949

Trendall, A.D., and Webster, T.B.L. *Illustrations of Greek Drama* London 1971

Turyn, A. *The Manuscript Tradition of Aeschylus* New York 1943

Van Nes, D. *Die Maritime Bildersprache des Aischylos* Groningen 1963

Vernant, J.-P., and Vidal-Naquet, Pierre *Mythe et tragédie en Grèce ancienne* Paris 1973

Vidal-Naquet, Pierre. See Vernant and Vidal-Naquet

von Fritz, Kurt *Antike und Moderne Tragödie* Berlin 1962

Webster, T.B.L. *The Greek Chorus* London 1970

Webster, T.B.L. See Trendall and Webster

Welcker, G. *Die Aischylos Trilogie Prometheus* Darmstadt 1824

West, M.L. *Studies in Aeschylus* Stuttgart 1990

Westphal, R. *Prolegomena zu Aischylos' Tragoedien* Leipzig 1869

Wilamowitz-Moellendorf, U. von *Aischylos Interpretationen* Berlin 1914

– *Griechische Tragödien* vol I, Berlin 1910

Winnington-Ingram, R.P. *Studies in Aeschylus* Cambridge 1983

Zeitlin, Froma *Under the Sign of the Shield: Semiotics and Aeschylus' Seven against Thebes* Rome 1982

Articles, reviews, etc.

Adkins, W.A. 'Divine and Human Values in Aeschylus' *Seven against Thebes*' *Antike und Abenland* 28 (1982) 32–68

Alexanderson, Bergt 'Darius in *The Persians*' *Eranos* 65 (1967) 1–11

Avery, H.C. 'Dramatic Devices in Aeschylus' *Persae*' *AJP* 85 (1964) 173–84

Bacon, Helen 'The Shield of Eteocles' *Arion* 3 (1964) 27–38

Baldry, H.C. 'The Dramatization of the Theban Legend' *G&R* 3 (1956) 24–37

Bamberger, Joan 'The Myth of the Matriarchy' in *Women, Culture and Society* ed M. Rosaldo and L. Lamphere (Stanford 1974) 263–80

Benardete, Seth 'Two Notes on Aeschylus' *Septem*' *WS* nf 1 (1968) 22–30

Bonner, C. 'A Study of the Danaid Myth' *HSCP* 13 (1902) 129–73

Burian, Peter 'Pelasgus and Politics in Aeschylus' Danaid Trilogy' *WS* nf 8 (1974) 5–14

Burnett, Ann 'Curse and Dream in Aeschylus' *Septem*' *GRBS* 14 (1973) 343–68

Caldwell, R. 'The Misogyny of Eteocles' *Arethusa* 6 (1973) 197–231

Cameron, H.D. 'Epigoni and the Law of Inheritance in Aeschylus' *Septem*' *GRBS* (1968) 247–57

Cavaignac, E. 'Eschyle et Themistocle' *Revue de Philologie* 45 (1921) 102–6

Conacher, D.J. 'Rapporte entre le choeur et la structure dramatique dans les tragédies d'Eschyle' in *Pallas, Revue d'études antiques* 38 (1992) 153–60

– 'Interaction between Chorus and Characters in the *Oresteia*' *AJP* 95 (1974) 323–43

– 'Aeschylus' *Persae*: A Literary Commentary' in *Serta Turyniana* ed John L. Heller (Urbana, Ill 1974) 143–68

Cunningham, M.L. 'Second Thoughts on *Ox. Pap.* xx.2251' *Rh Mus* 105 (1962) 189–90

– 'A Fragment of Aeschylus' *Aegyptioi*?' *Rh Mus* 96 (1953) 223–51

Dale, A.M. 'The Chorus in the Action of Greek Tragedy' in *Classical Drama and Its Influence: Essays Presented to H.D.F. Kitto* (London 1965)

Dawe, R.D. 'The End of the *Seven against Thebes* Yet Again' in *Dionysiaca: Nine Studies in Greek Poetry Presented to Sir Denys Page* ed R.D. Dawe, J. Diggle, and P.E. Easterling (Cambridge 1978) 87–103

– 'Some Reflections on *Atê* and *Hamartia*' *HSCP* 72 (1967) 89–123

– 'The End of the *Seven against Thebes*' *CQ* ns 17 (1967) 16–28

– 'Inconsistency of Plot and Character in Aeschylus' *Proceedings of the Cambridge Philological Association* no 189 ns 9 (1963) 21–62

Deichgräber, Karl 'Die *Persae* des Aischylos' *Nachr. d. Akad. d. Wiss. in Göttingen, Phil.-Hist. Kl.* (1941) 155–202

Diamantopoulos, A. 'The Danaid Trilogy of Aeschylus' *JHS* 77 (1957) 220–9

Easterling, P.E. 'Presentation of Character in Aeschylus' *G&R* 29 (1973) 3–19

Flintoff, E. 'The Ending of the *Seven against Thebes*' *Mnemosyne* 33 (1980) 344–71

Forrest, W.G.F. 'Themistokles and Argos' *CQ* ns 10 (1960) 221–41

Fowler, Barbara Hughes 'Aeschylus' Imagery' *ClMed* 28 (1967) 1–74

– 'The Imagery of the *Prometheus Bound*' *CQ* ns 10 (1960) 221–41

Garvie, A.F. 'Aeschylus' Simple Plots' in *Dionysiaca: Nine Studies in Greek Poetry Presented to Sir Denys Page* ed R.D. Dawe, J. Diggle, and P.E. Easterling (Cambridge 1978) 63–86

Hammond, N.G.L. 'Dramatic Production to the Death of Aeschylus' *GRBS* 13 (1972) 387–450

– 'The Battle of Salamis' *JHS* 76 (1956) 32–54

Herington, C.J. Review of Mark Griffith *The Authenticity of Prometheus Bound,* *Philological Quarterly* 58 (1979) 116–18
– Review of Mark Griffith *The Authenticity of Prometheus Bound, AJP* 100 (1979) 42–6
– 'Aeschylus: The Last Phase' *Arion* 4 (1965) 384–403
– 'Some Evidence for the Late Dating of the *Prometheus Bound' CR* ns 14 (1964) 239–40
Hermann, Gottfried 'De Compositione Tetralogiarum Tragicarum' *Opuscula* II, Lipsiae 1827
Holtsmark, E.B. 'Ring Composition in the *Persae* of Aeschylus' *Symbolae Osloensis* 45 (1970) 5–53
Ireland, S. 'The Problem of Motivation in the *Supplices* of Aeschylus' *Rh Mus* 17 (1974) 14–29
Jakel, S. 'The 14th Heroid Letter of Ovid and the Danaid Trilogy of Aeschylus' *Mnemosyne* 26 (1973) 239–48
Jocelyn, H.D. 'Greek Poetry in Cicero's Prose Writing' *Yale Classical Studies* 23 (1973) 61–111
Johansen, H. Friis 'Progymnasmata' *ClMed* 27 (1966) 39–64
Kirkwood, Gordon 'Eteokles *Oiakostrophos' Phoenix* 23 (1969) 9–25
Lattimore, Richmond 'Aeschylus on the Defeat of Xerxes' in *Classical Studies in Honor of William Abbott Oldfather* (Urbana 1943) 88–93
Lloyd-Jones, Hugh 'The *Supplices* of Aeschylus: The New Date and Old Problems' *AC* 33 (1964) 356–74
– 'The Guilt of Agamemnon' *CQ* ns 12 (1962) 187–99
– 'The End of the *Seven against Thebes' CQ* ns 9 (1959) 80–115
– 'Zeus in Aeschylus' *JHS* 76 (1956) 55–67
MacKinnon, J.K. 'The Reason for the Danaids' Flight' *CQ* ns 28 (1978) 74–81
Macurdy, G. 'Had the Danaid Trilogy a Social Problem?' *CP* (1944) 95–100
Manton, C.R. 'The Second Stasimon of *The Seven against Thebes' BICS* (1961) 77–84
McCall, Marsh, 'The Chorus of Aeschylus' *Choephori'* in *The Cabinet of the Muses* ed M. Griffith and D. Mastronarde (Chico, Calif 1990) 15–27
– 'The Secondary Chorus in Aeschylus' *Suppliants' California Studies in Classical Antiquity* 9 (1976) 117–31
Méautis, G. 'Notes sur *Les Eumenides* d'Eschyle' *REA* 65 (1963) 33–52
Moritz, Helen E. 'Refrain in Aeschylus' *CP* 74 (1979) 187–213
Orwin, Clifford 'Feminine Justice: The End of the *Seven against Thebes' CP* 75 (1980) 187–96
Otis, Brooks 'The Unity of the *Seven against Thebes' GRBS* 3 (1960) 153–74
Patzer, H. 'Die dramatische Handlung der *Sieben gegen Theben' HSCP* 63 (1958) 97–119

Peradotto, J.J. 'Some Patterns of Nature Imagery in the *Oresteia*' *AJP* 85 (1964) 378–93

Podlecki, A.J. 'The Character of Eteocles in Aeschylus' *Septem*' *TAPA* 95 (1964) 283–99

Porter, David H. 'The Imagery of Greek Tragedy' *Symbolae Osloensis* (1986) 19–42

Quincey, J.H. 'Notes on the *Persae*' *CQ* ns 12 (1962) 182–6

Robertson, D.S. *Proc. Cambr. Philol. Soc.* 171 (1938) 9–10

Rösler, Wolfgang 'Danaos à propos des dangers de l'amour (Eschyle *Suppliantes* 991–1013)' *Pallas, Revue des études antiques* 38 (1992) 173–8

Sansone, David 'Aeschulus' *Persae*, 163' *Hermes* 107 (1979) 115–16

Schenker, D.S. 'The Queen and the Chorus in Aeschulus' *Persae*' *Phoenix* 48 (1994) 283–93

Scott, William, C. 'Wind Imagery in the *Oresteia*' *TAPA* 97 (1966) 459–71

Sealey, R. 'Ephialtes' *CP* 59 (1964) 11–22

Sheppard, J.T. 'The Plot of the *Septem contra Thebas*' *CQ* 7 (1913) 73–82

– 'The First Scene of *The Suppiants* of Aeschylus' *CQ* 5 (1911) 220–9

Sicherl, Martin 'Die Tragik der Danaiden' *Mus Helv* 43 (1986) 81–110

Smith, Ole 'Observations on the Structure of Imagery in Aeschylus' *ClMed* 26 (1965) 10–72

Solmsen, F. 'The Erinyes in Aeschylus' *Septem*' *TAPA* 68 (1937) 197–211

Sommerstein, Alan H. 'Notes on Aeschylus' *Supplices*' *BICS* 24 (1977) 67–82

Stinson, T.C.W. '*Hamartia* in Aristotle and Greek Tragedy' *CQ* ns 25 (1975) 221–54

Stoessl, Franz 'Die *Phoinissen* der Phrynichos und die *Perser* des Aischylos' *Mus Helv* 2 (1945) 148–65

Thalmann, W.G. 'Xerxes' Rags' *AJP* 101 (1980) 260–82

– 'The Lille Stesichorus and the *Septem contra Thebas*' *Hermes* 110 (1982) 385–91

Thomson, George 'The Suppliants of Aeschylus' *Eirene* 9 (1971) 27–8

Van Looey, H. 'Mélanges Varia, Tragica I, Aeschyli *Supplices*' *AC* 38 (1969) 489–96

Wardman, A.E. 'Tactics and Tradition in the Persian Wars' *Historia* 8 (1959) 49–60

Winnington-Ingram, R.P. '*Septem contra Thebas*' *YCS* 25 (1977) 1–45

– 'Zeus in *Persae*' *JHS* 73 (1973) 210–19

– 'A Word in *Persae*' *BICS* 20 (1973) 37–8

– 'The Danaid Trilogy' *JHS* 81 (1961) 141–52

Wolff, E. 'Die Entscheidung des Eteocles' *HSCP* 63 (1968) 89–95

Zeitlin, Froma 'The Politics of Eros in the Danaid Trilogy of Aeschylus' in *Innovations of Antiquity* ed Ralph Hexter and Daniel Selden (New York 1992) 203–52